UNOFFICIAL HISTORY

Field-Marshal
SIR WILLIAM SLIM

K.G., G.C.B., G.C.M.G., G.C.V.O., G.B.E.,
D.S.O., M.C.

Pen & Sword
MILITARY

First published in Great Britain in 1959 by Cassell & Company Ltd
Re-published in this format in 2008 by
PEN & SWORD MILITARY
an imprint of
Pen & Sword Books Ltd
47 Church Street
Barnsley
South Yorkshire
S70 2AS

Copyright © Sir William Slim, 1959, 2008

ISBN 978 1 84415 791 4

Printed and bound in Great Britain
By CPI UK

Pen & Sword Books Ltd incorporates the Imprints of
Pen & Sword Aviation, Pen & Sword Family History,
Pen & Sword Maritime, Pen & Sword Military, Wharncliffe Local History,
Pen & Sword Select, Pen & Sword Military Classics, Leo Cooper,
Remember When, Seaforth Publishing and Frontline Publishing

For a complete list of Pen & Sword titles please contact
PEN & SWORD BOOKS LIMITED
47 Church Street, Barnsley, South Yorkshire, S70 2AS, England
E-mail: enquiries@pen-and-sword.co.uk
Website: www.pen-and-sword.co.uk

UNOFFICIAL HISTORY

This Book
is
gratefully dedicated
to
all those who read it

FOREWORD

I HOPE no one will be misled by this book's title and expect to find in it one of those fashionable keyhole chronicles of what went on behind closed doors in the councils of the great. In these simple narratives there are no great men—that is, great in the historical sense—and the actions described took place almost invariably in the open. Sometimes when I was compelled to share in them, I thought too much in the open.

The little battles and unimportant skirmishes I write of here have received scant notice in Official Histories and Government Records. Against the scale of world events and of mightier combats elsewhere, they have rightly and of necessity, when mentioned at all, been dismissed in a few sentences. Yet to those who took part in them they were, even if only temporarily, important enough, and the thought occurred to me that for interest if not for value, for amusement rather than instruction, it might be worth while to recall some of the events and feelings, grave and gay, that lay behind the dry phrases of official history.

These accounts are not, as official history should be, photographs taken through the lens of a camera, completely accurate and untouched by emotion. They are instead the more individual and freer canvases of a man trying to paint things seen, felt and remembered; a shade blurred here, a trifle out of perspective there, and perhaps a little, in this corner and that, consciously arranged to hold the design together. Yet withal true impressions of actual happenings as he saw them. Such as it is then, this book is by no means meant to be a very serious contribution to military history.

The earlier of these chapters appeared, long ago, in *Blackwood's Magazine*; the rest were written more recently. In a few I have changed the names of persons and places, and in one, 'Aid to the Civil', I have combined three or four separate incidents into one narrative.

Some readers may think I have at times, whether as subaltern or as general, treated too lightly, even when in this minor key, the grim and tragic business of war. If they do, I can only plead guilty to a fault—or is it a virtue?—that has for centuries marked the British soldier. There would be fewer battle honours emblazoned on his colours had he lacked it.

W. J. SLIM

Canberra   FIELD-MARSHAL

CONTENTS

		Page
I	TIGRIS BANK	I
II	THE INCORRIGIBLE ROGUE	23
III	ELIZABETH SUCCEEDED HENRY	51
IV	AID TO THE CIVIL	73
V	STUDENT'S INTERLUDE	99
VI	COUNSEL OF FEARS	125
VII	IT PAYS TO BE BOLD	149
VIII	PERSIAN PATTERN	177
IX	CAVIAR TO THE GENERAL	211

MAPS

	Facing page
Gallabat	127
Deir-ez-zor	151
Persia	179

I

TIGRIS BANK

Contact with the enemy which had been lost for some hours had been established about half an hour earlier, but little opposition was encountered until 4 p.m., when the vanguard was checked by the enemy—apparently his rear-guard—holding a line of trenches which ran north-east from Um-ul-Baqq for about two and a half miles.

British Official History of the War: Mesopotamia

TIGRIS BANK

SOME years ago I found myself, with half an hour to wait, in the library of a great government department. My eye wandered over the shelves seeking a book to while away the time, but ponderous tomes on international law and economics have never attracted me. I was just going to ask the librarian for the unexpurgated *Arabian Nights* that I know he keeps tucked away on some discreet shelf, when I caught sight of a long row of red volumes. They stood in ordered ranks, uniform and soldierly: the *British Official History of the War*.

'The Campaign in France and Flanders'? No, I went to France with the Conscientious Objectors. You might write a book about that extraordinary collection of exhibitionism, idealism, courage and cold feet, but not an Official History. I doubted if the non-combatant corps would be mentioned, and I was after something personal, something I had seen myself. 'Gallipoli'? No, the Peninsula held memories I was in no mood for now. 'Mesopotamia'? Why, yes, I would dip into that. Not the cruel battles before Kut, but some lesser action that I could look back on with a smile instead of with an ache for lost friends. Say the capture of Um-ul-Baqq on the dusty Tigris bank. There would not be a long account, enough for a quarter of an hour or so, but my battalion would be there—I might even find my own name. It would be very satisfying to find oneself a bit of official history.

I pulled out the volume, sank into an armchair, and, thanks to the admirable system of dates in the margin of every page, soon found the place I wanted. I glanced at my watch—I could not afford to miss that appointment—and settled down to read.

Contact with the enemy which had been lost for some hours had been established about half an hour earlier, but little opposition was encountered until 4 p.m., when the vanguard was checked by the enemy—apparently his rear-guard—holding a line of trenches which ran north-east from Um-ul-Baqq for about two and a half miles.

And that was all! Um-ul-Baqq, the only battle I ever, up to that time, enjoyed, dismissed in those few lines. Scandalous!

know Um-ul-Baqq was not one of the seven, or should it be seventy, decisive battles of the world, but.... It was very quiet in that library. I rested the open book on my knee and slipped back through the years.

*   *   *

I do not believe Napoleon himself ever felt so Napoleonic as I did that early spring morning in 1917 when I watched the first mixed force I had ever commanded defile before me. The khaki-clad British infantry trudged past, two companies of them, with a grin and a joke, as they have trudged across history. After them came a section of machine-guns on pack, with here and there a bobbish mule swinging sideways from the ranks; and then, O pride of a subaltern's heart, two jingling, rattling, rumbling 18-pounders!

I was happy. We were winning; the fatality that had hung like a pall over Mesopotamia had lifted at last. The Turk was on the run, and we were after him. The men sang as they marched—and they had not done that for a year. On the other bank of the great mud-coloured Tigris the dust-storms of the night still hung menacingly, but on ours the cool dawn breeze that came rippling across the dead flat plain raised no dun clouds between us and the pearly horizon. It was like sunrise at sea; it woke you up and put you on your toes. I suppose if I had been one of those wartime subalterns who have since written so prolifically and pathologically of their reactions to such scenes, I should have psycho-analysed myself into a desperate gloom, swallowed half a bottle of whisky, and laughed bitterly. But I had never heard of psycho-analysis, I had not seen whisky for a fortnight, and if I laughed it was from anything but bitterness.

I watched the tail of my little column—some stretcher-bearers from the field ambulance—go past, and then cantered to the front. We were just approaching a cutting which led steeply down to a pontoon bridge across a hundred yards' wide tributary of the Tigris. This bridge had been completed under fire the previous night; it looked none too secure, and the sappers were still busy on it. Their officer asked me to send the men across in parties as the current was strong. No engineer will ever admit a bridge he has built might break, but there was a look in that sapper's eye which warned me that the less weight we put on his bridge the better.

I dismounted and led my horse, Anzac; he came quietly enough, snorting a little as the loose boards moved under his feet and the pontoons swayed to the rush of water. Infantry, by sections, came over all right, and only one machine-gun mule played the fool. At one time it certainly looked as if he, his load, and the three men clinging to him would all go overboard together. However, being a mule, and therefore full of common sense, he realized that if he did it would be the end of him; so he gave a final shake that nearly rattled his load off, and minced demurely across. The guns gave more trouble. They and the limbers skidded down the slope with locked wheels on to the bridge. The horses hated the dip and swing of the pontoons as the weight came on them, but after some hair-raising moments all were over and the column halted to close up on the far bank.

The colonel rode across the bridge and gave me my final instructions. My little force was the vanguard to the advance on the Tigris east bank. The Turks, so the aeroplanes had reported, were digging hard on a line running back from the river at the village of Um-ul-Baqq, several miles ahead. I was to shove on for Um-ul-Baqq, clear away any opposition and, if possible, seize the village itself. There followed some brief directions about casualties, replenishment of ammunition, and sending back information. 'And', concluded the colonel, fixing me with a steady eye, 'and remember the first duty of an advance-guard is to advance!'

Rather sobered by this grim injunction, I called up my officers. They stood in a semi-circle before me. It was a young man's war, at least the *fighting* of it was, and, with one exception, we were all in the early twenties. The exception was the gunner, and he looked strangely out of place among us, with the big grizzled moustache of the old regular soldier, and a face like Foch's. He had a single star on his shoulder, but battery sergeant-major all over him.

I had not much to give them in the way of orders, but I repeated what the colonel had told me. 'And', I ended, trying to look as much like him as I could, though in that nature gave me little help, 'and remember, the first duty of an advance-guard is to advance!' It went very well, I thought, and they all seemed rather impressed.

Five minutes later we were off, a line of scouts ahead, the platoons of 'A' Company in blobs behind them, then my own 'B' Company, with the machine-guns on the leeward flank to save us from dust, and last of all the 18-pounders. Turning in my saddle, I could see dust clouds beginning to rise far behind, and knew the main body was on the move. Although we were near the Tigris, the *bund*, an earthwork embankment, hid it from us, and it was only in the distance that we could follow its course by dark masses of palm groves and gardens. For the rest, the country was as flat as a table and bare to the horizon, now drawing nearer as the dust haze increased.

We passed evidences of the desperate fight at the bridge, all the litter of a battlefield—torn clothing, scattered equipment, abandoned ammunition, broken rifles, and the bodies of a good many Turks. There was one Arab, a huge man, amongst them, shot, I suppose, as he crept from the river to loot the dead. However, the sight of dead Turks caused us few pangs, and of dead Arabs none at all.

This disorder was soon behind us, and we advanced steadily until the palm groves on the river bank began to take shape. Nothing had happened so far, and I rode forward to Bateman, commanding 'A' Company, to see how he was getting on. He had wisely sent a platoon rather wide on his left flank to move through the trees, and I could see it, well extended, moving steadily towards the first grove, not more than half a mile away. Beyond these fellows ran the high bank of the *bund*, and as I looked I saw to my surprise, marching along it in file, rifles at the slope, about a dozen men.

'What's that damn fool of yours doing on top of the *bund*?' I asked Bateman. 'If there are any Turks about, he'll be a cockshy for half Asia in a minute!'

'He must have moved pretty briskly to get there, anyway,' said Bateman, raising his glasses. He stared silently at the group, which continued to march, with good order and military discipline, along the skyline.

'They aren't our chaps at all,' he announced at last. 'They're Turks!'

'What!' I shouted, focusing my glasses.

He was right. There, about fifteen hundred yards away, going steadily, left right, left right, along the *bund*, was a squad of unmistakable Turks, and, between them and us, the platoon of 'A' Company marched happily along parallel to them. Neither party seemed to be taking the slightest notice of the other; there was a sort of 'too proud to fight' atmosphere about the whole thing. Indeed, the battle of Um-ul-Baqq was beginning in the rather fantastic and ludicrous manner that it maintained to the end. Still, it was all wrong, I felt. Something had to be done about it. Just as we were agitatedly discussing whether a Lewis gun could reach the Turks without hitting our own men, the little party on the *bund* suddenly vanished. I suppose they had spotted us, and as one man, with a gasp of horror, leapt off the top of the embankment.

Bateman sent a runner to warn the platoon commander of his dangerous neighbours and to tell him to keep his eyes a bit wider open. Then for the next five minutes all was peace as we walked steadily on, until we drew almost level with the nearest corner of the palm grove, a black rectangle about three hundred yards wide and a thousand long.

The flanking platoon was still some distance from the edge of the grove when there came a straggling *plick-plock*, *plick-plock* of Mauser fire. With astonishing unanimity the line of scouts sank into the ground as if pulled by one string. The sections shook out and began to double, little black figures against the brown earth, with spurts of dust here and there among them. No one seemed to fall, however, and they soon reached the scouts, where they too dropped into an almost invisible fold in the ground.

Meanwhile I had sat still on my horse while the rest of my force moved stolidly forward, not without some nervous glances towards the dark line of trees, now just on our flank and about six hundred yards away. Through my glasses I could see the 'A' Company platoon, in a ragged line, firing at the corner of the grove; of the enemy there was no sign, except the noise of their rifles and the strike of bullets. It looked to me as if that platoon had given up all idea of advancing, and I did not blame them. I followed the line of trees and, about half-way down it, caught the twinkle of sun on metal. Twenty or thirty little greyish figures were scurrying about behind a small bank on the edge of the palms. As I watched there came the unmistakable slow *knock, knock, knock* of a Turkish machine-gun and the giant whip-cracks of bullets close overhead.

Now we had had some experience of trying to walk over the plains of Mesopotamia—like billiard tables in all but greenness—with that *knock, knock, knock, crack, crack, crack* in our ears, and to most of us who survived there was, I fear, only one reaction to the sound—we lay down. Unfortunately I was on a horse. I have often felt conspicuous on a horse—people who ride like me do—but never as conspicuous as I did then. I dismounted in most undignified haste. Private Bronson, my groom, who had followed me on foot, stepped forward and took the reins. I felt a little ashamed as I met the quizzical eyes in his leathery, clean-shaven face—my scramble from the saddle had been so obviously dictated by funk —but he made no comment; only his lantern jaws moved steadily. He had the detestable habit of chewing gum, and never seemed short of the vile stuff; bits of it must have lasted him for weeks.

'Take the horse back,' I said. 'I shan't want him for a bit.'

'Very good, sir.'

Jaws still working, he slung his rifle, and proceeded methodically to shorten the stirrup leathers. Then he unconcernedly swung himself into the saddle and sat looking down at me. A bullet went overhead with an almighty crack. His jaws stopped working for a moment. 'Any messages?' he asked laconically.

Then I realized that if I sent him away I should be left standing alone in the middle of my command with no means of controlling it. This, I felt, was not generalship; I wished I had thought of it before.

'Er . . . er . . . yes . . .' I said.

I wrote a message giving as near as I could the location of the Turkish machine-gun, and telling our 18-pounders and half a section of machine-guns to get on to it, and the other half-section to come forward.

'Show that to Mr. Bowes with "B" Company, then to the M.G. officer and the gunners. Afterwards come back to "A" Company.'

'Very good, sir,' and Bronson cantered away, still chewing, while I hurried to rejoin Bateman.

'The duty of an advance-guard is to advance', but. . . . Truth to tell, I was getting flustered. We could not walk past that machine-gun, and it might be a sticky business turning it out. I pictured the rest of the brigade, then the division, and finally the whole blessed Army piling itself up behind us while we dodged about in front of those beastly palm trees.

I found Bateman perfectly calm and, as usual, slightly bored with the war. It is very galling for a commander to realize that one of his subordinates is a great deal better fitted to do his job than he is himself. But short of handing over, which I had not the moral courage to do, there was nothing to be done about it, so I told Bateman what I had done.

'I thought you'd do that,' he said, 'and I've got it all fixed to advance on the trees as soon as the guns get going.'

Almost as he spoke there was a *Whoosh! Whoosh! Bang! Bang!* and two little white clouds appeared just level with the palm tops and about thirty yards from them. More followed—a most reassuring sight.

'The guns, thank God, the guns,' quoted Bateman. He blew a whistle and gave a signal. 'A' Company rose to its feet and walked briskly towards the trees. Bateman nodded at the shrapnel bursts.

'Old Daddy seems to have got the spot—he can generally hit anything he can see with the naked eye. I hope he remembers to cock his spouts up a bit when we get in. I'll push "A" Company straight up through the trees and winkle those chaps out. I'll keep my H.Q. on the near edge so you'll see how we get on. Cheerio!'

With his thumbs stuck under the braces of his web equipment, Bateman strolled off, his company headquarters extended on each side of him. It was not at all the lady artist's idea of a young officer leading an attack, but Bateman always did go into an attack like that, and somehow he always got there. I found it much more reassuring than any '*Floreat Etona!*' business.

'I want your horse and groom,' I yelled after him.

He waved a hand in acknowledgment. Then once more I found myself standing alone in the middle of Mesopotamia, and once more I realized that there was something wrong with me as a commander.

When Bateman's groom arrived with his horse I felt less lonely but decidedly more conspicuous. However, only a few overs came our way. The firing began to die down. Whether this was due to Daddy's guns, which were firing so rapidly that I wondered if the ex-sergeant-major had remembered such trifles as ammunition expenditure, or to Bateman's steady but nonchalant advance, I do not know. Whatever the reason, the Turks were evidently going. I watched 'A' Company vanish among the dark palm trunks, and it was only an occasional flash of steel on the edge of the grove that showed where Bateman's headquarters was pushing forward. In a few minutes complete peace had descended on the scene. 'B' Company under Bowes, who ought to have been in a sanatorium for consumptives but seemed to prefer Mesopotamia, had arrived. I kept two of his platoons in reserve and sent the rest on to continue the original advance in place of 'A' Company. I was feeling much better now. We were getting on nicely, and I had collected a headquarters of sorts; Bronson had come back with my horse—I still had Bateman's—and from 'B' Company I had seized three runners and my own orderly, Francisco Ferrero.

Francisco was the son of an Italian hairdresser, and in looks he favoured his father, with his big brown eyes, olive skin, and wavy black hair, but his English mother's blood ran strongly enough in his veins to have made him enlist in August 1914. In one breast pocket of his tunic were his scissors, in the other his mouth-organ, and he was an artist with both. From the Persian Gulf to the Caspian the snip, snip of his scissors and the lilt of his mouth-organ never failed us, and I shall remember those cheerful sounds long after more pretentious music has faded from my memory. Good old Francisco! He had a quick wit, an eye for beauty, and a most contagious gift of laughter. On the march he was tireless, in action dependable to the last. For all his foreign name no stouter British soldier than Francisco Ferrero ever humped a pack. Even the saturnine Bronson allowed a wintry smile to flit across his working features as Francisco described, no doubt libellously, how the stretcher-bearers had burrowed mole-like into the sand at the first shot.

We were all on the move again. The guns had limbered up and were following at a respectful distance. It really looked as if the Turks had cleared out for good. Then suddenly, inside the palm grove, there broke out a most awe-inspiring racket—rapid rifle fire, the drumming of Lewis guns, and the *knock, knock, knock* of our old friend the Turkish machine-gun. Evidently Bateman had bumped into something pretty formidable. The din died down, but there was still a good deal of shooting going on among the palms. 'B' Company in front had halted, under fire again from the edge of the grove. I sent one of the grooms off at a gallop to Bateman to find out what was happening. In a few minutes he was back.

'Mr. Bateman says, sir, he's held up by Turks behind a wall all across the garden. They've loopholed it and he can't rush it.'

On the spur of the moment, without, I am afraid, any very clear idea of what I meant to do, I took my two reserve platoons and doubled off to Bateman. When, rather puffed, we reached him, he told me he had just got a report from his left that the wall did not seem to be held on the river bank.

'All right,' I said, 'I'll try and get through there,' and once more we panted off through the tall bare palm stems. The ground was all cut up with ditches taking to water the tree roots, and we soon lost sight of 'A' Company. When I caught the gleam of the river through the trees I turned right and advanced cautiously, feeling for that wall.

Sure enough, there it was, a mud-built wall about eight feet high, running up from the river. Opposite us there were no loopholes and nothing to show it was occupied, though to our right we could still hear firing. We edged cautiously forward from tree to tree, expecting every minute to feel the blast of rifles in our faces, but there came neither sound nor movement. A small wooden door, rough and unpainted, showed in the blank face of the wall. Revolver in hand but heart in mouth, I crept towards it, Francisco Ferrero close at my heels. We reached the door together, and paused. There was a crack in the weather-beaten panel, and I placed my eye to it, leaning with one hand against the door. At that gentle pressure it swung slowly open.

In one spring Francisco and I were back under cover at each side of the opening, but no bullet cracked through. Cautiously our heads came forward again, and we squinted round the door-post. The date palms had ended, and we looked into a garden of orange trees. Nothing stirred. All was quiet; even the firing on our right had stopped. But I had no desire to step through that door. My eyes met Francisco's, and I knew he felt the same. We looked again. Then I saw him push forward the safety-catch of his rifle and brace himself for a spring. That shamed me. I could not let him give me a lead—and I leapt. So did Francisco! We jammed ridiculously in the narrow doorway. I damned him, and I rather think he damned me as we struggled wildly, both of us frightened to death. Then we were through. Nothing had happened—yet; but the deserted garden, so silent, so still, seemed full of menace. I took a stealthy step forward, peering through the trees that shut us in, every nerve strained.

Suddenly Francisco seized my arm.

'Look! Look!' he cried.

'Where?' I gasped, my revolver describing agitated circles.

'There!' he pointed.

I looked, my heart pounding, my eyes starting from my head, but I could see nothing. He was pointing straight down an avenue of orange trees. Against the dark glossy foliage the golden globes of fruit stood out, with here and there a splash of waxy blossom, but no foeman lurked in the shadow or peered between the leaves.

'What is it?' I demanded.

'Oh, sir,' answered Francisco rapturously. 'Oh, sir, isn't it *be-autiful!*'

The men came pouring through the door. We extended and began to push through trees planted in long orderly lines. All at once there was a rustling and a crashing ahead of us, and we caught a glimpse of half a dozen nondescript figures in tattered grey uniforms dodging through the trees. With whoops and yells we plunged after them like boys after a rabbit.

We broke out of the trees on their heels into a little irrigated vegetable patch. Under a spatter of wildly aimed bullets the Turks splashed across it, and made for a small two-storeyed house that stood in its centre. They bolted into the lower room, followed closely by a mob of our men, and from within came sounds as of a couple of packs of hounds worrying half a dozen foxes. As I watched, the first wretched Turk shot out, evidently propelled by a lusty boot behind, and stood shivering with his hands above his head. His comrades were following with similar abruptness when I caught a flicker of movement in the top storey. A large,

dirty white flag was thrust out suddenly through a hole in a
shutter, a second followed, and yet a third. Then, incredible as it
seemed, from another window two tiny Union Jacks, such as
children have, fluttered agitatedly.

I suppose the soldiers of some nations would have cheered
wildly at the unexpected sight of their country's flag so dramatically displayed; being English, we laughed. The explanation came
when, in the wake of the somewhat battered Turks, appeared a
little man in a black coat, striped trousers, and yellow boots, who
politely raised a velour homburg and assured me he was 'Ver'
glad you 'ave gome!' This was about the total of the little
Armenian's English, but I gathered that he was the owner of the
garden, had been having a pretty thin time with the Turks, and
was, indeed, as he repeatedly assured us, 'Ver' glad you 'ave gome!'
Where he got his Union Jacks from I couldn't think. While we
were watching the Armenian's antics, Bateman arrived with 'A'
Company, and after sorting ourselves out a bit we went on.

As I followed our advance I could not help feeling there was a
lack of smartness about it. If you have ever tried to peel an orange
and at the same time carry a loaded rifle with a fixed bayonet at
the ready you will understand what I mean. Luckily the Turks
made no attempt to hold any of the other walls that crossed
the garden, and, leaving a trail of orange-peel in true British style,
we passed into date palm groves again. Very abruptly these ceased,
and the realities of a world at war were brought to our attention
by the bullets that smacked into the tree trunks. With a half-
sucked orange in one hand I peered round the fattest date palm I
could find. It was not too cheerful a view. Three hundred yards
of dead flat *putt*, hard, sandy stuff, then the broken edge of a
nullah, and behind that a flat-roofed mud village which I guessed
from my map—it was one of the few things marked on it—was
Um-ul-Baqq. The Turks were holding the *nullah*—not many of
them, but enough to discourage adventures in the open. 'The duty
of an advance-guard is to advance. . . .' I withdrew behind my
Falstaff of a tree and thoughtfully sucked my orange.

Meanwhile the two platoons of 'B' Company and the whole
of 'A' Company worked up to the edge of the palms, and as
oranges were munched to a finish our rifle fire began to kick up
the dust merrily all along the Turkish *nullah*. A couple of Lewis

guns joined in, and we began a good old 'fire fight' that would have rejoiced the heart of a South African veteran. The enemy fire died away, and I passed the word to rush. We rushed.

As we pounded, a wild mob, across the open there came a splutter of musketry from the *nullah*, but first one, then another, then a dozen, then a whole crowd of grey-glad figures went scrambling out on the far side. We hurrooshed after them; our ragged charge became a race. When we were fifty yards from the *nullah* all the Turks were legging it hard for the village. That is, all except one, and he, as luck would have it, was right opposite me. This fellow, whether more stout-hearted or slower-witted than his pals, still hung on. I could see his hand working the bolt, and I was quite sure he was aiming at me. I realized, with a nasty sinking feeling, that this was not at all the place the commander of the show should be in, but it was too late now. I was running as hard as I could, but after about three hundred yards in full equipment that was not very fast. He fired. I yelled with terror. Where the bullet went I do not know; anyway, it did not hit me. I was within a few yards of him now, and I fired my revolver twice at him as I ran. I do not know where those bullets went either, but, thank heaven! his nerve broke at last, and as I tumbled into the *nullah* he was out on the other side. There is nothing like seeing the other fellow run to bring back your courage! I emptied my remaining four shots after him, but all they did was to make him go a little faster.

Francisco Ferrero arrived with a crash beside me. I grabbed his rifle, took a hurried aim at the scurrying Turk, and fired. My first shot hit the ground about five feet in front of the muzzle and went *wheeping* off into the blue; my next *phutted* into the earth about three yards to the left of my man. He slipped his pack as he ran— oranges bounced out of it in all directions.

'Oh, sir! Oh, sir! *Please* let me have a go!' Francisco was dancing up and down beside me. I steadied myself, aimed carefully, and fired. I suppose it is brutal, but I had a feeling of most intense satisfaction as that wretched Turk went spinning down.

Our men lining the *nullah* were now firing rapid or standing up taking pot-shots at the flying Turks as they bolted for the village, but our shooting was rotten, for the men were puffed and wildly excited. A few Turks dropped. I marked where my man had fallen, but most of them covered the three or four hundred yards to shelter in remarkably good time. The ground between us and the village was littered with packs—German pattern, hide-covered, with hair outside—and a good many had been left in the *nullah*, most of them filled with oranges. I looked back. A couple of our fellows were limping into the trees, but I could see none lying. We had got off lightly so far.

Um-ul-Baqq was a fair-sized village made up of the usual mud hovels all thrown higgledy-piggledy together. A nasty place to tackle, especially as it looked as if the Turks meant business; they were firing pretty briskly from all parts of it, and any heads showing in our *nullah* drew unpleasant attention. The chances of another wild rush across the cultivated ground between us and the village were not promising. On the outskirts of the village, nosing about in the rubbish for a few poor tufts of grass, were half a dozen scraggy goats. Bullets whistled over them and smacked into walls around them, but those imperturbable animals continued to graze. Occasionally one of them would raise a head and look at us in a slightly indignant way, but they made it quite clear that our bickerings were no concern of theirs; an attitude not without its admirable aspects and, indeed, one that many worthy people have suggested should be adopted on wider fields than Um-ul-Baqq. Yet a dangerous one, as those poor goats would have found had they been allowed to persist. But they were not. Out of one of the village alleys darted two old Arab women. Their black garments fluttered wildly, their skinny brown arms waved, and we could hear their shrill screams as, regardless of the quite respectable battle we were working up, they rushed to save their flock.

And save them they did.

As soon as our fellows saw they were women they stopped firing, and, to their credit, so did the Turks. Or, perhaps I flatter our enemies; for them, interest may, as it so rarely does, have marched with honour. I rather think it did. Anyway, in spite of exhortations from our side to 'Bring 'em over 'ere, mother', the old hags, still screaming, drove the goats into the village.

We resumed the battle.

Now once more, 'The duty of an advance-guard' . . . but not so easy. Having allowed myself to get swept up into the front like this, I began to realize that we are all wrong to laugh at that accomplished soldier the Duke of Plazo-Toro; the right place to lead an army *is* from behind. Try leading it from where I was and you will realize this. True, I had a company and a half with me, but the guns and machine-guns, which were what we wanted, were God knows where. I was contemplating trying to get back to them and funking that open ground to the trees when, twenty yards down the *nullah*, a flag, signaller's, began to flutter out its dots and dashes. Some of the 'A' Company signallers had joined in the rush and were with us. Through them I got in touch with Bowes, the machine-guns, and old Daddy, and told them to strafe the front of the village as hard as they could from two-twenty-five to two-thirty, when we would up and at it.

At two-twenty-four we were all teed up, and at two-twenty-five to the second there came a heartening *bang, bang, tat-tat-tat* from our right rear. Two 18-pounders and a few machine-guns would not have made much show in France, but in Mesopotamia the smoke of the shell was magnified a hundred times by the dust. All across the front of the village a brown curtain was drawn, not very opaque perhaps, but enough to make accurate shooting by the Turks impossible. At two-thirty the guns stopped, and we went over.

It was a much more orderly charge than the previous one, and this time I followed discreetly behind the second line. The Turks were blinded, and, though bullets spat and hummed viciously among us, we were on them before they knew it. There were scuffles and hide-and-seek round the houses, but in a very short time there were no living Turks but prisoners in the village. The bulk of them were all out on the other side legging it hard for a low line of mounds some four hundred yards away.

A Lewis gun team of 'A' Company was well up, and I joined them as they pushed through the village. They were under Corporal Kelly, six feet of American-Irish, a deserter from the United States Marine Corps, who had arrived in the British infantry via the Merchant Service—another desertion, I fear. I had never met the U.S. Marine Corps, but if the men in it were as good as those who deserted they must have been a pretty useful crowd. We went through at the double and at the far side Kelly heaved the numbers one and two of his team up on to a flat roof, tossed them their gun, and hauled himself up. I scrambled up, too, just in time to see them coming into action.

It was a Lewis gunner's dream. Scuttling across the bare fields in front of us were a couple of hundred Turks. It looked rather like the start of one of those big cross-country races—a target impossible to miss.

'Now, boy,' urged Kelly, 'give 'em a drum! Sock 'em in the pants!'

Nothing loath, the Lewis gunner flicked up his sight, jerked his cocking handle, and let drive. A solitary report was the only result. The gun had jammed. In vain he lugged furiously at the cocking-handle; no cartridge was ejected. Kelly hurled the fumbling gunner aside, dropped to the roof, and like lightning, twisted off the butt and took out the bolt.

'Broken extractor!'

He hooked out the obstinate cartridge-case, and the disgruntled gunner caught it. The corporal fitted another extractor and re-loaded the gun, but it was too late. The last of the Turks was just vanishing. Corporal Kelly and the outraged gunner both sat up and glared at one another.

'Call yourself a Lewis gunner?' snarled Kelly. 'I've spat better Lewis gunners,' and he suited the action to the word.

The gunner looked thoughtfully at the cartridge-case in his hand.

'American made!' he said bitterly. 'It 'ud bust any ruddy extractor!'

I left them bickering and joined Bateman where he had established his headquarters at the back of the village. I collected mine, such as it was, in the same place. Well, here we were in Um-ul-Baqq. What next? Obviously the first thing was to sort out the men a bit; they had been searching the houses and were all over the place. Incidentally they never found the old Arab women or, what was more important, their goats.

While the reorganization was in progress I was getting into proper touch with the other parts of my force. I sent out a patrol to see if it could work along the river bank towards the mounds which the Turks were obviously holding. This patrol drew such heavy fire that I hurriedly recalled it, being quite convinced that the whole Turkish rear-guard was now confronting us in a properly entrenched position, which would require a set-piece attack by at least a brigade. I was confirmed in this by the number of machine-guns they had firing, and by the fact that for the first time that day their artillery began to take a hand. A couple of batteries of 77-millimetre guns opened, not on us, but on the dust clouds that marked our advancing main columns.

Looking back at them I suddenly remembered, with a guilty start, that I had not sent a single message to the colonel. I should be for it when we met! Still, I had something to tell him now, and rather above myself with the achievements of the day, I wrote my one and only message in something of the style of Napoleon addressing the Grande Armée. I remember it began: 'I have carried Um-ul-Baqq at the point of the bayonet'. A very grandiloquent message which, I fear, tailed away a bit at the end, where I pointed out that a further advance without strong reinforcements was out of the question. Just as I had sent it off a very brusque one arrived from the colonel, demanding information, but telling me to stay in the village as the rest of the brigade would come up on the right.

Very pleased with ourselves, 'A' and 'B' Companies settled down in Um-ul-Baqq. Settling down in the Army means first of all having a meal. Our thoughts turned to tea. Luckily we had lots of tea. My excellent quartermaster-sergeant had 'found' a complete chest of tea during an evening stroll in bivouac the night before. We had hurriedly issued the tea at a handful a man and burnt the tell-tale box. Yes, we had plenty of tea, and there was plenty of water in the river fifty yards away, but the Turks were on the opposite bank, and it looked as if we should have to wait for darkness before we could connect the two essentials. However, we called up our section of machine-guns and fairly plastered that bank, until the Turk decided it was too unhealthy, and we got our water.

While all this was going on I got the casualty reports. We had been extraordinarily lucky, only nine men wounded and two killed. One of these was Simpson, a signaller, a first-class fellow; his death, I felt, took the shine out of the day. He had been knocked over in the attack on the village, and I was thinking of him when two 'B' Company stretcher-bearers passed with a wounded Turk. I asked them if they had seen Simpson's body.

'Yes, sir,' one of them answered, ''e were laying on 'is face. We turned 'im over, but 'e were a goner.'

'Stone dead,' confirmed the other sorrowfully. 'So we picked up this Turk instead.'

'You would!' said a voice.

We spun round, and there was Simpson, dusty, dishevelled, and deathly pale, rifle in one hand and neatly rolled signal flag in the other.

'You *would* leave me,' he went on with heavy sarcasm, 'and pick up a lousy Turk! Thought he had more in his ruddy pockets, I suppose!'

A ricochetting bullet had hit one of his pouches, gone through the first clip of cartridges, and embedded itself in the second, luckily without exploding any of them. The effect was very much that of a punch on the solar plexus from Jack Johnson. Simpson took a count of about half an hour. He said he would be all right, but I did not like the look of him and sent him off, protesting, to the field ambulance.

The sight of the wounded Turk, who had been dumped with some prisoners nearby, reminded me of the one I had knocked over with Francisco Ferrero's rifle. I felt a proprietary interest in that unfortunate and, while tea was being got ready, I walked back with the stretcher-bearers to see if we could find him. Behind the village was all dead ground to the enemy, so we strolled in safety. I had marked down the place where my fellow lay, and we found him easily. He was only a youth. My bullet had smashed his leg rather messily below the knee.

One of the stretcher-bearers produced a cut-throat razor and sawed off the blood-stained trouser. Then he put on a dressing, using a discarded bayonet as a splint, and bandaged up the leg. The other stretcher-bearer produced a wide-mouthed water-bottle and held it to the Turk's mouth. He gulped at it, and as he finished, the man who had bandaged him removed his own helmet, extracted from it a rather part-worn cigarette, stuck it in the Turk's mouth, and lit it. The boy automatically drew two or three breaths. He took the cigarette from his lips and looked, first, at it, then at us—and burst into tears. We were dreadfully embarrassed.

The last I saw of the prisoner he was smiling with the tears still on his cheeks, the cigarette in his mouth, as he was borne away by the two British soldiers, one of whom was reassuring him as to his destination by a reiteration of 'No more this war for you! See? Bombay, Johnny, Bombay!'

When I got back I found tea almost ready for me outside a house.

'Why not inside?' I asked Bateman.

'Look!' he said, pointing to the door.

I looked through, and when my eyes were accustomed to the gloom I saw what seemed to be dust on the floor blowing about.

'What's that?'

'Fleas!' said Bateman.

And so it was. I backed out quickly, but not before a dozen or so had pounced on me. I spent the next five minutes slapping and shaking, the invaluable Francisco assisting to track down the more elusive ones. They were the biggest and fiercest specimens of *Pulex irritans* I had ever met. Finally the last and most active of all was rounded up. Francisco held him between finger and thumb.

'Cor, what a whopper!' he said in admiration. 'I'll keep him and teach him to carry my pack!'

On all sides slappings, writhings, and cursings; but although we did not realize it, the fleas had served us well. Suddenly the Turks began to shell our village. The first salvoes crashed through roofs or walls, exploding inside the houses. The shells always pierced one wall before detonating, but never seemed to come through the second. As the fleas had driven everyone outside no one was harmed in spite of the noise and dust. The shelling lasted about ten minutes and then died down. We officers sat with our backs to a house wall having tea. It was rather like a picnic during a shoot, but with cruder food and appliances. We balanced hot mess-tins of tea on our knees and munched bully and biscuit—a very peaceful scene.

Then, without warning, a shell slammed into the roof just above our heads. There was an almighty bang, clouds of dust, chunks of roof sailing in all directions, and the horrid sound of bits of shell slurring past. Cooke, a subaltern of 'B' Company, who was sitting next to me, let out a blood-curdling screech and collapsed. 'My God', I thought. 'I knew the luck wouldn't hold. That's done for poor old Cookie!'

But it had not! He had just been gingerly raising a tin of almost boiling tea to his mouth, when a couple of pounds of mud roof had come *plop* right into it, and he got a pint of scalding tea in his face. That was the last shell they fired at us that day—a good day and one to chuckle over.

As we were fishing the mud out of our tea, the colonel's reply to my bombastic 'I-have-carried-Um-ul-Baqq-at-the-point-of-the-bayonet' message arrived. All he said was: 'How many Turks have you killed?'

Come to think of it, we had not killed many, so perhaps the Official History was about right after all.

II

THE INCORRIGIBLE ROGUE

The police are anxious to get into touch with anyone who saw a black Austin saloon car, number JIQ648, being driven rapidly in a westerly direction away from the scene of a robbery at 63 Rampart Row, S.W.2 at about 9.30 p.m. yesterday. Information should be given as soon as possible to any police station or to New Scotland Yard, telephone Whitehall 1212.

Broadcast Message, B.B.C. News

THE INCORRIGIBLE ROGUE

ONE of the disadvantages of living in London is that you hardly ever see the stars. The real stars are so dimmed by theatre signs advertising the Hollywood variety, by shop windows, street lamps, and a thousand man-made lights, that a glimpse of them is rare. Besides, people in cities do not raise their heads much, and so they cannot expect to see the stars. Yet on that particular night, as I walked through the monotonous Kensington streets, I did raise my eyes and I did see the stars. In the strip of sky, clear after rain, between the tall black houses they shone, calm and tolerant as always. The same stars that I had watched, night after night, four or five years before, as I lay on the hard desert sand. But they had seemed nearer then, when Orion had swung so magnificently close that I felt I had only to raise a hand to tug him by the belt.

Head in air, I turned to cross a deserted square, and promptly learned one reason why star-gazing is not a city pursuit. A saloon car shot round the corner, missed me by inches and, with a screech of brakes, jerked to a standstill against the kerb a few yards ahead. I was angry. I might have been killed; I had been splashed.

As I drew level with the car, a man scrambled out of the driving seat, a great, burly fellow in rough clothes with a cap and a muffler. His back was towards me, but there was a vague familiarity about the broad, rather rounded shoulders and the suggestion of clumsy strength that he gave. He heard my step and swung round like a flash. Then I knew him. There was no mistaking that broad face with its high cheekbones, the small widely spaced eyes, the broken nose and big slit of a mouth. My anger evaporated.

'Why, Chuck!' I exclaimed. His figure relaxed and a half-sheepish smile spread over his ungainly features.

''Ullo!' he said in not too exuberant welcome. We shook hands.

'Funny meeting you,' I went on: 'I was just thinking of old times. I've often wondered what became of you. What have you been doing since the war?'

'Oh, jus' gettin' along like,' he answered non-committally, his eyes wandering over my shoulder, round the top of my head, anywhere but meeting mine—a habit of his I remembered.

'You've got a job now . . . ?' I persisted.

'I'll have to be goin'. Got a date,' he interrupted, jerking his head vaguely towards the other side of the square.

'Half a minute', I protested, but he was already edging away.

'See you some other time—p'raps,' he said.

'But, I say, what about your car?' I called after him. He looked back and grinned.

'Oh, somebody'll come for that,' he said as he turned the corner.

I was hurt. Even if he did not want to tell me much about himself—and I could well believe that—he need not have made it so obvious. He always was an awkward devil, but in his queer way I thought he had liked me. Well, I suppose I had flattered myself. I tried to shrug it off as I resumed my way. I had not taken twenty steps when, for the second time that night, I heard a furiously driven car turn into the square. I stopped and looked round. Regardless of tyres, this too drew up abruptly. Three men, one of them a uniformed police constable, sprang out and clustered round Chuck's deserted car. A large man in plain clothes separated himself from the group and sauntered towards me. He ran a keen eye over me, noting, I hoped, my air of respectability.

'You didn't happen to be hereabouts when that other car arrived?' he suggested.

'Er—yes. It passed me as I was walking through the square.'

'See anybody get out?'

'Yes—a man. Why?'

'Well, as a matter of fact, that's a stolen car and half an hour ago it was used in a smash-and-grab raid. What sort of a man got out? Could you describe him?'

I hesitated a moment.

'Describe him?' I repeated. 'No . . . no, I'm afraid I couldn't do that!'

*   *   *

'Light duty of a clerical nature,' announced the President of the Medical Board.

Not too bad, I thought, as I struggled back into my shirt. 'Light duty of a clerical nature' had a nice leisurely sound about it. I remembered a visit I had paid to a friend in one of the new government departments that were springing up all over London at the end of 1915. He had sat at a large desk dictating letters to an attractive young lady. When she got tired of taking down letters, she poured out tea for us. She did it very charmingly. Decidedly, light duty of a clerical nature might prove an agreeable change after a hectic year as a platoon commander and a rather grim six months in hospital. Alas, after a month in charge of the officers' mess accounts of a reserve battalion, with no more thrilling assistant than an adenoidal 'C' Class clerk, I had revised my opinion. My one idea was to escape from 'light duty of a clerical nature' into something more active.

Reserve battalions were like those reservoirs that haunted the arithmetic of our youth—the sort that were filled by two streams and emptied by one. Flowing in came the recovered men from hospitals and convalescent homes and the new enlistments; out went the drafts to battalions overseas. When the stream of voluntary recruits was reduced to a trickle the only way to restore the intake was by conscription, and this was my chance.

It had been decided to segregate the conscripts into a separate company as they arrived. I happened to be the senior subaltern at the moment and I applied for command of the new company. Rather to my surprise, for I was still nominally on light duty, I got it. The conscripts, about a hundred and twenty of them, duly arrived. They looked very much like any other civilians suddenly pushed into uniform, awkward, bewildered, and slightly sheepish, and I regarded them with some misgiving. After all, they *were* conscripts; I wondered if I should like them.

The young British officer commanding native troops is often asked if he likes his men. An absurd question, for there is only one answer. They are *his* men. Whether they are jet-black, brown, yellow, or *café-au-lait*, the young officer will tell you that his particular fellows possess a combination of military virtues denied to any other race. Good soldiers! He is prepared to back them against the Brigade of Guards itself! And not only does the young officer *say* this, but he most firmly believes it, and that is why, on a thousand battlefields, his men have justified his faith.

In a week I felt like that about my conscripts. I was a certain rise to any remark about one volunteer being worth three pressed men. Slackers? Not a bit of it! They all had good reasons for not joining up. How did I know? I would ask them. And I did.

I had them, one by one, into the company office, without even an N.C.O. to see whether military etiquette was observed. They were quite frank. Most of them *did* have reasons—dependants who would suffer when they went, one-man businesses that would have to shut down. Underlying all the reasons of those who were husbands and fathers was the feeling that the young single men who had escaped into well-paid munitions jobs might have been combed out first.

One man, however, did not plead overruling responsibilities. The first thing I noticed about him as he stepped through the door was that he nearly filled it; even the ill-fitting khaki could not hide the strength of his shoulders and his huge muscled thighs. There was a weather-beaten look about him too which the other men lacked, and he seemed much more sure of himself. As he looked down on me with a strong-featured face, reddened and roughened by exposure, his keen blue eyes, their smallness strongly emphasized by the distance they were set apart, met mine with a glance in which amusement verged on insolence. Then his gaze went wandering off over my head and round the room. I had a feeling that our roles were reversed—that I was the recruit waiting to be interviewed. Almost in self-defence I decided to be as brisk and official as I could.

'Name?' I snapped at him. The suddenly barked question startled him. His eyes swung back to mine; he stiffened.

'Chuck, sir,' he answered crisply. Then his figure relaxed, and he was once more the undrilled conscript. His eyes flickered warily over my face and went on their travels again.

'Christian name,' I went on.

'Richard.'

'Age?'

'Say twenty-five.'

'What d'you mean, *say* twenty-five? Don't you really know how old you are?'

'No.'

'Didn't your parents ever tell you?'

'Never knew 'em.' I felt I was getting out of my depth. Age twenty-five went down in my book, and I tried again.

'What was your job when you were called up?'

''Adn't got one.'

'Unemployed?'

''Sright,' he nodded.

'Well, what was your trade when you were employed?'

''Adn't got one.'

'But how did you get your living? You must have done something?'

'I walked.'

'Walked?'

''Sright.' This was getting beyond me.

'You walked? Where did you walk?'

'The roads,' he said simply.

'Walked the roads? You mean you were . . . a tramp?'

''Sright.'

'Well, there doesn't seem much reason why you couldn't join up. Why didn't you?' His eyes strayed back to mine; he shrugged massive shoulders.

'I knew they'd fetch me as soon as I was really wanted,' he said. Not a bad answer when you come to think it over.

'Ever been in the Army before?' I resumed.

'No'.

'Quite sure?'

'Yes.' I looked at him baffled as he stood there, his great red hands hanging loosely in front of him. Then on one wrist I saw tattoo marks.

'Pull up that sleeve.' Reluctantly he did so and displayed on his forearm the crude design of an unclothed female draped round an anchor.

'Sailor?' I asked.

'Stoker,' he admitted with a slow grin.

'Got your discharge certificate?' He shook his head.

'Tore it up.'

'Why?' I asked.

''Cause I was discharged as "an incorrigible rogue".'

And that was my first meeting with Private Richard Chuck, the Incorrigible Rogue.

The more I saw of my conscripts the better I liked them. They gave no trouble, and, physically, they were undoubtedly a big improvement on their immediate predecessors, the rather pathetic dregs of the voluntary system. Of course there were misfits among them, and Chuck was one. As his platoon sergeant put it: 'That Chuck 'e don't mill in at all. 'E won't play football, 'e won't box —though 'e's a darned sight too ready to fight—and as for work 'e just does what you might call the legal minimum. 'E's that stupid, too, you can't teach 'im nothink, not even 'is left from 'is right. It's my belief 'e's wantin', not right in the 'ead.'

As time went on these reports became more frequent. The men left Chuck to himself as a morose, dangerous fellow, the N.C.O.s disliked him, accusing him of that elusive military crime 'dumb insolence'; his platoon commander urged his discharge as mentally deficient. I was inclined to agree with him.

We had now advanced far enough in our training to introduce the company to the mysteries of the Mills bomb. There is something about a bomb which is foreign to an Englishman's nature. Some nations throw bombs as naturally as we kick footballs, but put a bomb into an unschooled Englishman's hands and all his fingers become thumbs, an ague afflicts his limbs, and his wits desert him. If he does not fumble the beastly thing and drop it smoking at his—and your—feet, he will probably be so anxious to get rid of it that he will hurl it wildly into the shelter trench where his uneasy comrades cower for safety. It is therefore essential that the recruit should be led gently up to the nerve-racking ordeal of throwing his first live bomb; but as I demonstrated to squad after squad the bomb's simple mechanism, I grew more and more tired with each repetition, until I could no longer resist the temptation to stage a little excitement. I fitted a dummy bomb, containing, of course, neither detonator nor explosive, with a live cap and fuse. Then for the twentieth time I began!

'When you pull out the safety-pin you *must* keep your hand on the lever or it will fly off. If it does it will release the striker, which will hit the cap, which will set the fuse burning. Then in five seconds off goes your bomb. So when you pull out the pin *don't* hold the bomb like this!'

I lifted my dummy, jerked out the pin, and let the lever fly off. There was a hiss, and a thin trail of smoke quavered upwards.

For a second, until they realized its meaning, the squad blankly watched that tell-tale smoke. Then in a wild *sauve qui peut* they scattered, some into a near by trench, others, too panic-stricken to remember this refuge, madly across country. I looked round, childishly pleased at my little joke, to find one figure still stolidly planted before me. Private Chuck alone held his ground, placidly regarding me, the smoking bomb, and his fleeing companions with equal nonchalance. This Casabianca act was, I felt, the final proof of mental deficiency—and yet the small eyes that for a moment met mine were perfectly sane and not a little amused.

'Well,' I said, rather piqued, 'why don't you run with the others?' A slow grin passed over Chuck's broad face.

'I reckon if it 'ud been a real bomb you'd 'ave got rid of it fast enough,' he said. Light dawned on me.

'After this, Chuck,' I answered, 'you can give up pretending to be a fool; you won't get your discharge that way!'

He looked at me rather startled, and then began to laugh. He laughed quietly, but his great shoulders shook, and when the squad came creeping back they found us both laughing. They found, too, although they may not have realized it at first, a new Chuck; not by any means the sergeant-major's dream of a soldier, but one who accepted philosophically the irksome restrictions of army life and who, at times, even did a little more than the legal minimum.

Chuck completed his training just about the same time as I was passed fit, and he was in the draft I took to rejoin the battalion in Mesopotamia. We endured the usual horrors of mass sea-sickness as the transport, a big converted cargo liner, rolled through the Bay. Chuck, slinging a hammock and then contemptuously heaving a green-faced soldier into it, was, to me at any rate, one of the few stable things in a revolving and revolting world.

The Mediterranean brought us internal peace, but a keener realization of the danger without. We studded the ship with amateur look-outs, who identified as an enemy submarine everything from a dead mule to a school of porpoises. When Crown and Anchor palled we amused ourselves by sing-songs, and in these we were lucky, for we had on board a draft of a couple of hundred Welsh Territorials bound for India. They sang magnificently as one great choir, and to listen to their Celtic harmonies rising to the calm evening skies while the ship's mast drew lazy arcs across the stars was to realize how and why music can be part of the fabric of a race.

Just after early dinner one evening I was climbing into a bath—not the time one would normally choose, but in a crowded transport junior officers take their baths as they can get them—when, above the generous rush of sea water from the tap, I heard the familiar clanging of bells. Cursing another practice alarm, I wrapped a towel round my middle and pulled on the Burberry that served me as dressing-gown. As I made for my cabin and a lifebelt the alleyways were full of men swarming up to the decks. Suddenly over all the din sounded a dull thud; the gun at our stern was firing. This was no practice alarm. With the lifebelt under my arm I dashed for my boat station. The watertight doors were closing slowly as I leapt through them.

I found my men already fallen in along the rail on the forward deck. They stood in two lines, very silent in their lifebelts, while the deck beneath their bare feet vibrated to the beat of straining engines, and all round them, packed close, crowded the tense ranks of other drafts. An officer told me he had seen the greenish track of a torpedo cross our bows a few minutes before, and our gun was firing rapidly, but the superstructure of the bridge towering above us prevented us from seeing its target. Then, without warning, over the top of the bridge something rustled through the air, cleared our crowded deck, and fell into the sea far ahead with a white splash—the submarine had surfaced and was firing at us. Again and again a shell passed over us, small shells judging from the sound, and aimed at the bridge, but the effect of one of them plunging into the solid mass jammed tight on the foredeck would not bear thinking about.

I looked at the men. They were steady enough, but faces were white and drawn. No one spoke. The uncanny silence was broken only by the *thud*, *thud* of our gun astern, the rush of water past the ship, and that sinister rustle overhead. For minutes we stood with nothing but our imaginations to occupy us, waiting the shell that would find us. All around me I could feel in the crush of men a pent-up emotion struggling for outlet.

Then the Welshmen fallen in beside us began to sing. It was not a case of one or two starting and the others joining in; they began suddenly altogether as one man. They sang 'Nearer My God to Thee', and they sang it just as beautifully as they had on calmer evenings when no shells whispered overhead. I turned and watched them, row after row of pale faces, upturned and absorbed. They stopped as abruptly as they had begun. As an example of steadiness and discipline it was strange and moving, yet somehow the hymn with its melancholy cadences made me think of the sinking of the *Titanic*. I shivered.

Again that horrible rustle, this time so low over our heads that men ducked and the ranks swayed. An uneasy murmur went up from the crowd. Then behind me a solitary voice began suddenly to sing. It was Chuck. Hoarsely and without much regard for tune he roared out the chorus of a pre-war music hall ditty, with the refrain, '*I don't care if the ship goes down, it doesn't belong to me!*' A coarse, silly song, but Chuck put into it such a ring of reckless defiance, of vitality, of humour, that jangled nerves were steadied, imaginations mastered. Some laughed, some joined in. We were ourselves again.

The shelling ceased; we had shaken off our pursuer. For another hour the ship drove through the deepening dusk, while the men sang, and then the bugles blew the 'Dismiss'. As I walked back to my cabin I was cold, and I tried to believe that was why my knees trembled.

Once through the Suez Canal we passed from a world at war into a world seemingly at peace—but if peaceable it was hot. Canvas wind-scoops sprouted like mushrooms all over the ship, but it was only when we circled on our course to defeat the following wind that they sucked down any air to the sweltering troop decks, and when a call came for volunteers to reinforce the stokehold I expected no great rush. I was wrong. The only man in my draft who did not volunteer was Private Chuck. I asked him why.

''Ad some,' he explained briefly.

'Well,' I said, 'this is another of the times you're wanted badly enough to be fetched'. He looked angry for a moment, then shrugged as a shadowy smile drifted across his face.

'Orlright,' he agreed.

I was not sure what that smile meant, and I was even more suspicious when I saw Chuck that evening in earnest conversation with a group of grimy stokers at the entrance to the crews' quarters in the forecastle. Next day, as we clambered down oily steel ladders to the stokehold, I half expected to find him missing, but he was there. A ship's engineer officer received us, and I found myself partnering Chuck at a furnace door, under the bleary but cynical eye of a grizzled old stoker. Immediately above us was a great duct from which a fan beat down air, and I was surprised to find that the stokehold was no hotter and certainly fresher than many other parts of the ship.

The old stoker thrust a great shovel he had already obligingly filled with coal into my hands, and jerked down a lever which opened the furnace door. I found myself staring into the red-yellow heart of a great fire. The heat of it stung my eyes as I heaved the coal at the opening. It was not a very good shot. The ship chose that moment to heave, too. Most of the coal went wide, and it was only Chuck's huge hand on one shoulder that saved me from lurching against the hot iron. The old stoker spat accurately over my other shoulder and the door fell with a clang.

'First footin'!' announced Chuck in a loud voice.

''Sright,' agreed the old man. I looked suspiciously at them.

''Sright,' repeated the stoker. 'Orficers allus pays their fust futtin'.'

I gazed round the stokehold. There seemed an extraordinary number of people in it, and they were all looking at me with expectant and thirsty grins. From them my eyes came back *via* the old stoker, still nodding his grey head and mumbling ''Sright', to Chuck's broad face. Then I knew why he had smiled the day before. I laughed.

'All right,' I said. 'How many of you are there?'

In due course we bumped over the bar at the mouth of the Shatt-al-Arab, and landing at an incredibly confused, congested, and primitive Basra one sweltering afternoon, found ourselves in the British Reinforcements Camp, Indian Expeditionary Force D.

There was something wrong with I.E.F.D.; one could not be a day in the Reinforcements Camp without feeling that. In Gallipoli we had clung precariously to a few miles of shell-swept beaches; we knew we were in an almost impossible tactical position, yet we were cheerful. In France we knew, if we were infantrymen, that it was only a question of time before we stopped something in one of the offensives that were always going to end the war but only succeeded in making it more unpleasant; yet we were cheerful. In Mesopotamia, very definitely, we were *not* cheerful. The climate played its part and the humid summer heat in the fly-infested tents was almost unbearable. Comforts and amusements there seemed none. Rations were poor in quality, unsuited to the time of year, and deadly in their monotony. Bully-beef—I can still hear the sickly *plop* with which, half liquid, it oozed from the tin—and biscuits, unearthed from some long-forgotten surplus of the South African War, washed down by over-chlorinated water, were our staple food. It seemed to us that I.E.F.D. was a dump for everything that was too old, too worn out, or too bad to be used elsewhere. Even the ammunition we loaded into barges for the front was labelled: 'Made in U.S.A. To be used for practice only'.

All this men could have endured, and still have mustered a grin, but Kut had fallen—fallen in spite of those repeated, desperately gallant efforts that had bled I.E.F.D. white. Its shattered units were exhausted in body and soul. Failure lay heavy on them. A campaign that had once been carried forward on a wave of optimism was now sunk in stagnant despondency. In Mesopotamia in that summer of 1916 men felt they were far, very far from home, forgotten of their friends and deserted by God.

The only hope was to get up the line. It is at the base that extremes of despair and optimism prevail; with the battalion, I knew, things would be better. So when orders came to proceed up-river and we marched out of camp to embark, the whole draft was heartily glad to see the last of Basra.

But the gladness rather fell from us as we marched on and on, while the sun got hotter and hotter and the road dustier and dustier. Eventually we reached our embarkation point, a crude wharf of roughly-shaped palm logs, alongside which were tied two big iron barges. An immaculate lieutenant of the Royal Indian Marine met us.

'Your barges,' he said with a flourish, as if inviting me to take over a couple of *Mauretanias*.

I looked round. The two rust-stained barges, with their dirty awnings; the deserted wharf; the muddy banks running up to the black palm groves and the dull river flowing sullenly past were all the melancholy prospect.

'When do we sail?' I asked. The lieutenant hesitated.

'Well,' he said at last, 'you ought to sail now, but the "P" boat that's due to tow you isn't here yet.'

'Where is she?'

'There,' he answered, pointing across the wide stretch of the Shatt-al-Arab.

I followed his arm and could see, apparently buried among the palm trees on the opposite bank, a small paddle-steamer.

'What's she doing there? Picking dates?' The lieutenant seemed pained at my flippancy.

'She's aground,' he explained, 'but I expect they'll get her off this afternoon. I hope you'll be comfortable.'

'I hope so,' I said, as he climbed down into a motor-boat and chugged away.

By three o'clock that afternoon I had given up the attempt to make the men comfortable—I was concentrating on keeping them alive. The iron deck of a barge under a single awning in the fantastic temperature of a Mesopotamian summer is about as near hell as one can get this side of the Styx—and our 'P' boat was as firmly embedded in the palms as ever. No relief was to be expected from there. I searched our bank. It seemed completely deserted until I caught a glimpse of tents among the trees about half a mile downstream towards Basra. This looked more hopeful. I decided to explore.

I found a couple of large E.P. tents inside a barbed-wire enclosure that was stacked with crates, boxes, sacks and supplies of all kinds. I passed an Indian sentry at the gate and made for one of the tents. Inside, seated at a packing-case fitted roughly as a desk, was a lieutenant-colonel of the Supply and Transport Corps. He was a tall, cadaverous, yellow-faced man with a bristling moustache. He looked very fierce and military—officers who dealt with bully-beef and biscuit in the back areas so often did— and he gave short shrift to my timid suggestion that his dump might possibly provide something in the way of additional awnings or tents for us. No, his Supply Depot contained nothing but supplies. Then, perhaps, a little something extra in the way of rations . . . ? I was informed that his supplies were not for issue to any casual subaltern who cared to ask for them, and, if my detachment had not got everything that was necessary for its comfort, it was because either:

(a) I was incompetent,

(b) The staff at the Reinforcement Camp was incompetent, or

(c) A combination of (a) and (b).

I gathered he rather favoured the first alternative. He ended with the final warning: 'And don't let your fellows come hanging round here. The British soldier is the biggest thief in Asia and his officers encourage him.'

It is not a very profitable pastime for subalterns to quarrel with lieutenant-colonels, so I swallowed all this as best I could; besides, I wanted to use the field telephone on his packing-case desk. He could hardly refuse the request, and after some difficulty I got through to the Reinforcement Camp. To my suggestion that I should march my detachment back to the camp and remain there until the 'P' boat tore itself away from its sylvan retreat, I received a peremptory order to remain where we were, for we should certainly sail next morning. The only satisfaction I got was the promise of a couple of bullock *tongas* to take away my sick, and authority to draw rations from the colonel's supply depot.

We did not sail in the morning; in fact we spent two more infernal nights on those moored barges. We had, however, one pleasant surprise. On the evening of the second day our rations, which up to then had been limited strictly to the regulation bully, biscuit, dried vegetables—horrible things—tea and sugar, were suddenly supplemented by a liberal issue of tinned fruit. As I squatted on my valise, making a leisurely choice between pineapple and peaches, I thought of the kind heart that S. and T. colonel must hide beneath his fierce exterior. Next morning when we all breakfasted off first-class bacon, followed by admirable Australian quince jam, while tinned milk flowed in streams, and every man seemed to have a handful of cigarettes, I meditated on how one could be misled by first impressions.

I will not deny that certain suspicions did flit across my mind. There was a tinge of apprehension on the mahogany face of my acting quartermaster-sergeant when I suggested it would be a graceful act of courtesy if he would accompany me to thank the good colonel for his generosity. Well, well; perhaps the colonel was one of those splendid fellows who rejoiced in doing good by stealth and thanks might be embarrassing—most embarrassing.

On the last afternoon of our stay another subaltern and I were standing in the stern of a barge, clad only in our topis, heaving buckets of tepid water over one another, when an agitated quartermaster-sergeant interrupted our desperate attempt to avert heat-stroke.

'They've caught 'im, sir!' he panted, as if announcing the fall of a second Kut.

'Caught who?'

'Chuck, sir!'

I groped for a pair of shorts.

'Who's caught him and why?' I demanded.

'The colonel at the dump, sir. Says Chuck's been pinchin' 'is comforts, sir. There's a warrant officer and a gang of natives come to search the barges, sir.'

'Search the barges?'

'Yes, sir, to see if any of the stuff's 'idden.'

One look at my sergeant's face told me what to expect if the search took place.

'How long do you want?' I asked.

''Arf an hour, sir,' he answered hopefully.

With as much dignity as I could muster I walked to the gangway and confronted the warrant officer, who informed me with the strained politeness of a hot and angry man that his colonel had sent him to search the barges. With the utmost indignation I spurned the idea that any unauthorized supplies could be concealed on my barges. Did he think my men were thieves? He made it quite clear that he did. I shifted my ground. What authority had he? No written authority! I could not think of permitting a search without written authority until I had seen the colonel. We would go back to the colonel.

I dressed, and we went to the supply depot. It was in an uproar. Indian *babus* and British N.C.O.s were feverishly checking stores in all directions, while from the office tent came roars of rage as each fresh discrepancy was reported. I entered in some trepidation to be greeted by a bellow.

'Do you know how much those Birmingham burglars of yours have looted from my hospital comforts? Look at this!'

He thrust a list under my nose, item after item: condensed milk, tinned fruit, cigarettes, jam.

'But—but how do you know *my* men have taken all this, sir?' I gasped.

'Caught 'em! Caught 'em in the act! Bring that hulking great lout who said he was in charge!'

Chuck, seemingly quite unmoved, and if anything slightly amused by the uproar, was marched in between two British sergeants.

'That's the feller!' exploded the colonel, stabbing a denunciatory pencil at Chuck. 'Caught him myself, marching out as bold as brass with a fatigue party of your robbers and a case of lump sugar—the only lump sugar in Mesopotamia! Lifting it under my very nose! Said he'd picked it up by mistake with the other rations, blast his impudence!'

Chuck stood there stolidly, his jaws moving slowly as he chewed gum—more hospital comforts, I feared. His eyes roamed over the tent, but as they passed mine they threw me a glance of bored resignation.

'He'll be court-martialled,' continued the colonel, 'and'—he glared at me—'you'll be lucky if he's the only one that's court-martialled! Now I'm going to search those barges of yours.'

Chuck grinned ruefully as I passed and I caught a whisper of, 'It's a fair cop, all right.' I was afraid it was. We left him chewing philosophically while he and his escort awaited the arrival of the provost-marshal's police.

The colonel, to give him his due, searched those barges thoroughly. He even had the hatches off and delved among the sacks of *atta* that formed the cargo. He and his men grew hotter, dustier, and more furious, but not an empty condensed milk tin, not the label of a preserved pineapple could they find. He turned out the men's kits, he rummaged in the cooks' galley; he even searched the sick-bay we had rigged up in the bows for the sick awaiting removal by bullock *tonga*.

It was empty, except for one man, who lay stretched out flat on his blankets, under a mosquito-net. The colonel glared through the net at the wretched man who with closed eyes was breathing heavily.

'Suspected cholera!' the quartermaster-sergeant whispered hoarsely.

The sick man groaned and clasped his stomach. I thought his complexion was rather good for a cholera case, but then I am no clinical expert. Nor was the colonel. He called off his men, and, breathing threats, left us.

That evening we sailed. After much chuffing and chugging, to the accompaniment of a great deal of yelling in good Glasgow Scots and bad British Hindustani, a squat little tug had hauled our steamer out of the palm grove. We were lashed, a barge on each side, and staggered off up-river. But we left Chuck behind us, and I was thinking, rather sadly and not without some prickings of conscience, that we should miss him, especially at mealtimes, when the quartermaster-sergeant interrupted my gentle melancholy.

'Will you 'ave peaches or pineapple for dinner, sir?'

'Good lord, Quartermaster-Sergeant, I thought you'd chucked it all overboard?' I gasped.

'So we did, sir,' he grinned 'But we tied a rope to it with a bit of wood for a float, and when the colonel 'ad gone we pulled it up again. Some of the labels 've come off the tins, but that's all.'

'What about the cigarettes; they weren't in tins?'

'Oh, that chap in the sick-bay, 'e lay on 'em!'

We found the battalion out of the line, resting. Resting in Mesopotamia meant that, instead of sitting in trenches dug in the desert, one sat in tents in the same desert. It was just as hot, just as uncomfortable, just as depressing, and more monotonous. But it was something to be back with the battalion again and to find myself commanding my old company.

I still missed Chuck. I had come to look for his clumsy figure on parade and to catch the understanding twinkle in his wandering eye, but no news of him reached us and we pictured him sweating out the sentence of his court-martial in some detention camp. The popular conception of a court-martial is half a dozen blood-thirsty old Colonel Blimps, who take it for granted that anyone brought before them is guilty—damme, sir, would he be here if he hadn't done *something?*—and who at intervals chant in unison, 'Maximum penalty—death!' In reality courts-martial are almost invariably composed of nervous officers, feverishly consulting their manuals; so anxious to avoid a miscarriage of justice that they are, at times, ready to allow the accused any loophole of escape. Even if they do steel themselves to passing a sentence, they are quite prepared to find it quashed because they have forgotten to mark something 'A' and attach it to the proceedings.

Still, even a court-martial could hardly acquit Chuck, and we were astonished when one day he joined us, without a stain, or at least any more stains, on his conduct sheet.

'Acquitted? But, dash it all, the colonel caught you red-handed, carting off his sugar!' I protested as soon as I got him alone.

''Sright,' he grinned, 'and 'e weren't 'arf wild, that colonel! Wanted me charged with pinchin' a list of things as long as your arm.'

'Well, you had pinched 'em, hadn't you?'

'Oh, I'd pinched 'em orl right. Easy. You only 'ad to march up in fours like you was a proper ration party and the Indian sentries 'ud let you in. The British N.C.O.s always slept of an afternoon, lazy 'ogs, and so we could take what we liked. 'Orspital comforts mostly—tinned fruit, milk, you know.'

'I know!' I agreed guiltily.

'But at the court-martial they told the old colonel 'e 'adn't any evidence I'd pinched anythin' except the sugar. No more 'e 'ad!'

'And what about the sugar?'

'Well,' Chuck thoughtfully rubbed his nose, 'that was a bit orkard. But "Cube Sugar" was written on the case, and I said I wouldn't steal sugar. Why should I? We get sugar as a ration. If I'd been stealing I'd 'ave taken tinned fruit or somethin' not in the ration.'

'And they believed you?'

'Must 'ave.'

'But tell me, Chuck, why *did* you take sugar?'

'I thought it was tinned fruit.'

'But it had "Cube Sugar" written on it.'

'Ah,' said Chuck, 'but *I can't read.*'

It seemed as if Chuck brought luck. No sooner had he rejoined than things began to improve. Rations, comforts, replacements of worn-out equipment arrived on a scale previously unheard of; new steamers appeared on the river; convoys of Ford vans rattled across the desert. The shock of the fall of Kut had galvanized Whitehall and Simla into an interest in our sideshow. Maude was in charge, and there was not a man in the Force who did not feel the renewed energy and hope that were vitalizing the whole army. To watch an army recovering its morale is enthralling; to feel the process working within oneself is an unforgettable experience.

The temptation to supplement our rations by unorthodox means grew less, but habit dies hard, or perhaps with Chuck it was nature, not habit. Our weekly issue of meat on hoof would mysteriously increase in numbers during the night, and bitter lamentations would rise from neighbouring units. There was, too, the painful incident of the corps commander's private stores, unloaded by a fatigue party which had included Private Chuck. But suspicion alone will not avail a lieutenant-general against even a private; and besides, the corps commander was so rude, even for a corps commander, about the whole affair that we hardly felt it necessary to inquire too closely into the origin of the delectable tinned *hors-d'oeuvres* that lent such welcome variety to our simple fare.

After his encounter with the corps commander, Chuck very wisely avoided senior officers, and it was some time before he again brought himself to the notice of Higher Authority. The war was in full blast again, but for the moment we were enjoying a comparatively quiet spell of trench warfare between attacks on the formidable Turkish positions round Kut. Three hundred yards separated us from the Turkish trenches, and the usual struggle to dominate no-man's-land was going on between patrols at night and snipers by day. Chuck had proved himself an exceptionally fine shot, and spent his days curled up in a cunningly hidden lair just behind our trench bumping off unsuspecting Turks. A slight rise in the ground gave him a view over the enemy lines, but he could neither see into our trench nor be seen from it, although he was within easy speaking distance.

At this time our brigadier, a somewhat anxious officer, was

notorious among the troops for his constant warnings, repeated and groundless alarms, and sudden orders to stand-to against attacks that never materialized. One morning my company headquarters was rung up by the adjutant, who asked me if I had noticed the enemy cutting lanes through their barbed wire just after dawn. I said I had not; had anybody? Yes, the brigadier himself had, and was convinced it portended imminent attack. I suggested that at the distance brigade headquarters was from the enemy the light must have played tricks, and the brigadier's well-known imagination done the rest. The adjutant agreed: we cursed senior officers who would not leave us in peace to get on with the war, and I went to my breakfast.

I had hardly begun it before I was hurriedly called to the head of a communication trench to meet an imposing procession. First came my colonel, who, I suspected from his expression of suppressed fury, had been interrupted at *his* breakfast; then the tall bent form and eager face of our brigadier, followed by the staff captain, who threw me a friendly wink over his general's shoulder. A straggle of orderlies brought up the rear. The brigadier acknowledged my salute and stalked majestically to the fire-step. Taking off his *topi*, he peered over the sandbags. The colonel, the staff captain, the orderlies and I followed suit. The two sentries in the bay were crowded out, and resigned it to us.

As I knew, the Turkish wire was uncut—not the sign of a lane. Nothing daunted, however, the brigadier waved aside the question of lanes, but persisted that at dawn he had seen, with his own eyes through field-glasses, Turks working on their wire under our very noses. It was no use my saying we had had patrols up to the wire just before dawn; that from the first glimmer of light until now the wire had been under observation. He had seen Turks working there that morning. I called up the men who had been on sentry; they had seen no Turks. The brigadier was not convinced.

'I've had a sniper up there, sir, since before dawn. He would certainly see any movement on the Turkish wire,' I said in a last effort to settle the matter.

'Well, ask him!' snapped the brigadier.

'Chuck!' I shouted.

''Ullo,' came back the answer.

'Did you see any Turks working on their wire just after dawn this morning?'

'No; they wouldn't be such ruddy fools!'

'But the brigadier says he saw them himself.'

'The brigadier!' came the answer in tones of ineffable contempt. 'The brigadier's got Turks on 'is flickin' eye-lashes!'

There was nothing more to be said. In frigid silence the procession moved on.

Trench warfare when it is not the most terrifying is the most monotonous form of warfare. In the intervals between attacks we spent our time shovelling the sandy soil of Mesopotamia into bags, and it was this interminable shifting of what he called 'dirt' that proved Chuck's undoing.

One night he was digging himself a sniper's post; being something of an expert at the job he liked to design and build his own. Every shovelful of earth went into a sandbag, and when the sandbag was full Chuck carried it down the communication trench to empty it where the fresh earth would not betray his position. Along came Corporal Galbally, an ex-elementary schoolteacher, a precise, conscientious little man, a shade over-mindful of the dignity that should hedge a non-commissioned officer and a schoolmaster. The corporal, noting the number of man-hours Chuck expanded in removing the earth sandbag by sandbag, bethought him that the process should be speeded up.

'You're wasting time, carrying all that earth away,' he said, shortly. 'Scatter it around. It'll be dry by morning and won't show.'

'Sez you!' responded the sweating Chuck, resting on his spade.

'Don't talk like that to a non-commissioned officer,' snapped Galbally, 'or you'll find yourself in trouble!'

'Look,' said Chuck, his anger rising, 'I've got to get into that 'ole, not you. I'm the judge of what sort of trouble I'd be in to-morrow with all that flippin' fresh earth around me—a flippin' bulls-eye I'd be. Buzz off, you little so and so, and let me get on with the job!'

'You're under arrest for using insulting and insubordinate language to your superior officer,' announced the corporal, standing up bravely to the now furious Chuck.

'Superior officer? Aw, 'ell, you little black bastard!' said Chuck, and punched him on the jaw.

I attended the court-martial. My sympathy went out to poor Corporal Galbally, a most conscientious man with the highest conceptions of duty, but such a nagging voice. The scales, not perhaps of justice but of inclination in my mind, dipped however towards Chuck, when he was asked by the prosecutor, 'Why did you call the corporal "a black bastard",' and replied, 'I can't think! He's not *black*!' But this time there was no loophole of escape, and Chuck came back to us from the court-martial under a suspended sentence of six years' imprisonment for, when on active service, striking his superior officer in the execution of his duty.

These suspended sentences were unsatisfactory things, introduced to prevent men from committing offences in order deliberately to exchange the hardships and dangers of active service for the not much greater hardships and the safety of prison. The men rejoined their units under the threat of having to serve their sentences after the war, unless by exemplary conduct they earned remission. Usually a suspended sentence had little effect on a man; it was a waste of time, especially for an infantryman, to bother about what was going to happen *after* the war.

Chuck took his indifferently enough; he became a shade more morose and quick-tempered—N.C.O.s were more careful in their dealings with him—and took to grousing a good deal. This was not very serious; all good soldiers grouse, and Chuck had a way of giving his bitterest and most profane grouses a picturesque turn that took away their sting.

Immediately we had retaken Kut, we pelted so hard after the bolting Turk that, while we never caught him, we did outstrip our supplies, and received, instead of our bully and biscuit, the only rations available, those of the Indian troops alongside us. Private Chuck, muttering to himself, regarded the heaps of strange foodstuffs piled up on the river bank for issue to the company. He filled one great hand with *atta*, the rough Indian flour, and the other with a mixture of the grain, *gur*, turmeric, and what-not dear to the sepoy's stomach.

'Fourteen flickin' miles and an empty belly yesterday,' he growled; 'twenty-two flickin' miles and a flickin' battle today!

They marches us like buckin' mules; they loads us like buckin' mules; and now'—he raised his full hands to an outraged heaven—'now, by cripes, they *feeds* us like buckin' mules!'

However, whether 'they' fed us like mules or not, we took Baghdad. It was an extraordinary feeling to find oneself there. For a year Baghdad had been for us the Unattainable City, a mirage on the distant horizon. And now a sudden rush and it was ours. The slackness that follows achievement, the physical and mental reaction after prolonged striving, descended momentarily on us. There seemed no more to be done; there was an unreality about everything as we bivouacked beyond the city and looked wonderingly about us.

Through the evening dust haze I caught the gleam of a blue-tiled dome above date-palms. Forgetful of everything but curiosity, I wandered towards it, and found myself on the outskirts of a large village. The Arabs streamed out to greet me in the most friendly way. They patted me on the back, they made signs inviting me to enter their village, they urged me forward, in every way demonstrating their delight at my arrival. My chest, under its sweat-stained shirt, swelled. This was the sort of thing I had read about, but never expected to see—the liberated populace welcoming the Conquering Hero! I strode confidently forward to increasing applause.

Suddenly it dawned upon me that a score of energetic brown gentlemen were all trying at the tops of their voices to tell me the same thing, all continually pointing in one direction. Their excitement increased. So did the closeness with which they hemmed me in, the speed with which they swept me along. I grew uneasy. There was rather too much urgency about all this. I felt myself exchanging the role of Conquering Hero for that of Unwilling Captive! A grubby little boy in a dirty nightshirt squirmed through the mass.

'Good-night, Tommy,' he said affably in American.

'Good-night—I mean, good evening. You speak English?'

He nodded.

'Sure.'

'Well, what are these fellows saying?'

'They say—Turks!'

'Turks! Where?'

'Right here!'

'How many?'

He shrugged indifferently.

'Twenty, thirty,' he hazarded, and added with relish: 'You fight them!'

'Here, I say!' I protested. 'Stop!'

But it was no use; the mob bore me on. Without warning it melted away and I found myself standing alone in the mouth of a lane opening into a small square. The space in front of me was empty, the booths surrounding it deserted. Only in one, an Arab coffee shop immediately opposite me, did I detect a sign of movement. There, through a rough barricade, I saw a glint of steel; half a dozen rifles were covering the square.

I dodged quickly into a doorway and stood there sweating gently. The silence of expectation had fallen on my once vociferous allies; a hundred eyes watched me from sheltering doors and windows. I was conscious, too, of eyes behind those rifle barrels across the square. The noble exhilaration of a Conquering Hero had evaporated completely; all I wanted to do was to bolt back to camp for help, but I doubted if my brown friends would let me.

I had just decided to run for it, when, above the buzz of voices that was beginning to rise again in every alley, I heard drawing nearer a rumbling metallic sound—*jangle, jangle, bump, jangle, jangle, bump*. It was a sound heard often enough over Flanders *pavé*, on Gallipoli beaches, along Frontier tracks, in East African jungles, in a dozen odd corners of the world at war—the unmistakable rumbling rattle of an Indian Army transport cart. Some unsuspecting native *drabi* was driving his cart right up to those threatening rifles.

Sure enough, as I watched, into the square from my right debouched a pair of mules, and clattering behind them the familiar two-wheeled cart. Seated nonchalantly on the board that served as driving-seat, a rifle slung over his shoulder, was not an Indian *drabi*, but a British soldier.

'Get back!' I yelled, showing as much of myself as I dared. The soldier pulled up his mules and looked towards me. It was Chuck.

'Get back, you idiot!' I shouted again.

'Why?' he roared back.

'Turks!' I shrieked, pointing.

Chuck turned deliberately and looked at the barricade. Then he stood up in the cart so that he could see over the top.

'Oi, you!' be bellowed, with a sweep of his arm. 'Come out of it! *Jaldi, imshi, idarao!*'

A dirty white rag fluttered over the barricade. A swarthy, bearded man in bedraggled khaki stepped out with his hands above his head. Another followed him, another, and another. I walked across and joined Chuck as he clambered down from his cart and unslung his rifle.

'My God, Chuck,' I said, 'you took a risk!'

'Risk! With them?' He jerked a contemptuous thumb at the increasing group of ragged prisoners. 'All they was waitin' for was to surrender to the first white man they saw—these lousy Arabs was after 'em!'

He slammed the butt of his rifle hard into the ribs of an Arab who was prancing round the wretched Turks brandishing a murderously curved knife. This gentleman and his friends fell back to a respectful distance.

'Rifles in there, Johnny,' said Chuck to the Turkish N.C.O.

Their rifles clattered on to the iron slats of the cart, and we counted our bag. There were ten Turks in all, two of them in dirty blood-stained bandages, too weak to walk. These went into the cart after the rifles.

Chuck climbed back on to the seat; the prisoners formed up. The Turkish N.C.O. saluted me.

'March!' I ordered.

'*Chelo! Imshi!*' translated Chuck, and the procession moved off amid the mingling of cheers for us, and curses for the prisoners.

'Chuck,' I called out, 'how did you get that cart?'

'Borrowed it.'

'And what were you doing with it?'

'Scroungin',' he answered expressively.

I looked into the cart. One of the wounded Turks was reposing on a sticky mass of dates, the other on a sack half-full of oranges; a couple of fowls with hastily wrung necks were in a corner.

But the campaign was not over with the capture of Baghdad. Within a few days we were off again, marching north, and it was not long before we found ourselves launched in another of those frontal assaults on an entrenched enemy so typical of the first World War. On whatever front these attacks took place they were, at least for the infantry, uniformly uninspiring and unbelievably bloody. The only difference in Mesopotamia was that there was less cover than elsewhere, the distances to be crossed under fire longer, and the artillery support less.

In long thin lines we plodded forward across a plain, flat and bare as a tabletop. My company advanced, steadily but wearily, with two platoons extended in the front line and two in the second, with my headquarters, a little knot of men, centrally between them. Two thousand yards away, glimpsed now and then through the smoke and dust of a bombardment that was the best our one and only artillery regiment could do for us, stretched the enemy position.

The lines of my company were continued far to the left and right where the other battalions of the brigade moved forward too. Soon, here and there, a man fell or started to hobble back, but the long khaki lines went doggedly on. As we drew closer to the enemy the whining of bullets overhead changed to sharp claps at more and more frequent intervals in our ears; shells began to crump among us, not as yet doing very much harm; the lines became more unevenly spaced. We began to walk a little faster.

Ahead of me, I saw one of my leading platoon commanders, a fine young Australian, stumble to his knees. I hurried forward; he was sitting on the ground, face towards me. I knelt beside him for a moment, my hand on his shoulder.

'Where are you hit?' I asked him. He looked at me wonderingly.

'I don't know,' he said. 'In the body I think.' And then he was dead. I lowered him to the ground.

As I rejoined my headquarters, Chuck, whom I had attached to myself as an extra runner so that I could keep an eye on him, jerked his head with a question towards where the platoon commander lay.

'Dead,' I answered.

'Pity, 'e was a good bloke,' said Chuck—the soldier's requiem for a comrade.

Our bombardment suddenly stopped. The dust curtain drifted up into the air, and there about a hundred yards away across our front stretched a shattered wire entanglement and behind it a line of newly turned earth, the enemy parapet. At that moment we must for the first time have become fully visible to the Turkish gunners. With a horrible slurring screech there slammed down on us a slanting blizzard of steel. Shrapnel shells burst in salvos twenty feet in the air ahead of us and hurled their heavy bullets in our faces, blasting whole sections from our lines. Men ducked their heads as they cringed against the storm. Many fell—I lost more than half my company in the next two minutes, only one officer remained alive and unwounded—some stopped dazed, a few turned back. The lines hesitated, wavered, in a moment they would have broken in rout. I ran forward shouting to the leading platoons to get on, but it was not I who rallied them. In a voice like the last trumpet, Chuck at my side roared, 'Heads up the the Warwicks! Show the —— yer cap-badges!'

Even in that pandemonium a few men heard him as his great form came bullocking through them. They had no cap-badges for we wore Wolseley helmets, but they heard the only appeal that could have reached them—to their Regiment, the last hold of the British soldier when all else has gone. The half dozen around Chuck heard, their heads came up, they lurched on again. Other men feeling them move came too; in a moment the whole line was running forward. We cursed the wire as it tore at us, but we were through, looking down on brown faces, grey uniforms, raised hands and dirty white rags held aloft.

*   *   *

I have tried to describe Chuck to you. Do you wonder that I could not describe him to the policeman in that Kensington Square?

III

ELIZABETH SUCCEEDED HENRY

The Armoured Cars of the Light Armoured Motor Battery were also in observation ready to take advantage of any favourable opportunity.

British Official History of the War: Mesopotamia

ELIZABETH SUCCEEDED HENRY

THERE are many ways of estimating progress. Some people do it by blue-book figures, by trade statistics, census returns, or the number of telephones per head of the population; some by a less concrete yard-stick, the health of the United Nations or the attendance at the last Surrealist Exhibition. Long ago I did it by motor-buses.

Every three or four years I used to come home from a country where we still estimated progress by the decrease in tribal raids on the settled districts. Like all my kind, whatever I proposed to do with the rest of it, I spent the first week of my leave within a mile of Piccadilly Circus. There I would renew my acquaintance with the London bus. Since last I saw it, it would have grown in size, in impressiveness, in dignity; it would be less noisy and more smoothly running; it would carry more passengers in greater comfort, and it would have added another two or three miles an hour to its speed. My bus would register for me, neatly and by no means inaccurately, the material progress civilization had made since I last visited it.

I stood on the kerb outside the Cavalry Club one spring morning in 1920 as an old General omnibus, flung out from the whirlpool at Hyde Park Corner, came rattling up Piccadilly. Alongside the great six-wheelers that now sweep past like liners, this bus of years ago would look ramshackle and spidery, but then, compared with its 1915 predecessors, the last I had seen, it represented progress. The world was moving. Civilization, like that bus, was bearing along more people in greater comfort, faster than ever before, but—the people in the bus knew where it was taking them. Morbid thoughts for a spring morning, and perhaps better interrupted. Anyway, interrupted they were. A motor-horn blared at my elbow; one of those pestilential, pretentious horns that start with a shriek and end with a bellow. I leapt around.

A mustard-yellow Rolls with the most sportive of sporting bodies had crept up to me as I meditated on the destination of civilization, and lounging in the driving seat, his lazy-lidded eyes gleaming with amusement at my fright, a smile on his lean face, was Tony Ayrton. I had no idea Tony was in England, but he had a habit of turning up at apposite moments whether in Piccadilly or in the desert.

'Hullo, Tony,' I said, adopting that casual attitude to the unexpected fashionable among the youth that survived the war. 'Rich uncle dead?'

I nodded at the car.

'No,' he grinned. 'Spoils of war! How d'you like Elizabeth?'

'Elizabeth?'

'The car, you old ass, the car!'

'Oh, it seems a pretty average cad's car to me—but why Elizabeth?'

'I'll tell you. You ought to know, for you were in at her birth, as you might say. You don't remember her?'

I shook my head.

'Well, come along to my pot-house and I'll refresh your memory.'

★   ★   ★

When I was about eight years old a kind aunt gave me *The Boy's Book of Battles*. It was a splendid book, and on its shiny cover, printed in the most glowing colours, was the picture of a battle. The artist had fairly let himself go. On the right, squadrons of cavalry galloped across the plain; in the centre cannons roared; behind them dense columns of infantry massed for the attack; and to the left, floating on an incredibly blue ocean, the British Fleet joined in the fun. Altogether a magnificent picture. Magnificent, but, of course, as I realized when I grew older and more superior, not war. An army could not advance to battle like that in these days.

And then, just after dawn one pearl-grey morning in Mesopotamia, I suddenly realized that my *Boy's Book of Battles* had come to life and I was in the middle of it. There on my right were the cavalry, a whole division of them, lance-points gleaming, pennons fluttering—yes, they *had* got little red-and-white pennons—as squadron after squadron moved forward across the brown plain. Beside me two batteries of 18-pounders, their guns beautifully aligned, were in action ready to fire. I looked back; the infantry were on the move, black columns advancing on a broad front with the dust already beginning to rise. I turned to my left. It could not be true! There was the British Fleet steaming along in exactly its right place. Through the early morning mist the silhouettes of the little river gunboats pushing up the Tigris might have been Dreadnoughts. The picture was complete: war *was* like that.

The sun grew hotter, the dust thicker, as the whole array moved steadily forward. The stage was set for the Boy's Battle; only one thing was wanting—an enemy. In the night the Turkish rearguard had slipped away and now our imposing entrance was to empty stalls. As if petulant at this fiasco the cavalry halted and the gunboats, following some bend in the river, turned away from us. We infantry, with our friends the gunners close behind, were left, as usual, to carry on.

Once over the abandoned Turkish position, when the force closed up to continue the pursuit, I found myself with my company far out on the right as flank-guard to the leading column. It was our first experience of following up a defeated enemy in full retreat, and we had plenty of evidence of how headlong that retreat had been. The desert was littered with all the debris of flight—torn clothing, packs, bits of harness, scattered shells, and smashed carts. Once we came across an abandoned gun, its breech missing and its muzzle shattered. In one place we marched for a couple of hundred yards through a sea of paper, where some headquarters had jettisoned its records before joining or perhaps leading the stampede. We had long outgrown the passion for collecting souvenirs; we had enough to carry without adding useless junk to our load, but I made one exception from that vast rubbish-heap. This was a neat steel attache-case, containing what seemed to my inexpert eye a very complete set of German surgical instruments, all new and beautifully kept. As I put it into our Lewis-gun cart I felt that the surgeon who had thrown this away must have been very hard pressed indeed.

The only enemy we met was a dejected party with two mountain-guns dragged by wretched sore-backed mules. The Turks squatted apathetically waiting for us, dirty white rags tied to the cleaning rods of their rifles. They looked as if they had been wandering in circles all night, and, as far as we could make out, had been pretty thoroughly harried by Arabs.

The march was again becoming monotonous when far out on the flank I saw, conspicuous in the empty desert, a square black object. My glasses showed it to be a huge saloon car, stationary and solitary on the sand. Out of sheer curiosity, but telling myself that for military reasons it should be inspected, I decided to have a closer look. The ground was dead level and even a mile away I should still be in view of the company, so I was taking little risk. I told Private Bronson, my groom, to come with me, and we started off. Both he and I were mounted; I because I was entitled to a horse, he because he was a perfect genius at scrounging one. We left the company plodding on and rode out. It was farther than I had thought and we approached with some caution—after all one never knew—but the car was deserted. There it stood, a great Mercédès, certainly the biggest car I had ever seen in Mesopotamia, and apparently in perfect order.

'Run out of petrol?' I suggested. 'The old general and his harem or whoever was in it must have had a long walk.' Bronson, his long jaw working as usual at a piece of last week's chewing-gum, contemplated the scene.

'They didn't walk,' he said, pointing to tracks alongside the car, 'they pinched somebody's cart. Shall I 'ave a dekko inside?'

I nodded and we both dismounted. Bronson was the quicker and I was still a few steps away when he seized the handle of the driver's door and wrenched it open. Immediately there was a blinding flash and a great puff of smoke shot up into the air. My horse plunged wildly, jerking me backwards, and it was a few seconds before I was able to see what had happened to Bronson. He still held his horse and his jaws still moved steadily but a trifle more quickly. Beyond a singed eyebrow he was unhurt.

'That,' he said, after profound thought, 'that must 'a' been one of them booby traps we've 'eard about!'

'It must,' I agreed, 'and you're lucky the chap that set it was in a hurry, or else it might have done you no good. There's nothing inside the car; we won't mess about with it any more. Come on.'

I threw a last look around the horizon, and my intention of

returning forthwith to the company was greatly strengthened by what I saw. A dozen scattered horsemen were cantering across our front about half a mile away.

'Arabs!' I exclaimed, beginning to mount in some haste. Bronson regarded them with interest.

'What are they doing?' he asked.

'Doing? Coming after us, you idiot.'

'No, they're not,' contradicted the imperturbable Bronson, 'they're chasing somebody—somebody white.'

At that I took my foot from the stirrup and got my glasses. They *were* chasing somebody. A short distance ahead of the horsemen a little naked figure was running desperately. Every now and then one of the Arabs would spur forward, turn the fugitive, and fall back while the pack hunted him on the new line. It was like a gang of brutal boys chivvying some wretched animal. As I watched, it suddenly struck me that the running figure was very small and slight.

'My God, Bronson,' I exclaimed, 'it's a child!' He did not answer, but even his jaws had stopped working for once.

I looked back at the company, still trudging doggedly on—too far for any help from them to be in time. Bronson had a rifle, I a revolver; we were in no shape to take on a whole bunch of Arabs. The only hope was to make a diversion at once and trust it would both draw off the Arabs and attract the attention of our own people.

'Give them five rounds rapid!' I shouted at Bronson, grabbing his horse.

He was just loading and I was leading the horses to cover behind the car when a strange sound, as if a huge rope were being dragged across acres of straw matting, made us both turn. Two Rolls-Royce armoured cars were bearing rapidly down on us; the noise we heard was made by their tyres cutting into the hard, brittle surface of the ground. A steel door in the body of one swung open and a pair of long legs in beautifully creased shorts appeared, followed by the rest of my friend, Tony Ayrton. He slid out languidly but neatly, careful to avoid soiling his immaculate khaki.

'Hullo!' he remarked. 'We saw some smoke over here and I thought we'd have a look-see'. He eyed the Mercédès with an expression of as near enthusiasm as he ever allowed himself. 'Natty little runabout you've got there! You wouldn't. . . .'

'Never mind that now,' I interrupted. 'Take your two rattle buggies and get after those Arabs. They're chasing somebody; I believe it's a child!'

Ayrton's gaze followed my pointing finger. There was no languor about the way he got back into his car, and it was moving before the door clanged to. Two minutes later the only Arabs still capable of movement were fast-vanishing dust-clouds on the horizon.

We rode forward in the wake of the cars, and arrived to find them halted with their crews grouped round someone on the ground. As I peered over their heads, one of them, putting a great brown arm round the slight shoulders, raised the pathetic little figure and I saw its face—a small face, haggard and dust-stained, but which ended in a grizzled, pointed beard! My child was an elderly man. He could have been little over five feet in height, and his scraggy, almost emaciated body was stark naked, but the fairness of his skin showed that he was undeniably a European. His eyes were open, but with the vacant gaze of the semi-conscious.

'*Wasser . . . wasser*,' he murmured. '*Die Araben. . . .*'

Somebody produced a water-bottle and held it to his lips. With the water, understanding came slowly back to his eyes.

'Poor ruddy little 'Un!' said a sympathetic soldier. Ayrton, whose German was much as mine, none at all, leant over him.

'*Deutscher?*' he asked doubtfully.

The little man showed further signs of animation. He shook his head vigorously.

'*Nein! Nein! Osterreicher, Osterreicher!*'

'Austrian?'

'*Ja*, yes,' he broke into fluent but guttural English. 'Austrian, *doktor*-major. Two days ago wis my 'ospital I join. Yesterday, all day, I work, many, many vounded. At night in my tent I sleep, most tired. In the morning I vake—no 'ospital, no army, no Turk! Only me wisin my tent. I am abandon!'

He seemed to think his Turkish colleagues had left him behind on purpose, but it would have been quite in accordance with Turkish staff work for the newly arrived foreign doctor to be forgotten in the confusion of a hurried retreat in the dark.

'Then I valk,' he went on. '*Mein Gott*, how I valk!'

Soon after it grew fully light he was seen by Arabs who were scavenging on the Turkish rear, but he had escaped them by making for the river. He swore he swam across, only to find more Arabs on the opposite bank and to be compelled to swim back. It seemed very doubtful if so frail a man could swim the Tigris twice in this way, but he was convinced he had, so we let it go at that. He had then seen the dust of our advance and was hiding on the river-bank waiting to surrender when another gang of marauding Arabs caught him. They stripped him naked and amused themselves by hunting him. To do justice to his opinion of Arabs the little doctor had to fall back on German, but we gathered that he disliked them.

One of Ayrton's men produced from the 'tray', the un-armoured space at the back of an armoured car, a pair of khaki drill trousers they carried to wear after sunset as a protection against mosquitoes. The Austrian was carefully inserted into them and they certainly did cover his nakedness. Even when he dragged them up to his armpits and they hung in folds round his chest, they still flopped over his ankles. We all laughed, and he laughed too; the inevitable cigarette was stuck in his mouth and lit for him. Finally, he was lifted into the 'tray' and made as comfortable as tool-boxes, spare ammunition, water-bags, petrol tins, and a primus stove would allow.

Meanwhile Ayrton in the other car had, with due precautions, examined the stranded Mercédès. He returned disappointed. Not only was its petrol tank empty but someone had thought-fully removed the magneto and one or two other essential bits of mechanism. So, with the two cars moving slowly while we trotted alongside, we rejoined my company. Before the cars left us to hand over our Austrian prisoner, I gave him the case of instruments we had picked up. His beady eyes glistened and his cropped head nodded emphatically.

'*Ja, ja*, mine, mine!' he exclaimed, opening it and lovingly fingering scalpels, clips, forceps.

When we waved him good-bye he was curled up in the back of the car like some quaint little monkey, his pointed beard wagging up and down as he shouted farewells, one skinny arm clutching those ridiculous trousers to his chest, the other clasping his precious instrument case. I do not know whether he was allowed to keep it, but I like to think of him in some comfortable prisoners' camp where in a nice whitewashed hospital he could again handle those shining horrors. I only hope for their own sakes that none of his patients were Arabs.

A rather notorious general, whose language was as florid as his complexion, once told the somewhat sceptical remains of a battalion that had been shot to bits in an attack that 'the offensive spirit is the British infantryman's brightest jewel'. It would have required a clear eye to discern any sparkle about us when late afternoon found us still trudging across that interminable flatness. Looking at the men one would have sworn that nothing would rouse them. But time and again the British soldier has startled his enemies and surprised his friends by staging a come-back when both thought he was down and out. Towards evening, with little warning, we bumped a weak enemy rear-guard holding a hastily occupied line straggling up from the river. An aeroplane dropped a message on our battalion headquarters reporting that a Turkish heavy battery drawn by bullocks was struggling to escape some two miles ahead. The infantry before us had been hurriedly halted and turned about to cover its withdrawal.

The news of the battery spread rapidly among the men; its effect was electrical. The old general's heart would have been warmed to the Crimean charge-for-the-guns scramble that followed, and, I am sure, he would have got off a splendid piece about the irresistible sweep of the dauntless infantry, company vying with company, platoon with platoon, in noble rivalry to be the first to plant the British colours on the enemy cannon. But the regrettable truth is that it was not honour we were after, it was not even the guns—it was the bullocks! Unless you have lived for goodness knows how long on salt bully—and not too much of that—you cannot appreciate the primitive feelings roused in a healthy Englishman's breast at the prospect of getting his teeth into a juicy beefsteak. Those Turks were between us and our beefsteak. No doubt they had relied on the three hours that, as a Turkish officer once told me, the British always spent in reconnaissance before they did anything. This time they hardly got three minutes before we were on them, over them, and going hard on the other side.

Between us and the guns, which we could at last see as long black caterpillars crawling slowly over the brown earth, stretched a last obstacle, a *nullah*, one of those ancient disused canals that score the face of Mesopotamia in unexpected places. Twenty feet wide and nearly as deep, it was crossed by a crude bridge of palm trunks, laid side by side and covered with beaten earth. Our ragged lines were still short of this *nullah* when four of Ayrton's armoured cars came rushing in from the flank, making for the bridge. The first three cars took the crossing cautiously, but the fourth, anxious I suppose to be in at the death, came round in a wide sweep and fairly charged at it. Something went wrong. The near front wheel went over the edge of the bridge, the whole car swerved right off it, pushed its nose into the far bank and disappeared. A cloud of dust shot up and hung hovering over the bridge.

'I'll bet that 'asn't 'arf bent something!' remarked Bronson.

By the time we were scrambling out of the *nullah*, no easy task in full equipment even where the sides had fallen in, Ayrton's three surviving cars had beaten us handsomely to the battery. The Turkish guns, strung out one behind the other at irregular distances, were old pattern Krupps with peculiarly high mountings; but ancient as they were they looked infinitely more serviceable than the wretched oxen that drew them. The poor beasts were lying on the ground, their long-horned heads drooping mournfully, driven to a standstill. Sharp bones threatened to break through their ill-conditioned hides in all directions, and I doubt if a pound of honest beef could have been found anywhere on one of those gaunt carcases. Steak was 'off'. Even our chances of stew disappeared when the brigadier arrived and forbade the slaughter of these innocents. All transport animals were urgently required for army use, he declared. We drew off from the victims with dark mutterings about midnight feasts at brigade head-quarters. However, the great ones decided to call it a day; another battalion passed through us to take up outposts, and steakless we went into bivouac. I strolled back to the bridge to see what had happened to the armoured car. It was jammed across the *nullah* almost at the bottom, and from the look of it I was inclined to agree with Bronson that something ''adn't 'arf got bent'. Ayrton, who was superintending the salvage, confirmed this.

'Bit of luck that all four chaps in that car weren't killed,' he said. 'As it was they got away with nothing worse than the father and mother of a shaking, but the car's a complete write-off. Even if we had the tackle to raise her, which we haven't, her chassis was buckled to blazes by the weight in the middle when the ends jammed. We'll pick up all we can—the engine's more or less all right—and indent for a new car.'

During the next three weeks, as we marched and fought our way up the river, more than once Ayrton's armoured car battery lived up to its reputation for turning up at critical moments, but there was one occasion when we missed him. The Turk had suddenly the impertinence to turn round and advance against us. Two brigades were turned out to meet the threat, and after one of the longest, dustiest, and most unpleasant marches we had ever had, we reached at nightfall a little oasis of irrigated palm groves in the bare desert that is Mesopotamia without water. The brigadier told us that the Turks were digging in at a village five or six miles farther on and that he would reconnoitre tomorrow with a view to attacking. Several of us were detailed to accompany him as unit representatives.

At dawn next morning we started off, the brigadier, the four colonels of battalions, a gunner or two, and an assortment of us smaller fry, escorted, rather inadequately, I thought, by a troop of British cavalry. We left the palm groves, still dark against the lightening sky, and trotted out into the flat, featureless plain. It was a lovely morning, the air fresh with almost a nip in it, the sky a gentle, unclouded blue with the last pale rear-guard of the stars retreating as the red rays of the advancing sun, straight as sword blades, pierced the misty curtains of the horizon. As we rode, the dull brown earth ahead seemed to take on a faint opalescent sheen, and then, suddenly, our horses' hoofs were among flowers— tulips and tiny blue grape hyacinths. I had not seen a flower, hardly a green thing, for a year; it seemed unbelievable that the Mesopotamia I had known, so arid, harsh, and cruel, should suddenly grow gentle with spring flowers. I slipped from the saddle and picked a little bunch. When I caught up with the rest again they had passed beyond the flowers and were back to the bare brown earth. As the sun climbed, the freshness went out of the air, and I felt an increasing stickiness between my bare knees and the saddle. I looked at my flowers; they had wilted in my hand. Regretfully I let them fall. We were back in the old Mesopotamia, and I had better begin thinking of other things than flowers.

Personally, I did not like it a bit. We moved, about half a dozen of us, officers and orderlies, in a group with our own escort, little blobs of mounted men, four or five hundred yards ahead and on the flanks. We seemed to me pathetically few, completely without concealment, getting farther from support every moment, and riding straight into the arms of a considerable Turkish force waiting to receive us. This, I felt, was a job not for us but for Ayrton and his cars. However, the brigadier did not share my misgivings. At any rate he rode steadily on until at last we saw rising out of the plain a low mound, the Turkish position. Field-glasses were produced, and we all gazed at it. My horse would not keep still, and looking through glasses that jog up and down and keep on giving you sharp raps on the bridge of your nose is not very informative.

The brigadier did not see enough either, and to my alarm decided on a closer look. We rode on again until, even with the naked eye, we could see that a village straggled up the mound; in fact, most of the mound was village, houses piled on the remains of older dwellings. There was, too, clearly distinguishable in front of it, stretching away to either side, a line of earthworks. Neither in the village nor in the trenches was there any sign of life. We must have been plainly visible and easily within field-gun range, yet nobody took the slightest notice of us.

'I suppose those trenches *are* occupied?' said the brigadier, letting his glasses hang round his neck. He showed every sign of pressing still nearer to find out, when a trooper of the escort rode up.

'Enemy cavalry working round our right flank,' he reported in a matter-of-fact way.

'Eh, what? Where?' said the brigadier, wheeling his horse and getting his glasses into action again.

We all followed suit and saw, about three-quarters of a mile away on our flank, a body of horsemen sweeping steadily round us with the obvious intention of cutting off our retreat. I could not make out what the brigadier was waiting for. I had no doubt what the next word of command should be: 'Home, James, and don't spare the horses', or words to that effect. And then the subaltern commanding our escort rode up. Now, I had all the wartime infantryman's prejudice against the cavalry—people who hovered about the edge of a fight until it really got dangerous and then went off and watered their horses—but, as I watched that young cavalryman approach, I began to wonder whether they were really like that. He was a large, raw-boned, eager young man, and he seemed very earnest about something. I edged up to hear what he was saying.

'. . . you see, sir, if I took the troop round there'—he swung his arm back across the front of the Turkish position—'we could easily get behind them and cut them off.'

'And what then?' asked the brigadier.

'Oh, then,' said the cavalryman simply, 'we'd charge 'em.'

'And what do you suggest that I and these officers should do while you are charging?' The subaltern surveyed us doubtfully, then he brightened up.

'Oh, you could form a second line behind my troop and charge too. It would make us look like a squadron. And it *might* add weight to the charge.'

A groan of mingled apprehension and protest arose from the assembled infantry officers. For myself I knew that if my *waler* got going in a charge we should not stop this side of Mosul, unless, of course, I fell off or got impaled on a Turkish lance. My only weapon was a revolver, and with that even on foot I am not much of a danger to the enemy; on a horse I should be only a peril to my friends. No, cavalry charges were all right—for cavalry. Even the brigadier hesitated.

'There seem to be rather a lot of them,' he hazarded.

'Only about a squadron, sir,' that fire-eater assured him airily, already adjusting his sword-knot round his wrist.

'How many do you think there are, Colonel?' the brigadier asked his senior battalion commander.

'At least two squadrons, sir.'

'A regiment surely,' corrected another.

'For the love of Mike, tell him it's a brigade,' whispered someone. By that time the cavalry subaltern was giving little tugs to the hilt of his sword, drawing it out a few inches and reluctantly letting it fall back into the scabbard.

'Oh, sir,' he begged, 'we've never got into 'em, and this *is* a chance!' And his sword was half out.

'What about it, Colonel?' demanded the brigadier. There was a breathless pause.

'Well, sir, the duty of a reconnaissance is to collect information, not to engage in unnecessary shock action.' Never before have I more heartily agreed with any senior officer's tactical dictum. The brigadier turned to the cavalryman.

'I'm afraid the colonel's right. We'll withdraw.'

'But, sir,' wailed the heartbroken cavalier, 'we've never got into 'em. Can't we try, just this once?'

The brigadier shook his head, and the subaltern, muttering mutinously, rode back to his men, where he trailed his coat before the Turks in a most outrageous fashion, determined, if he was not allowed to charge them, to make them charge him. But they were not to be tempted, and after following at a respectful distance they halted and let us go unmolested.

We had got away with the reconnaissance; the actual attack would be another matter. The prospect of furnishing for several miles a perambulating target to the nicely entrenched Turk filled me with gloom. The more I thought of it the colder my feet became, until at last I had frightened myself into an unshakable premonition that this attack would be the end of me. I have never been more convinced of anything in my life. The correct thing to do on such occasions, I felt, was to put my affairs in order. In my case this consisted of paying Bronson the arrears I owed him. The money was of little use to him, there was nothing he could spend it on, but he took it cheerfully enough and showed a complete understanding of my motives by saying: 'Oh, well, sir, we'll 'ope it won't be as bad as all that!'

But that night, when we marched out from our friendly little oasis into the dark plain, I was still sure it would be. Even when I saw among the trees the dim shapes of armoured cars—Ayrton had come up after dark—it cheered me very little; all I thought was how much nicer it would be for him tomorrow behind half an inch of armour-plate.

We marched by compass. As chief guide the staff captain went ahead of the centre column, and everybody took direction from him. To check distances two officers paced solemnly behind him counting their steps; four non-commissioned officers surrounded them in a square to protect them from interruption or distraction. To make the guide faintly visible in the darkness he had been decked out in the chaplain's surplice. As he moved slowly forward, his head sometimes bowed over his compass, sometimes raised to the star on which he marched, he might have been a priest leading some strange pilgrimage, with his acolytes, muttering prayers, beside him, and the rest of us innumerable penitents silent and mournful. Anyway, the general effect was funereal and depressing, the more so as I was sure our staff captain, a cheerful bungler, would misread his compass and mix up his stars. The course he had to follow was not a straight one; it had two angles in it, so that, instead of advancing directly on the enemy, we should, just before dawn, arrive at a deployment position somewhere on his left flank. Whether we reached this spot or not depended therefore not only on the accuracy with which we kept our bearings but on advancing the correct distances before each change of direction.

The first turn was quickly made; the second seemed hours later, but eventually it was reached. While the brigade was forming up on the new alignment and the staff captain juggling with his compass, the brigade major came over with our colonel and in a stage whisper told me: 'According to the map there ought to be an old canal running across our line of advance, about a couple of hundred yards ahead. There may be an enemy picket or something in it. Take a platoon and see if there is.'

Off I went, the platoon extended on each side of me. I felt a little more sympathy for the guides when the star I was marching on persisted in modestly effacing itself among its fellows, and I kept on forgetting how many paces I had counted. We had come well over two hundred, yet there was no sign of a canal. At three hundred, none; the same at four. I began to think I must have lost direction. I paused for a moment to check on my star; the platoon moved slowly on. I could see the line of black figures, fading away on each side, flitting soundlessly forward. One instant it was there, the next it had vanished, and the silence was shattered by one explosive word. My platoon had found the *nullah*! Each man, as he fell, had gasped that one word, the only swear word the British soldier ever seemed to know. Luckily there was no Turkish outpost to be scandalized by our profanity. Here we dropped the guns, since by all calculations we should now be in easy artillery range of the Turkish position. The infantry crossed the *nullah*, and took up a formation that would allow them to deploy rapidly for the attack. Then, after mysterious rites by the High Priest with the compass, the advance was resumed. It was now what well-trained staff officers, who dislike using the perfectly good word 'dawn', would call 'first light', or vulgar subalterns 'sparrow cheep'. A greyish tinge diluted the darkness; columns to the left and right could be dimly seen; gradually those beyond began to appear. The staff captain doffed his surplice—it was day.

We continued to move forward, but there was a certain uneasiness visible among those who directed us. Anxious officers swept the widening horizon with glasses, there were hurried consultations with fluttering maps much in evidence. But all to no purpose; of the Turkish position, which should have been right under our noses, or of the conspicuous village mound behind it, not a sign. We might have been in the middle of the Atlantic Ocean for any landmark we could discover. Had the High Priest followed a wrong star? Had his acolytes mistold their beads? Were we still short of the enemy or had we lost him? The Lord alone knew.

'Halt!' said the brigadier.

The troops sat down, and, as is the invariable custom of the British soldier, promptly went to sleep. We must have looked excessively silly sitting there, three thousand men with not the least idea of what to do next or where to go. Our hopes were raised when Ayrton, who had made a wide detour to avoid the old canal, arrived with his whole battery of eight cars—his recent casualty replaced—and reported.

'Where are those blasted Turks?' the brigadier asked him.

'Search me!' replied Tony affably.

The brigadier was not amused, and the elegant Anthony was only saved from something pretty astringent in answer by an unexpected interruption. Away to our left came a dull report—high in the air an unmistakable rustle, a shrill crescendo, a thud, and *cr-rump!* a five-nine shell landed two hundred yards short of us. Its black smoke had hardly begun to drift before the brigadier rapped out his order: 'Change direction left. Forward!'

We swung slowly round, and in good old Prussian fashion

marched towards the sound of the guns, or, in our case, gun; for there seemed to be only one firing at us, and that in a most leisurely fashion. We got into 'artillery formation', which left a great deal of sand for the shells to fall into without hurting us, and pressed on. After a few minutes the haze or mirage or whatever it was that had limited our view lifted, and there, straight ahead of us but still a long way off, was the village-topped mound. We shook out into looser formation but, if we could see the Turks better now, so could they us, and it would have been most unpleasant had it not been for our own guns. We had the bulk of the divisional artillery back at the *nullah*, and they came down with a grand slam. The smoke and dust they kicked up all along the front screened us almost entirely, and the enemy fire became very wild.

The battalion was on the right of the attack, and I could see the long, straggly lines, of which we were part, stretching interminably to the left. On the right they ended abruptly with the last man of my company. I had a nasty feeling that our old friends the Turkish cavalry might suddenly swoop round the edge of the dust curtain and take us in flank. I looked apprehensively over my shoulder and was reassured. Out beyond my right-hand man were the swiftly moving shapes of armoured cars.

So far so good, but soon our guns would have to lift their barrage and with it our dust screen, then the Turkish machine-guns would come into their own. My premonition of a sudden end to a promising junior officer descended on me again in full force. When our guns did lift, sure enough an anti-British gust of wind rolled back the curtain while we were still a few hundred yards away. It was a case of the British grenadier at Fontenoy— for what we were about to receive might the Lord make us truly thankful! With the idea of getting it over as soon as we could we began to double, and I hunched my shoulders and ducked my head waiting for the storm. It never came. At the moment our barrage lifted, the armoured car battery swept between us and the enemy. It was beautifully timed. The eight cars, one behind the other, ran down the Turkish line, not more than a few yards from his front trench, their machine-guns firing continuously. The Turks ducked for shelter; in another minute we were in among them, and it was all over.

Nothing remained but to collect the prisoners. I watched them shuffling past, the usual docile, at first frightened and then thoroughly cheerful, ragged Turkish prisoners. At the head of one nondescript group walked a figure of almost startling spruceness, a dapper little officer in patent-leather field-boots and pale-blue breeches of the horsiest cut. Behind him staggered a soldier, evidently his servant, carrying an old-fashioned gladstone bag. Every now and then the officer would cast an anxious glance behind him to make sure the precious bag was following. He seemed so concerned about it that I began to wonder what was in it—papers, plans, orders, marked maps, whole archives of the Turkish General Staff? I stopped him and ordered the bag to be examined. After much unbuckling of straps and fumbling with catches, the servant laid it open at our feet. We craned expectantly forward and saw, neatly folded and piled one on the other, a dozen stiff-fronted white dress-shirts. The little Turk regarded them with pride.

'*Je suis officier!*' he explained.

I moved along the parapet of the captured trench, getting reports from my platoon commanders, and congratulating myself on how lightly, in spite of premonition, we had escaped, thanks to the armoured cars. They, however, had not saved us without some loss to themselves; one car stood battered and forlorn, victim of a direct hit from a shell. Its whole body was wrecked, doors blown out, turret twisted drunkenly to one side, the armoured bonnet torn off. Another car was standing alongside while its commander, a sergeant, ruefully poked about in the shattered engine.

'Cor,' he said to no one in particular, 'we ain't got much money but we do see life! She's a proper write-off!'

She certainly looked it.

*   *   *

'Well,' said Tony Ayrton, leaning back in his armchair in the club, 'we salved the chassis of that car—about all there was to salve—and slipped into it the engine of the one that fell into the *nullah*, you remember? We'd carted that engine about with us for weeks. Our mechanics made a good job of it. There was no difficulty about spares and oddments; by that time Mesopotamia was bulging with spares for everything, and when our carpenter had fitted a box-body, made from wood looted from the Inland Water Department, we had a perfectly good extra car. And the beauty of it was that it wasn't on the strength—pure buckshee!'

'But it must have been discovered some time?' I protested.

'As a matter of fact we had no trouble at all until the battery was due to embark for home in 1919. You know how narrow-minded these embarkation wallahs are: anybody'd think another half-ton would sink the blooming ship to hear 'em talk! They said an armoured car battery had an establishment of so many vehicles, they'd ship that number but not a car, not a bicycle, not a perambulator more—and would I please note the ship was sailing in two hours.

'It was time for action, old boy, not words. I put my sergeant-major at the wheel of a Ford van and I took the spare Rolls myself. We drove hard for ten miles out into the desert and there we left that Ford van. I daresay some old sheikh found it and still drives his Friday hawking party round in it. Anyway, the Rolls went into the hold and the Ford stayed in the desert. Everybody was happy, especially the Embarkation Staff; for the battery had sailed with its exact establishment of vehicles—in numbers at any rate.'

'But what about the other end?' I asked. 'What about handing over in England?'

'Ah!' said Tony, '"ver difficile but I arrange", as they say at Port Said. I've got a brother. Not a bad bloke as brothers go, I wired him from Aden, and when we tied up at Southampton, there was Brother Bill with a nice part-worn Henry Ford sitting on the quayside. You could get 'em pretty well for nothing from surplus stores: they almost paid you to take 'em away in those days. When the spare Rolls was lifted out Bill drove her away and I trundled old Henry into her place. Battery present and correct, sir! We fitted a decent body to the Rolls, and *voilà*—Elizabeth!'

'Yes, but why Elizabeth?' I asked.

'Don't you see? Brush up the old history, my dear chap. Think of the jolly old Tudors. Didn't Elizabeth succeed Henry?'

'No,' I replied, feeling rather superior; 'as a matter of fact she didn't: Edward VI did.'

'Oh, well, you couldn't call a car Edward the Sixth; every-body'd think you'd had five others. Besides, it would have to be a girl's name anyway, love interest and all that.'

'Then it ought to have been Mary, she came next.'

'Did she?' said Tony, slightly crestfallen. Then he cheered up. 'Oh, but you couldn't call a peach of a car like this Bloody Mary!'

IV

AID TO THE CIVIL

Inter-communal rioting broke out between Hindus and Moham-medans in Gurampur on Thursday. A number of both communities were injured and three killed. On Friday the disorders increased in extent and a military detachment, called in to support the police in their efforts to restore order, was compelled to fire to disperse violent mobs near the Juma Masjid. Five civilians were killed and several wounded. Order has now in general been restored but sporadic assaults continue in the city.

Government of India Communique

AID TO THE CIVIL

IN the days when Aurangzeb Alamgir still held a grip on his Empire, he built a fort at Gurampur; one of those lovely, rose-tinted Mogul forts, with great gates bristling with spikes to discourage butting elephants and with over-hanging machicolated galleries from which further discouragement could come sizzling down on beast and man below. For two hundred years after Alamgir had gone to reward in the highest heaven or torment in the lowest hell—to which destination you consign him depends on whether you are a Mussulman or a Hindu—his fort remained, a thing of beauty but, oh, so insanitary!

Then came a new race of rulers and, in their train, a be-whiskered colonel of sappers. He took one sniff at the fort, and the painted ceilings were whitewashed, the marble-channelled fountains gave place to galvanized pipes, and the picturesque, ramshackle, incredibly smelly bazaar that filled the central courtyard was swept tidily away. In its stead rose the British infantry barracks. They, too, were red; not the sun-soaked, mellow red of Mogul sandstone, but the garish red of good, honest Victorian brick. If their colour screamed a discord, so did their architecture—a Lancashire cotton-mill dumped in the midst of the Arabian Nights.

Yet, as the old sapper could have pointed out, had anyone in his day been so blind to progress as to question his taste, these barracks had some advantages over their more artistic predecessors. For instance, you did not die quite so quickly in them. Then, some fifty years later, when the Military Works Department put in electric light and mosquito-proof fittings, what, asked the old sapper colonel, or at least his very image minus the whiskers, what more could the heart of the British soldier desire?

All the same, sitting in the bare whitewashed room that was

Note.—This narrative, unlike the others of this series, is a composite one, made up from the events of three occasions on which the military aided the civil power.

my office, I did not like the place. Perhaps the thermometer, steady at 105°, or the prickly heat around my waist, had something to do with it.

The fan that beat waves of hot air down on me clicked monotonously, and a sparrow twittered maddeningly from an iron strut in the roof. Sparrow? Did I say the barracks were mosquito-proof? No, the Military Works said that, but neither I nor the sparrows believed them. I grabbed the pincushion from my barrack table and hurled it. With an indignant squawk the sparrow flew to another strut and twittered more maddeningly than ever. My *babu* replaced the pork-pie hat that he had surreptitiously removed, rose from his table, and retrieved the pincushion. Without a word he put it back in its exact position on my table. No, I did not like Gurampur Fort, and I did not relish this standing by, day after day, with my company. Internal security duty might be all right if anything ever happened, but this waiting. . . .

I resumed my consideration of an objection-statement to a barrack damages claim returned by some minor deity in the financial pantheon: 'Ref. two panes glass, alleged broken by storm on 3 April. Meteorological reports indicate dead calm 3 April. Kindly explain.'

Rather a fast one, that, in the hot weather tournament between the unit and the Military Finance Department! Still, the great thing in these games is to keep the ball in play.

'When was our last earthquake, *babu*?' I asked.

Then the telephone rang.

I reached for it, the objection-statement clinging to my sticky forearm in the infuriating way papers have in the hot weather. An agitated voice in clipped English demanded: 'Hello? Hello? Why you not answering? Hello? Hello?'.

'Gurampur Fort,' I replied in a pause in the babble.

'Is that O.C. Troops? Yes?'

'Speaking.'

'I am Personal Assistant to Deputy Commissioner Sahib. Assistance of British troops is urgently required!'

'What's the trouble?'

'There is riot. Mob is committing violences at meat market.'

'Where's the Deputy Commissioner?'

'At market, confronting multitude in peril of life and limb.'

'Did *he* tell you to ask for troops?'

'Yes. He says come Kotwali at once.'

'Kotwali? The Government Offices, not the market?'

'Yes, Kotwali. He wants you there. Kindly arrive with prompti-
tude and despatch.'

'All right. Tell him we're coming.'

Ten minutes later my company, less one platoon left behind
under the only other officer, was ready. The men, as is the way of
British soldiers, had cheered up at the prospect of action, and I
shared their feelings until I suddenly remembered all the snags of
this internal security business. I hurriedly checked over the contents of my haversack—sandwiches, chocolate, torch, map, note-
book, field dressing, and, most important of all, in the pocket of
my grey-back shirt, Indian Army Form D.908.

I.A.F. D.908 is a neat folding card, headed *Instructions to Officers
Acting in Aid of the Civil Power for Dispersal of Unlawful Assemblies.*

Its three closely printed pages held the concentrated essence of
the four bulky legal volumes that should control the soldier's
action in such circumstances. While some of its instructions, such
as 'The Military are not to be used as Civil Police', were puzzlingly
vague, it was a very serviceable handrail to steady one among the
pitfalls of the law. It had, also, a detachable fourth page which
should be signed by the magistrate, if one were present, before he
authorized the officer to take action. Altogether, D.908, unlike
many army forms, was a useful thing to have about one.

I climbed into the leading lorry, and we were off.

I had not had much experience of the Salisbury Plain refine-
ments of mechanization, but I had done a good many miles over
bad and winding roads in lorries packed with soldiers and their
gear, and I had sometimes wondered if the infantryman would be
decanted on the battlefields of the future after a sixty-mile journey
in quite the state of eager freshness some people expect. Perhaps
he will, I thought, if somebody designs an army lorry in which
all the exhaust fumes do not come up through the floor. As it was,
even after the short run to the city I was glad enough to get out.

The Kotwali, headquarters of the civil and police administration, stood in a square at the very centre of the city. A gloomy,
buff-coloured building with a veranda round the first storey,
supported on brick pillars, from which the plaster was beginning

to peel. In the centre of the ground floor an arched tunnel led from the street to an interior courtyard. On the opposite side of the square was the Imperial Bank, an imposing pseudo–classical portico with a huddle of ramshackle godowns behind, and a much bewhitewashed telegraph office. Hemming in these official buildings rose high, narrow, flat-roofed houses which looked as if they remained standing only because they were jammed so tightly against each other. Two or three wide thoroughfares of shops led out of the square, and, in turn, branched into narrow streets and dark alleys where wheeled traffic could not go. A typical Indian city stewing in the unsavoury heat.

There were a good many people moving about, but no signs of any disturbance, although I noticed that the shops were closed and shuttered. As we arrived, Cornwall, the deputy commissioner, drove up in his open car. I knew him fairly well; a slight, dried–up man of about forty, with the stoop of a student and an unhealthy pallor bred of too many hot weathers. With strangers he was shy, almost diffident, and this, added to his appearance, often deceived people into thinking he was less a man of action than a deputy commissioner should be. Those who acted on this assumption received a rude shock, for Cornwall in his official capacity was a live wire. The Government of his Province used him as a sort of fire brigade. When the incapacity of a deputy commissioner caused a conflagration in any particular district, the incumbent, as was the kindly custom in the Civil Services of India, was promoted to the secretariat, and poor old Cornwall was rushed off to replace him in the ruins. By the time he had rebuilt the edifice of Government there, the fire alarm was pretty sure to be ringing elsewhere, and so he went from district to district cleaning up the messes of men who were promoted over his head. He had a sense of humour, but by the time he reached Gurampur it was getting strained.

'Hullo,' he greeted me. 'Thanks for being so prompt. I've left Marples tidying up at the market. That spot of bother is all right for the moment, but things aren't too promising. I'd like your chaps to stay here tonight, anyway. Come along and we'll see what can be done to make you comfortable.'

I got the men out, piled arms in the courtyard, and let them sit in the shade. The lorries went back to the Fort for kit, mosquito nets, beds, rations, and everything else required for a possibly prolonged stay.

Marples, the police superintendent, arrived within half an hour with about twenty native police armed with buck-shot Martini-Henrys. His khaki shirt was black with sweat between the shoulders and round the belt, while his clean-shaven face looked thin and fine-drawn under its lank black hair. However, he grinned cheerfully enough at the sight of my fellows sprawling about.

The three of us then retired to Marples's office, a big untidy room on the first floor. There, over three 'John Collinses', which a police orderly produced from a big ice-box, we began the conference between Civil and Military that all good soldiers know is the orthodox opening to co-operation. Cornwall explained the situation.

'It's the usual hot weather communal trouble, only it's boiled up rather badly. The immediate cause is the new meat market. For some reason my predecessor allowed it to be built on the edge of the Hindu quarter; it's a standing offence to them, and, of course, the Mohammedans have delighted to rub it in. A Hindu crowd tried to stop supplies going in early this morning, and if Marples hadn't turned up just in time with his fellows there'd have been a useful riot. As it was, some of the Mohammedan butchers were badly beaten up, and one Hindu killed. Crowds have been trying to collect there ever since and when I sent for you an hour ago it looked ugly. However, Marples again managed it after some pretty *lathi* work, and it's all quiet for the moment.'

'The trouble is', added Marples, 'that there have been minor clashes in half a dozen places, and my police are scattered in penny packets all over the city. My only reserve is the twenty men I have below.'

We discussed how I could help, and eventually to my relief, for at one time they rather pressed me to scatter my men in small detachments, they agreed that for the present we should remain concentrated as a central reserve.

'What about a magistrate if I'm called out?' I asked, remembering that I.A.F. D.908.

Cornwall laughed.

'Want your card signed? I'll get you a tame magistrate. Mind he doesn't vanish at the critical moment, though. Magistrates are a bit shy sometimes. I don't altogether blame 'em. It's a rotten job for us, but they have to live among the people afterwards.'

We finished the 'John Collinses' and the conference at the same time. Cornwall went off to his court in the Civil Lines and, while Marples spent an hour at his routine office work, I saw my men settled in and their dinners under way. I shared lunch with Marples, and afterwards he started on a tour of his police stations, leaving me with an Indian police inspector and the residue of the constables. I kept one of my platoons ready for immediate action and let the other two strip to their vests and get what rest they could under the nets.

It was fairly hot and I was standing in the archway where there seemed a suspicion of movement in the air, when an imposing figure approached me—a burly, six-foot Indian. He wore a starched white *puggri*, a long black alpaca coat stretched tight across his broad chest, and voluminous white Mussulman trousers pinched in at the ankles. His aquiline face ended in a neatly pointed beard streaked with grey and his dark eyes twinkled merrily as, slipping an ornate walking-stick under one arm, he held out a big hand.

'I am Jallaludin Khan, Special Magistrate,' he explained.

He was not at all the bespectacled, failed B.A. type I had been expecting. He looked as if he would have been more in his element leading an Afghan marauding expedition than dispensing justice in a stuffy court. He spoke some English, and with my halting Urdu we managed very well. I gathered he was a local landowner, not a regular magistrate, but one roped in by Cornwall for emergencies. He told me he had offered to bring a party of his own tenants to help preserve order.

'You know, sahib—twenty, fifty of my people, *sowars*, with horses. But Deputy Commissioner sahib say, "No, no, you Jallaludin are enough. You more than fifty men!" '—he laughed hugely and slapped a thigh—'Cornwall sahib, afraid I make *zulm*, oppression, on those Hindus, but'— he grew serious—'I am magistrate, I would be impartial. Yes, even with those sons of burnt pigs I would be impartial!'

We shared my tea. Jallaludin shovelled spoonful after spoonful of sugar into his cup, talking incessantly all the time, except when he sipped noisily at the boiling tea.

While we were at it, the police inspector came in and said he had just had word from the Juma Masjid that crowds were collecting and trouble likely. He was going there with all the reserve police. I wondered if I ought to go too, but he did not seem to think so; he told me he would telephone if things got serious.

The flap, flap of his men's shoes as they hurried off was very different from the tramp of soldiers, and as the sound died away the afternoon seemed very still. I sent a warning to the platoon on duty and resumed my tea. In a pause between Jallaludin's sips I heard, like wind in trees, a murmur that rose from silence and sank again. Jallaludin heard too. He jerked his head over his shoulder.

'The Juma Masjid,' he said. 'Crowds!'

The sound swelled up again. There was nothing menacing about it. It did not even seem human, more the sustained humming note of a distant machine.

'They are getting angry,' announced Jallaludin.

Suddenly the sound burst to a full-throated roar; I thought I could even distinguish shrill individual yells. Then it subsided again to a low growling mutter. I did not like the sound at all. The telephone rang.

'Come quickly, sahib,' said the voice of the police inspector. 'Juma Masjid!'

He sounded to me like a man in need and I ran into the courtyard. The platoon was ready and off we went at the double through almost deserted streets. As I ran, certain of the maxims on my I.A.F. D.908 crossed my mind: '*Keep your troops in a position to make use of their weapons . . . do not commit them to a hand-to-hand struggle . . . act in the closest co-operation with the civil authorities . . . get the magistrate to fill in the card. . . .*' Good Lord, where *was* my magistrate? But Jallaludin had not failed me; there he was, running extraordinarily lightly for a man of his bulk, just behind me.

Puffing and sweating, we reached a point where the street debouched into a wide open space, but the entrance to this square was blocked by a solid mass of people, their backs towards us. All I could see was the great white dome of the mosque towering up against a brazen sky on the far side. There was a tremendous noise, yells, cat-calls, shrieks, above a continuous din, and, every now and then, the crowd in front of us swayed backwards and forwards. Evidently something was going on in the square, and equally evidently I ought to do something about it. But what?

I had always pictured myself confronting a crowd, not standing behind it. It was very disconcerting. It was no use plunging into the mob; we should have been swallowed up. Besides, that would have committed us to 'a hand-to-hand struggle' with a vengeance. I could not fire on the backs of the crowd; as far as I could see those near us were mere spectators and not engaged in any violence. The first essential was to see what was happening. I looked at the houses—all barred and shuttered—it would take time to get in, and judging by the row, time was going to be precious. Then I saw a stationary motor-bus of the ordinary one-deck Indian type with a dozen people standing on its roof. I made for it, clambered up, helped by a huge heave from Jallaludin, who, with the platoon sergeant, followed me. The magistrate pushed the two nearest Indians violently off the roof, the rest took a startled look at us and followed them.

The bus made an excellent observation post. I looked out over the densely packed heads of the crowd, over a sea of waving arms and brandished sticks, to another crowd facing us, equally large, equally vocal, and just as formidable-looking. Between these two crowds was a narrow space along each edge of which I saw bobbing and swaying a thin fringe of scarlet *puggris*—the police. In the centre was a group of khaki figures among which I thought I recognized my friend the inspector. A constant rain of missiles sailed through the air as one crowd bombarded the other or the police indiscriminately.

As I watched, a khaki figure staggered out of the line and fell. The mob on that side surged inwards. The inspector with his little party flung himself into the breach. I could see their *lathis* going like flails as they beat the crowd back again. The stone-throwing increased; both crowds swayed ominously. Plainly the heroic efforts of the handful of police could not hold them apart much longer. Then not only would the mobs be at one another's throats, but the police would be overwhelmed and probably beaten to death.

'Shoot, sahib, shoot!' urged Jallaludin in my ear. 'Shoot *there*!'
He pointed to the crowd immediately below us. 'Shoot them.
The rest will run away!'

Even in the excitement I noticed, from the number of round
hats and *dhotis*, that this was the Hindu faction. Jallaludin's boasted
impartiality was weakening under strain.

I reckoned that if I did not act within three minutes there would
be wholesale murder in that square, so I got a section, five men,
on to the roof, as fast as I could, and told them to lie down ready
to fire. The bugler we had with us I ordered to blow the 'Com-
mence Fire', the call we use on the ranges. The bugle shrilled out
above the clamour, and many heads turned to look at us, but
beyond that it had no effect.

'Warn the crowd I'm going to fire,' I said to Jallaludin.

He plainly regarded this as an irritating delay, but, cupping his
hands, he raised a mighty voice. I could not follow much of what
he shouted, it seemed mostly abuse and threats at the Hindus
below, but he did say the soldiers were going to fire. A few people
near us began to slip away, but out in the square where they had
probably heard neither bugle nor voice, the noise increased,
stones flew more viciously, and a couple more police went down.
There was nothing for it but to fire.

I knelt down, tapped two of the men lying ready to shoot, and
roared in their ears:

'Two hundred. At the front of the crowd facing us, one round,
when I give the word.'

I gave a similar order to two other men to fire at the Hindu
crowd.

'And for God's sake don't hit the police!'

The four men raised their rifles and aimed with all the stolidity
of British soldiers in a crisis.

'Fire!'

The little volley crashed out, startlingly abrupt and shattering
even in that din. The crowd near us, terrified by the blast of
rifles just over their heads, broke back and streamed away, but out
in the square, whether they realized firing had begun or not, they
held their ground and even closed in on one another. I ordered a
further two rounds rapid from the same men. This time it had
some effect. The crowds swirled and eddied on themselves for a

moment. The police seized the opportunity, and hurled themselves on them. The mobs broke. In an instant they were making in wild panic for all the exits from the square. Luckily the roads leading away were wide and unobstructed, and in three minutes even the roof-tops had cleared. There was an extraordinary hush. The square was empty except for scattered knots of police, and eight or nine crumpled figures lying still on the ground.

Leaving one section beside the bus, I extended the rest of the platoon and marched across the square. The whole ground was littered with stones, bricks, pieces of iron, sticks, shoes, hats and bits of clothing. The police inspector, dabbing with a rag at a nasty cut above his ear, met me. Hardly any of his men had escaped minor injury, and four of them were seriously hurt, one still unconscious. I asked anxiously if there were any bullet wounds among them, and I sighed with relief when he answered: 'No, sahib, only the ordinary stones, sticks, and one knife-stab.'

We turned to see what could be done for the casualties of the crowd. Of the nine left behind, five were past aid, and the other four seemed badly wounded. It is always rather a pitiful business seeing men you have shot, even enemies in war, and it was doubly so with these misguided civilians. We began to patch them up, the men using their own field dressings, until a policeman brought bandages from a chemist's shop in the square. A little Hindu came out of this shop, announced that he was a doctor, and set to work. He seemed quite unmoved, intensely professional, and, as far as I could see, indifferent whether his patient was a Mohammedan or a Hindu. When the motor ambulance for which we had telephoned arrived, I asked the little doctor if he would go with the wounded to the civil hospital. He hesitated for a moment, and then said: 'If I am accompanied by British troops as escort.'

He evidently did not rely on his services to their wounded to protect him from his Mohammedan fellow townsmen. We commandeered the bus—its driver had vanished—and sent it off with the ambulance. I gave a section as escort to the party, and the little doctor went too. Before he left he very punctiliously gave me his card—a decent little man.

Then for the first time since I had left the Kotwali I had a moment to run over in my mind the action I had taken during the last half-hour. The soldier always knows that everything he does

on such an occasion will be scrutinized by two classes of critics—
by the Government which employs him and by the enemies of
that Government. As far as the Government is concerned, he is a
little Admiral Jellicoe and this his tiny Battle of Jutland. He has to
make a vital decision on incomplete information in a matter of
seconds, and afterwards the experts can sit down at leisure, with
all the facts before them, and argue about what he might, could, or
should have done. Lucky the soldier if, as in Jellicoe's case, the
tactical experts decide after twenty years' profound consideration
that what he did in three minutes was right. As for the enemies of
the Government, it does not much matter what he has done.
They will twist, misinterpret, falsify, or invent any fact as evidence that he is an inhuman monster wallowing in innocent
blood.

With some such thoughts in my mind I began to jot down in
my note-book the sequence of my action while it was still fresh
in my mind. I had reached the point at which Jallaludin had asked
me to fire—of course he was not entitled to do that, only to tell
me to disperse the crowd, leaving the method to me—when I
realized that, after all, he had not signed my precious card. I presented it to him. I do not believe he could read it, though he
pretended he could.

'You sign on the dotted line,' I explained.

He cocked his head on one side and looked thoughtfully at a
dead Mohammedan the police were lifting into the bus.

'I only asked you to disperse *one* crowd; you dispersed both.
Still'—he smiled magnanimously—'I am magistrate and impartial.
We will forget that.' His signature straggled all across the card.

By five o'clock in the afternoon one of my platoons was used
up in pickets at the mosque and the market, and I was left with
the other two at the Kotwali, where Cornwall and Marples had
their headquarters.

That night I had my first experience of patrolling a city in the
dark. The heat, between the tall houses, pressed down like something tangible as we tramped through deserted streets and peered
up dark gullies. It was all unreal and nightmarish, except for the
smells, which were only too horribly real. Once I began to play a
game with myself, counting them. I forget how many I had
totalled when one more revolting than the rest made me retch

and I lost count. The narrower lanes of an Indian city on a hot night have to be smelt to be believed.

I turned in on a camp-bed two hours before dawn, and awoke in broad daylight feeling beastly, with my bearer, who had followed me, offering the usual tepid tea. A shave and a hurried wash improved my outlook on life. Marples was still asleep; he had, in fact, just gone to bed, having been up most of the night making security arrangements for the funerals of the men killed the day before. Cornwall I found at work. He seemed amused by something.

'We are to have visitors,' he said while I breakfasted. 'Some of the leading Hindus have asked to see me, and hearing, I suppose, that they had done so, the Mohammedans want to send a deputation too. I've told both parties to be here at nine, that's in half an hour. You'd better attend the meeting, but don't be drawn into any argument.'

The Mohammedan delegation arrived first. It consisted of two members. One, addressed as Maulvi sahib, was a picturesque old gentleman in the black gown of a theologian, with a strikingly beautiful—there is no other word for it—face. He had the soft brown eyes of a contemplative, a beard like white spun silk. The other, an excessively fat man, was dressed in European clothes, but with a Mussulman *puggri*. He wheezed a little as he moved, but his small eyes were keen and roved everywhere. He was introduced to me as Khan Bahadur Mohammed Zaman; and his profession given as 'contractor', a term which in India covers a multitude of activities and sometimes sins.

They were quickly followed by the first of the Hindus, Mr. Bhagwan Dass, a wealthy merchant, almost but not quite as fat as Mohamed Zaman. He appeared to be a little put out at finding the rival faction present, but chatted with the Khan sahib in a friendly enough way. There was a more distinct tension in the air when the rest of the Hindus arrived. They came together, naturally enough, for they were father and son. Imagine a Roman senator with a brown face and sock-suspenders and you have the elder, Mohan Lal, lawyer-politician. The son, Debindra Lal, a leaner, taller edition of his father, was without his dignity, but had instead a sort of dynamic restlessness, the kind of repressed power that one feels in a wild animal pacing up and down behind bars.

Mohan Lal, as befitted a Roman senator, opened the proceedings with a sonorous broadside: 'As the mouthpiece of the Hindus of this city, nay, of all India, I protest against the callous massacre that occurred yesterday. I demand an impartial inquiry by non-officials. The Hindu crowd was a peaceful assembly, the funeral procession of a victim of Mohammedan outrage——'

This was too much for Mr. Mohammed Zaman; quivering like a coffee blancmange he burst out: 'Peaceful assembly! Mohammedan outrage! I, too, protest. I protest at the inactivity of the police who stood idly by while a Hindu mob attacked defenceless Mohammedans on the very steps of the Juma Masjid, and still more at the action of the military in shooting down innocent men defending themselves from this unprovoked attack.'

'Unprovoked!' exclaimed Mohan Lal, registering magnificent indignation; 'I——'

Cornwall cut short his eloquence.

'Gentlemen,' he said, 'in the first place, there was no need for the funeral procession to come anywhere near the Mosque; that was deliberate provocation'—gratified murmurs from the Mohammedans. 'In the second place, the attack was begun by Mohammedans.'

Both delegations tried to speak at once. Cornwall swept on, overriding them: 'Surely, gentlemen, you could combine to use your influence to prevent such provocations and responses to provocations. I suggest you form a joint conciliation committee. As educated men of affairs, you should not find it difficult to agree on this.'

The appeal was not too enthusiastically received, and the spare Debindra Lal leant forward: 'You forget, Mr. Deputy Commissioner,' he said sauvely, 'agreement has already been reached on one important point. Could we not start from that?'

'From where?' asked Cornwall cautiously.

'From the necessity for an unofficial inquiry into the shooting. Both Mr. Mohammed Zaman and my father insist on that. Could we not start from that very considerable basis of unity?'

'I have satisfied myself,' answered Cornwall, keeping his temper admirably, 'that the firing was necessary, carefully controlled, and that it was the minimum required to disperse the unlawful assembly and thus prevent serious disturbance and great loss of life.'

Debindra Lal inclined his head courteously.

'If that is your view, Mr. Cornwall, why object to an inquiry?'

'Because, as you know only too well, such an inquiry is the last thing likely to help towards what should be the object of us all, the restoration of order.'

'Nevertheless,' the elder Lal took up the running, 'unless such an inquiry is promised we cannot be responsible for the peace of the city.'

Cornwall's voice remained quiet, but there was cold authority in it as he answered: 'You're not, Mr. Lal. I am! And I shall restore it—I hope with your co-operation. Our business is not to increase friction between communities, but to avoid it.'

'The true way to avoid friction', proclaimed Mr. Bhagwan Dass who, I thought, felt he was getting left out of things, 'is to remove the cause. What is the cause? The meat market. Remove it!'

The obese Mohammed Zaman quivered again into protest, and communal feeling was running high when Debindra Lal made a diversion.

'There are guards of British soldiers at the market and the mosque. The sight of these men, responsible for yesterday's shootings, is a provocation to both communities. Unless they are withdrawn there will be bloodshed.'

'If anybody is so foolish as to attack the military, there will undoubtedly be bloodshed,' admitted Cornwall drily. 'But if you believe it likely, Debindra Lal, there are only two courses of action honourably open to you.'

'And they are?'

'Either you do your best publicly and honestly to dissuade these misguided people from attacking or—or you appear yourself in the very front rank of the attackers. Unless you do one or the other, we must doubt either your moral or your physical courage.'

Debindra laughed. He seemed genuinely amused, but his father watched him narrowly and, I thought, anxiously.

'*Touché*, Cornwall,' he conceded, 'but you know very well I do not lack courage, and it's no good your hoping I will oblige you by losing my temper and getting myself shot in a street brawl.'

The discussion went on for some time. It was obvious that any real co-operation between the two communities was unlikely, and, whenever there was a sign of anyone co-operating with Cornwall, Debindra Lal threw a spanner into the works. Both sides seemed to be more occupied in scoring points in a three-cornered debate than in tackling any concrete question. The only exceptions were the old Maulvi who took no part at all—I discovered afterwards that he could not speak English—and Debindra Lal, who was out for trouble, not talk.

The deputations departed in large American motor-cars, and I asked Cornwall: 'What's Debindra Lal really like?'

'Brilliant at Oxford. Fine athlete. He's quite right, we know he's got courage, tons of it; drive, organizing ability, and brains—first-class brains. It's hard for a fellow like that to keep his head in India; he gets much more excitement, attention, and real power if he's ag'in the Government than if he's for it. Perhaps that's our fault. Anyway, Debindra was blackballed from some potty station club, saw red—and went red. His old father's terrified he'll go and get himself shot or hanged one of these days. I doubt it myself; he's more likely to get a lot of his pals hanged and some of us shot.'

'He was pretty quick at switching communal into anti-Government feeling,' I ventured.

'Oh, anybody can do that. I'd guarantee to turn the tables by changing any anti-Government dispute into a communal one in twenty-four hours—only it's not what I'm paid for.'

Marples came in, looking tired. He had got his reports for the night from his inspectors. They showed that while there had been no major clashes, the disturbances were taking the form of isolated assaults on individuals, stabbings and bludgeonings in the back alleys—a very difficult business to suppress.

'Another Hindu has died in hospital,' he went on gloomily. 'His pals will try to make a *tamasha* of the funeral this evening. I shall want all available police, and other parts of the city will be denuded. I'm nervous about attacks on Europeans. There's a decided anti-Government—that means anti-European—tinge coming into things. We'd better get all the British out of the city before this evening.'

'I think you're right,' Cornwall agreed. 'There are only the fellows at the bank, Borman, the American missionary and his family, and the convent.'

'It's the convent I'm worried about,' went on Marples. 'There's been a bit of stone-throwing there. I've had to put a guard on it. I don't know exactly how many nuns and whatnots there are, but it's a fair crowd. We'd better use the army lorries.'

'Yes,' said Cornwall to me. 'Would you go alone and see to it, while I get on to civil lines and have the Circuit House ready for them?'

'All right,' I agreed dubiously.

Nuns, I felt, were rather outside my orbit, and I did not look forward to shepherding a mass of timid, cloistered women. As I rumbled off with a couple of sections in my lorries I practised reassuring phrases that would show the weeping nuns that I was gentle but firm. By the time we found the convent, after losing our way twice, I was feeling quite the little Sir Galahad. It was plumb in the middle of the Hindu quarter, packed in among rather better-class Indian houses. A high brick wall, pierced by an iron-covered door, fronted the street. A couple of constables lounged against it; not, I thought, a very effective guard, but no doubt all Marples could spare. One of them hammered on the door, and it was opened by a decrepit *chowkidar*. I followed him across a deserted playground towards a long, three-storeyed, red-brick building with pointed windows that gave it a semi-ecclesiastical air, and jangled a bell at the main door. After a little delay, a grille slid open and a face peered at me—a brown face framed in a nun's white coif.

'I wish to speak to the Mother Superior,' I said.

After much drawing of bolts, the door opened, and the little nun, her face very dusky against the starched linen, her hands hidden in voluminous sleeves, greeted me with a quick glance of big, rather frightened eyes. And then, as I live, she curtseyed to me. No one had ever curtseyed to me before, and it embarrassed me vastly. I removed my helmet and attempted a bow. I felt, and I am sure looked, a fool, but I need not have bothered, for the little nun's eyes were now modestly fixed on my boots.

'Please come this way,' she said in sing-song English, and ushered me into a room.

'Please to sit down. I will bring Mother Angela.'

'Thank you,' I said, sitting on the edge of a very hard horse-hair chair.

She curtseyed again. I rose hurriedly and repeated my bow as she fluttered away. I looked curiously round the room. Three severe upright chairs, a plain table, and a *prie-dieu* were all the furniture on the polished linoleum. The walls boasted a big crucifix, a couple of German religious oleographs, and in one corner a small bookshelf. I tiptoed across to it—why I tiptoed I do not know, but I did. There was a New Testament, Douai Edition, next to a gilt-edged *Grimm's Fairy Tales*, half a dozen odd volumes of some series of *Lives of the Saints*, and wedged between the last of these and a Latin devotional work, *Anima Devota*, a paper-covered book of crossword puzzles. There was something else odd about the room besides this assortment of books—its smell. Not a particularly pleasant smell, but at any rate, a clean one, the first clean one I had met for some time, the smell of soap. Not the strongly scented variety, beloved of Indian servants, but good, honest, plain soap, the stuff you buy in long yellow bars.

I heard a brisk footstep in the passage, the door opened, and a nun entered. I knew at once that she was the Mother Superior because it was quite impossible that she could be anyone else.

Some years before, while my Sam Browne sat newly upon me, I turned from inspecting my platoon and found myself suddenly confronted at a few yards range with Lord Kitchener. He looked straight over the top of my head and said in a low voice, 'You'll all be wanted soon enough.' One of the men in the ranks behind me said, 'My Gawd!' That was all. But from that moment I never doubted that Kitchener was a great man. Similarly, after seeing Mother Angela for a couple of minutes, I knew that she could not fail to be the Mother Superior of any community in which she found herself.

She was a tall, spare woman, and her black gown hung angularly about her, but the lean, brick-red face, with its deep set eyes of brightest blue, and the hooked nose that jutted out over her wide mouth, could only belong to a woman of breeding and character. She held out a large, well-shaped hand, and smiled, showing a gap in her strong white teeth.

'You wished to see me?'

As I shook hands I quickly revised my ideas of the timid, hysterical religious. Rather nervously I explained my errand. Mother Angela listened patiently.

'But', she said when I had finished, 'there's no real danger. The people round here are better-class Hindus, they send their daughters to our school, *they* won't do anything. A few hooligans from the bazaar may throw a stone or two, but we've had that before. Besides,' she went on, 'if we run away, who's to look after the convent? It'll be looted all right then!'

'Oh no,' I hastened to reassure her. 'I'll put a guard on it.'

'Then', Mother Angela counter-attacked triumphantly, 'why not let us stop and put the guard on us? If you give us half a dozen British soldiers, who will dare to molest us? Not that bazaar rabble!'

In vain I argued. She was very good-tempered, very reasonable, too reasonable almost, but she would not go. Finally, I temporized weakly and agreed to leave a section for the night pending a final decision. Mother Angela, waving aside my suggestion that the men could camp in the playground, showed me a large classroom where they would be comfortable.

'But,' I said, 'won't it be very—er—awkward having men in your convent like this?'

'Why?' asked the Mother Superior innocently.

I subsided in blushes.

The old lady saw my confusion and relented. Putting her hand on my arm she said: 'My dear boy, even an old nun sees something of the army in this country, and I should be very happy to entrust my community not only to the valour, but to the courtesy of British soldiers.'

I surrendered unconditionally.

In spite of the efforts of the police and our patrols there was a nasty crop of murders and assaults in the back streets that night. In the morning Cornwall promulgated a curfew order forbidding anyone to be abroad between sunset and sunrise, and we were fully occupied in preventing Mohammedan mobs from breaking in on the route of the Hindu funeral. This was our third day and, after two nights with little rest, we were all getting rather part worn. I relieved a platoon with the one from the fort, but the police had no such exchanges to make. They had been at it longer than we had and much more constantly; indeed they were approaching exhaustion. Luckily we were able to take on much of the patrolling required to make sure the curfew was obeyed. I used lorries for the main streets, every now and then going through the narrower lanes on foot with a police guide. Moving between the high, shuttered houses reminded me of those engravings of the Inferno; gloomy chasms, at the bottom of which a few forlorn mortals grope their way.

About an hour before dawn, I stopped my two lorries at the mouth of such an alley and let the headlights shine down it. A solitary figure in the middle of the road turned and faced the sudden glare. We scrambled out and surrounded him. It was the little Hindu doctor who had attended the wounded outside the mosque. He showed me his pass, signed by Marples, and said he was on the way to a case of childbirth.

'You're very near the Mohammedan quarter; better be careful,' I warned him.

'I am almost at the house,' he said confidently. 'That one.'

He pointed to a door a few yards farther on. I watched him walk up to it and knock. The lorry was backing into the main road again, and its lights swung off us, but I could still distinguish the little doctor by the white suit he wore. As he raised his hand to knock again a shadow detached itself from other shadows and flitted towards him. For an instant I saw a bare arm which rose and struck. There was a gasp, and the little doctor crumpled up.

The assassin slipped back into the shadows but, as we dashed up the lane, I caught a glimpse of a running figure as it whipped down a side turning. A couple of men and my police guide stopped with the doctor, the rest of us plunged in pursuit. The man jinked again and again but, clattering and panting, we hung on his heels. At last, gaining on him, we emerged from a narrow entry into a wider street, just in time to see him scramble over a high wall. I jumped for the top of the wall. Built of dried mud, it crumbled and I fell back. By the time my sergeant had given me a leg up again, the small courtyard into which I looked was empty, but a soldier, astride the wall already, called out excitedly:

'He's gone in there, sir! I saw the door open and he went in!'

I dropped into the yard and shone my torch on the door, a

stout enough one. A good shove showed that it was firmly locked. I kicked on it till my toes ached, but with no result. While I was thus rather futilely occupied, the sergeant, with more presence of mind, had posted men to watch the windows and the road outside. I left off hammering and made a quick reconnaissance. The house stood on a corner, so that it had the street on two sides, the courtyard on a third, and only the fourth abutted on another house, a much smaller one, its roof so much lower that it would have been impossible to drop from one to the other. If the murderer had gone in he must still be there. The obvious thing was to search the house. I returned to the door.

I remembered reading of Bulldog Drummond or some other hero, who, confronted with a locked door, whipped out his pistol and blew away the lock. I drew my revolver, presented it at the huge keyhole, told the men to stand back, and loosed off. There was a great deal of noise, and a bit of metal whirred back over my shoulder, but as for any practical result on the door—nothing. I had effected something, however, for a shutter on the first floor creaked open and an old man's head cautiously emerged.

'*Kaun hai?* Who's there?' he quavered.

'Open the door!' I yelled. 'I am a British officer. Open!'

'*Chabi nahin hai*, there's no key!' he piped.

'It's no use talking to him, sir,' interposed the sergeant. 'This'll do the trick.'

Four of my men appeared with a heavy wooden bench they had discovered in the yard, and began a thunderous assault on the door. At the third blow we heard someone removing bolts inside. The door opened to show the old man standing in the bright light of an electric lamp. He was protesting volubly, and could not or would not understand my inquiries about the fugitive. I had never searched a house, and this seemed a big one. By the time I had posted men to watch the outside and left two at the door, I had only the sergeant, myself, and four men left.

We started on the ground floor, offices, a kitchen, and a storeroom with no signs of a cellar. 'Old Methuselah', as the sergeant dubbed him, continued to wail his protests, and was joined by two more men, an old one rather like himself, probably a brother, and a younger one, possibly a son, fat and middle-aged. They both jabbered in Hindustani, but so fast that I could not follow. In due course, having drawn a blank, we moved up to the first floor. Here were the main living-rooms, filled with an incongruous mixture of Victorian oddments of the antimacassar period and purely Indian furniture. The effect was garish and untidy; the air was of an abominable stuffiness. Here we met a fourth Indian, a young one, and I was puzzled. The man we were after could not be either of the ancients; the middle-aged one was far too fat; but this young man? Finally, I decided he was too tall, and gave him the benefit of the doubt for the present.

After a search without result I made signs that I would move to the next floor. A storm of protest arose, but, ignoring it, I advanced to the foot of the stairs, and there I came to a full stop. A carpet hung across the steps. In front of this purdah stood an old woman, she might have been of any age from seventy to a hundred, who as soon as I approached began to scream imprecations and abuse in a high, cracked voice. She held a strip of muslin over her mouth, but, as she warmed to her tirade, it slipped, and she never bothered to replace it. Her face was the colour and texture of a walnut shell; nose and chin almost met over toothless gums, but her black eyes were bright and baleful enough. I tried to explain to her menfolk that she must let us pass. They only joined their outcry to hers. At last in desperation I gave the order: 'Shift her out of the way as gently as you can.'

The sergeant advanced on her making pacific noises. 'Now, now, mother,' he cooed ingratiatingly.

The fat, middle-aged Indian suddenly broke into good English. 'This is a Mussulman house,' he said. 'That is the *zenana*; you cannot go in.'

'But we must. How else can we search the house?'

'You cannot go,' he reiterated.

I began to feel I was not on quite so good a wicket. I pictured the outcry that could be worked up if I forced an entrance into the *zenana*, especially if I could produce no justification. I wondered what my legal position was. I hesitated. The pandemonium died down. I could hear whisperings and shufflings beyond the curtain. My own men, the Indians, all looked towards me. An uncomfortable moment, but I felt my name would be mud if I gave way now. I turned to the fat man.

'Tell all the women to come down and go into that room we

have left. You can put a purdah over the door. My men will not enter. We will then search the upper rooms.'

More protests, but by now I was growing angry. I issued an ultimatum. Either the women came down or I searched upstairs with them there. A hurried consultation between the menfolk and the old woman resulted in their giving way and she vanished through the curtain.

Soon a procession of about a dozen women of all sizes, muffled in flowing *bourkas*, shuffled down the stairs. The old hag placed herself on guard, and at last some of her abuse was diverted from us to the presumably younger and more flighty women who kept peeping out at the white soldiers. Leaving a couple of men to see that none of the women came out of the room into which we had herded them, the sergeant, the other two, and I began our search upstairs. The furniture here was almost all Indian; mostly low beds, covered in plaited webbing, some of them with elaborately painted legs. There were several heavy chests, rickety wardrobes, some good rugs, and untidy heaps of clothing. In one room stood a European dressing-table covered with sticky pots of cosmetics. The air was stale with heavy perfume, and what was once euphuistically described to Queen Victoria as '*esprit de corps*'.

We delved into every hiding-place that could have held a man and searched the roof, but without result. Yet my soldier was positive that he had seen the fugitive enter, and something in the manner of its inmates convinced me that he was still in the house. It followed then that he was either one of the four men we had seen—and I did not believe he was—or . . . he was among the women. The more I thought of it, the surer I was that that was the solution. For all I knew there might be half a dozen men among them. How I longed for one of those imposing policewomen who watch you take your ticket in the Piccadilly Circus tube! Or if only Mother Angela had been here she would have winkled the fellow out in two minutes; but it was no use wishing, something had to be done. To demand to see the ladies' faces was out of the question. Completely at a loss, I turned to my sergeant. As a married man he might have some ideas. Splendid fellow, he had!

'We might be able to tell, sir,' he suggested, 'if we looked at their hands and feet.'

This seemed an excellent scheme, but I was sure that if I simply demanded to inspect their hands and feet I should be met by another outburst of refusal. Guile was indicated.

'The man we are after may be among the women,' I said.

'Impossible!' snorted the middle-aged Indian.

'Nevertheless, I must be sure.'

He began to protest, but I cut him short.

'The man has a finger missing from one hand. If all the ladies as they pass out will show their hands that will be enough to satisfy me whether he is there.'

The men of the household held a hurried consultation in whispers. At last the spokesman said: 'All right. We will allow that, but we protest at the outrage.'

There was a great deal of chatter and shuffling among the women, but in a few minutes they began to come out, one by one, passing between the sergeant and me. The old woman came first, holding out gnarled claws and saying something particularly biting which luckily I could not understand. We inspected another half-dozen pairs of hands, most small and well-shaped, some with henna-stained nails, some not over-clean, but all unexpectedly fair and undoubtedly feminine. Then seventh or eighth came a muffled figure with hands that, though little, were a shade darker than any that had gone before. True, they drooped languidly from the wrists, yet those very wrists were by no means innocent of black hair, and there was a hint of sinewy forearm.

I looked quickly at the Indian menfolk. They were silent, and I saw anxiety in their strained intentness. I caught the sergeant's eye. He nodded almost imperceptibly. Still I hesitated. A mistake would be most unfortunate. How were we to be sure? The sergeant rose again to the occasion. With seeming carelessness he let the butt of his rifle fall sharply on a slippered foot. Instead of a feminine squeal, there burst from the *bourka* an undeniably masculine howl!

It was broad daylight when we got back to the Kotwali with our bag—for we had collected all the male members of the household as accessories after the fact.

When he heard of our exploits, Marples mustered a grin.

'The Military will not be used as Civil Police,' he quoted, 'and don't ask me how much of your action was legal! But we'll put that chap where he'll get what's coming to him.'

While he was speaking, the telephone rang to tell us that two more companies of my battalion had arrived by train during the afternoon to relieve mine in the city. I felt as if I were deserting Marples and Cornwall, both of whom had already been working longer than I had and under greater strain, but I must confess that after four days and nights of 'Aid to the Civil', I was glad to pack up.

That night, back in my old brick barracks in the fort, I crept under my mosquito curtain and lay with a towel around my middle under a slowly ticking fan. Drowsily I passed in review the varied figures of the past few days: Jallaludin the magistrate, Debindra Lal, Mother Angela, the little Hindu doctor, the old hag in the *zenana*, and the rest. My mind ambled on, but in the end I fell asleep raising a metaphorical topi to the man who had provided me with a place where I could lie in what I realized now was comfort, and breathe air that did not poison me—to that old bewhiskered colonel of sappers.

V

STUDENT'S INTERLUDE

A Brigade Column, operating from Thal in the Kurram, yesterday took punitive action against the village of Panch Pir in Waziristan. The village was destroyed, three towers demolished and considerable loss inflicted on the hostile tribesmen. Our troops suffered few casualties and, having successfully accomplished their mission, returned to their base without incident.

Government of India Communique

STUDENT'S INTERLUDE

AT five o'clock of a warm autumn afternoon in the year 1920 I sat in my eighty-pounder tent laboriously following the career of Rahman Buksh, a perfectly beastly little boy, whose doings were of necessity familiar to such unfortunates as had still to pass the Higher Standard Urdu Examination of the Indian Army—and in those days we were a pretty numerous band.

The Great War was over, and the army was getting into its peace-time stride again so quickly that some of us found it hard work keeping up. Four years of war had, as our seniors never wearied of impressing on us, lamentably interfered with our training, and now our education was to be resumed, or, perhaps one should say, begun. Hence examinations—examinations for retention in the Indian Army, for promotion, for admission to courses, for the Staff College, in languages; all with the grimmest of penalties for failure. Under the shadow of the axe we sweated at our books, and I and others like me, wrestling with the crabbed Urdu script, grew to hate Rahman Buksh and sometimes, perhaps, to think a little wistfully of those unacademic days of war when what your platoon thought of you was of more moment than the opinion of the most erudite board of examiners.

We studied under difficulties. The tranquillity which should surround the student was sadly lacking. On every village green in England monuments were rising which proclaimed that the war was over, yet here I had only to raise my eyes to see once more the piled sandbags, the rough stone parapet, and the writhing strands of the barbed wire. Along some hundred miles of bristling frontier, we studied as best we could, amid alarms, excursions, and interruptions.

One such interruption drew my thoughts from Rahman Buksh. A hoarse voice, that rose unaccountably to a squeak every now and then, was speaking rapid Gurkhali somewhere behind my tent. It was the subadar-major giving a few final hints to the camp night pickets before sending them off to their posts.

'. . . after dark no challenging. Shoot anybody who approaches the wire, but'—a squeak—'remember, no shooting the wind in the wire or the shadow of a cloud on the rocks! If you shoot you must have a body to show for it'—squeak—'or at least blood, lots of blood. . . .'

No, peace and tranquillity did not seem to be having much of a show here! I resumed my halting translation of the list of sticky sweetmeats Rahman Buksh was gorging—loathsome little glutton!—but not for long. Another voice was raised outside, asking, this time in Hindustani, unmistakably sahib's Hindustani, for the adjutant.

I groaned.

Next moment the brigade major's florid face peered into my tent, rather like the rising sun in the badges of the Australian Forces that he had worn until some twist of fate diverted him into the Indian Army.

'Ah, there you are, digger!' he greeted me.

I waved him to a seat on the camp bed.

'What is it?' I asked wearily. 'Have I failed to furnish on due date the bi-weekly return of Jews, orthodox, practising, in the battalion, or have we to detail two of our remaining six officers for a course in mine-sweeping?'

'Beany' Harkness shook his head.

'I will deal with those matters by correspondence through the usual channels,' he said. 'This is the big stuff. Shh-h! Are we alone?'

'Except for about three thousand men within a few yards of us, yes!'

'Good!' He leant towards me while the bed creaked uneasily.

'The war's on!' he announced.

'What war?'

'Never you mind, digger. It's secret. The brigadier's been writing the orders for it for ten days.'

'I thought that was your job, writing orders?' I ventured.

'So'd I, but the brig thought different. I dare say he's right; I'd never have thought of half the sub-paras he's got in. Wonderful! You'll hear 'em.'

'When?'

'This evening, six pip emma, at the civil rest-house, bring your Old Man. Not a word to anybody else. Got to get round to the others now. So long.'

Well, that was that! Something was in the wind, and it was pretty certain I should not have a chance to open a book for the next few days. With some satisfaction I pitched Rahman Buksh into a corner and went to warn the colonel.

In some fortunate lands the fact that rests depends on security may not be obvious, but on the North-West Frontier of India, at any rate, there can be no doubt about it. The civil rest-house was in reality a small fort, with the living-rooms opening on to an interior courtyard, where a dozen or so British officers had assembled to get their orders. It was the sort of group that has gathered in such places at any time during the last hundred years, and for the same purpose.

There was Bill Harris, tall, lank, and hard as nails, commanding the Frontier Force battalion; Ewart of the Sikhs, stocky and short as his own men were tall; Roberts, brown and hook-nosed as any Pathan of his Frontier Militia; and my colonel, broader than most and tougher than most. Add a cherubic gunner major, a serious-minded captain of sappers, and a sprinkling of adjutants, fussing with note-books, message forms, and maps, and you have the typical audience that the brigadier looked down on from his table on the low veranda.

The brigadier always reminded me of President Wilson. Not that I had ever seen President Wilson, but I pictured him as a tall, spare man, deliberate in manner, efficient, just, earnest and kind, but withal more than a shade, shall we say, academic. Put a moustache on that and you have our brigadier. To inflict on this military Wilson as his Colonel House a brigade major like Beany Harkness was a masterpiece of juggling with square pegs and round holes.

Still, there they were. The brigadier at his table with a map the size of a sheet spread over it, a neat little sheaf of typewritten pages in his hand, and Beany lounging against a post slapping his boot with a leather-covered stick.

'Don't do that!' snapped the brigadier.

'Sorry,' said Beany.

The brigadier addressed us. He spoke of a certain village, Panch Pir.

'Where the hell's that?' demanded my colonel in a hoarse whisper.

'I don't know,' I answered, searching a map.

It appeared that Panch Pir had committed pretty well every possible outrage from massacring a survey party to pinching the morning milk on its way to camp. It is true that the inhabitants of Panch Pir were Wazirs and the Wazir is not a very refined fellow, but the catalogue of their exploits would have made Chicago police records seem Sunday School reading.

'It has been decided, therefore,' said the brigadier, 'to take punitive action against Panch Pir.'

'Yes, but where *is* the damn place?' growled my colonel.

'I will now read the Operation Order,' announced the brigadier. 'Reference Maps——'

I have a theory that, while the battles the British fight may differ in the widest possible way, they have invariably two common characteristics—they are always fought uphill and always at the junction of two or more map sheets.

This battle was to be no exception. The brigadier named four separate sheets of the one-inch map, and you are to imagine half a dozen field officers in a restricted space, each trying to fit together four large squares of paper. Some seated themselves and tried to spread them over their knees, some to hold them against the wall. My colonel carpeted the ground with his and used them much as a devout Mohammedan uses his prayer-mat. There was such a rustling, flapping, and crackling, such an undertone of cursing, that we missed the paragraph of the order headed, '*Information, our own and enemy forces.*'

However, we did find Panch Pir, a couple of tiny red squares on the map about eleven miles south of us as the crow flies, but a good deal farther by the only practicable route.

The brigadier read on.

It was a model operation order, but it was a long one. At last even the *Appendix of Administrative Instructions* was finished. We straightened our aching backs. The brigadier laid down the order.

'If there is any part which is not clear I can read that portion again,' he volunteered.

There was no response.

'We get a copy?' whispered my colonel.

I nodded.

'Are you quite happy, Colonel?' pressed the brigadier.

'Quite, sir, er—quite,' mumbled the colonel.

'What about you, Harkness?' asked the brigadier, turning suddenly on his brigade major.

Beany roused himself from a reverie and answered sweetly: 'I should like you to read it *all* again, sir, *taking the funny parts slowly!*'

The brigade majors of those days were not the efficient machine-turned Staff College article of today, but they *did* add a spice of variety to a conference.

The brigadier's jaw dropped; then it closed, grimly. He glared at Beany. In another moment speech would have returned to him, but nature intervened. A dust-devil came spinning through the gate into the courtyard. The whirling yellow spiral burst into our midst, scattered our maps and, seizing the precious leaves of the Operation Order, sent them twirling and twisting fifteen, twenty feet up. The meeting broke up in pursuit of the elusive paper, and Beany's castigation was deferred.

The next night I stood with our battalion headquarters waiting for zero, the hour the brigade would move out from camp. Beyond mysterious rustlings, the occasional stamp of hooves, the rattle of a harness chain, and, once or twice, the distinctive sound of rifle-butts colliding, there was little to show that all round two thousand men were feverishly active. The shrill protesting bray of a mule was followed by the hollow smack of a hand across its nose, and suddenly near at hand there came an anguished whisper of '*Teri ama—Lato!* Blockhead, that's my foot!' hushed at once by some N.C.O's low growl of '*Chup!* Shut up!'

A minute still to go; then a muffled tramp, tramp, and the leading troops, the Sikhs, were approaching the gate in the perimeter. They flitted silently past like a moving black screen with a frieze of silhouetted *puggris* against the sky, rounded for the Sikhs, pointed for the Pathans and Punjabis who followed them. A sudden drop in the height of the screen and the Gurkha hats of two of our companies, picketing troops with the advance guard; then a bunch of British topis, a section from a machine-gun company with their mules; more mules, the mountain guns; *puggris* again and a stream of mules, the transport, rations, spare ammunition. Last, the ambulance, recognizable easily from the portly figure of our Indian doctor on his pony, bulking broadly against the stars.

Behind me two Gurkha signallers began to whisper: one, Jaspati, a youngster fresh from the depot; the other, Ranbir, a veteran of the Great and several small wars.

'O *sati*,' piped the youth, 'what are *we* going to do?'

'Rear-guard.'

'Rear-guard? And we are Gurkhas!'

'Wait, Jaspati, we shall also be rear-guard coming back; you'll get your bellyful of fighting.'

A brusque 'Silence!' from a Gurkha officer put a stop to this conversation between ardent youth and soured experience.

At last our turn came, and we tailed in behind the ambulance, but we had hardly passed the wire when some disturbance ahead held us up. Masses of mules, in strings of three, were swirling round in a sort of ring-a-ring of roses, while above all, spinning rapidly on his axis, loomed the doctor. I could hear him bleating above a rising clamour.

Shoving through the mob, I reached the rotating doctor; his words came in gusts, like beams from a lighthouse, as he revolved.

'... orders to go to Mukhi Khel ... brigade major told me ... this is not way ... *that*'—he risked a hand from the saddle—'that is way ... I am turning ambulance.'

Then I remembered that as a secrecy precaution in the orders issued to troops that afternoon Mukhi Khel had been named in place of Panch Pir. The real objective had been published only an hour before the start, but somehow it had not reached the doctor. I explained, but he was still doubtful, so I gave his pony a good slap over the rump when it was headed in the right direction, and it bore him rapidly after the column. His people sorted themselves out, and we resumed the march.

We soon left the road and turned south into a track described in the route-book as 'made camel road, passable for field artillery except at river crossings'. But it had been made in happier times; for more than three years no British foot had ventured far along it, and the ravages of the weather had destroyed its surface, while crumbling side ditches had encroached and wandering streams scored it deep every few yards. There would be a lot of work for pick and shovel before it was once more 'passable for field artillery'. Years afterwards, I was flown along this track. Beneath me, motor-buses did their thirty miles an hour over the macadam and across great girder bridges, where we had stumbled and floundered a decade before.

For stumble and flounder we certainly did, stubbing our toes against stones, tripping over ruts, and twisting ankles in pot-holes. At night, on such a track, the tail of a column, move the head ever so steadily, will advance in a series of jerks, more tiring than a much faster even pace. After a time we dipped downhill into the bed of the river which we had been following, and crossed to the other side. The actual stream was only about sixty yards wide, but it was three feet deep and running strongly. Three feet of water may not trouble a long-legged Pathan very much, but for a five-feet-two Gurkha it is over the waist. Luckily, what the Gurkha lacks in inches he makes up for in the qualities most required for river crossing, stability and cheerfulness.

We emerged on the far bank and trudged on, our boots squelching, for a couple of miles. We were now approaching the big village of Fakir Kot, inhabited partly by a section of Wazirs no longer openly hostile and partly by the same section that owned Panch Pir. The brigadier had decided to round up Fakir Kot not only because we could hardly expect to pass it unobserved, but because he hoped we might find some particularly wanted out-laws lurking there. Accordingly we halted while the Sikhs and some Militia put a cordon round the sleeping village. We hung about, feeling rather cold and miserable for an hour, enlivened once by a single shot from the village, some shouts, and much barking of dogs. However, the alarm died down, and, leaving the Sikhs sitting tight all round the village ready to search it at dawn, we moved on.

The track got worse, the night darker; all we could do was to keep the last mules of the ambulance in sight and follow trustfully. Soon there seemed to be a hitch in front, and we halted for twenty minutes. Suddenly the mules ahead of us moved off and disappeared as if the earth had swallowed them. So in fact it had. We could hear them sliding and crashing down into a deep *nullah* which here crossed our path.

We followed. The colonel, who was leading, slipped and tobogganed forty feet on his ample posterior to the bottom, where he broke my fall nicely. I murmured something about 'getting on to keep touch', and left him before he had recovered enough wind properly to express himself.

I crossed the sandy *nullah* bed, about forty yards across, splashed through a little stream, and climbed the steep bank. As I emerged I could see against the sky a dark mass of motionless mules, with to the flank a familiar silhouette.

'What's the trouble?' I asked the doctor. 'Why don't you get on?'

'Where to go?' he demanded plaintively. 'My horse makes a bother, and when I get to top—no one is here. Where to go?'

I looked around. There was not a sign of the rest of the column. It had marched on, happily ignorant that the natural protests of a fourteen-hand pony at having to carry as many stone of doctor up a cliff had deprived them of an ambulance and a rear-guard. The track seemed to fork in all directions, and in the dark it was not easy to discover which branch to follow. However, the colonel, by no means quite mollified, arrived and promptly ordered me to ride on and tell the main body to halt till we caught them up.

I took my old horse, Nigger, from the *syce* and trotted cautiously along the most likely track. Very soon I had lost all touch with the rear-guard and could hear nothing of the column. Nigger's hooves made no sound in the dust, and the faint starlight showed no bounds to the flat plain over which we moved except on the right where a denser blackness hinted at hills against the sky. It was rather uncanny and not at all comfortable. We were well within hostile limits and my thoughts wandered to the unpleasantness that I might bump into if I really were, as I was beginning to suspect, on the wrong track. I seemed to have ridden for miles. I *must* be on the wrong track!

I am afraid I am not very brave by myself in the dark. I pulled Nigger up and sat listening. Not a sound. Suddenly his twisted, country-bred ears went forward, and when I eased his reins he trotted on confidently enough. Soon we came up to a string of three mules led by a solitary *drabi*, a gap, then the straggling tail of the transport, half-running to keep up. Trotting briskly, I pushed past the column until the topis of the brigade staff showed up amongst their horses.

I was not welcomed. The brigadier asked me what I thought I was doing clattering up and down the column. I apologized and gave my message. He made a few uncomplimentary remarks about a rear-guard that could not keep up, and though I might have reminded him that the little red book says a column should halt to close up after crossing an obstacle at night, I had too much sense. Long ago I had learned that in conversation with an irate senior, a junior officer should confine himself strictly to the three remarks, 'Yes, sir', 'No, sir', and 'Sorry, sir'! Repeated in the proper sequence, they will get him through the most difficult interview with the minimum discomfiture.

I fell back on these, and the column halted. When I met the rear-guard closing up, I found relations between its commander and the doctor somewhat strained, and I arrived just in time for the colonel to work off some of his nervous irritation on me.

Had I found the unmentionable brigade? Had I asked them why the blazes they had not halted after crossing the *nullah*? I had been a hell of a long time about it!

'Yes, sir', 'No, sir', 'Sorry, sir'!

Reunited, the column resumed its march, and plodded on for a couple of hours, until turning sharp left it abandoned the track and struck across rough stubble fields, down a gradual slope, to the river again. The water which ran in several channels was nowhere more than a couple of feet deep, but it seemed icy cold as it filled our boots once more. Now, ahead of us, the stars began to fade, and against a greyish background a jagged line of low hills began to stand out. The grey was tingeing with the faintest lemon-yellow as we stumbled across a stony plain, and before we were at the foot of the hills, a reddish glow threw their crests into sharp silhouette. We still moved in the chilly shadow, but behind us distant peaks far beyond the river glowed in the light. The sun was up.

So were our pickets. As we clambered up from the river, semaphore flags jerked, with the spasmodic energy that distinguishes that form of communication, from the summits on our flanks. It was full daylight by the time we had urged the last mule on to the plateau and we saw the promised land spread out before us—and it did not look too promising!

A boulder-strewn plain stretched for more than a mile until it met the low, broken hills that formed its far boundary. Rocky outcrops thrust through its surface in all directions, limiting the view and giving it a wild, grim look that a few isolated wind-swept trees and some poor efforts at cultivation did little to soften. The only sign of habitation was the square top of a frontier tower that showed, half a mile away to our right front, above the end of an intervening outcrop.

'Panch Pir!' announced the colonel, and as he said it we heard the first shot.

The first shot of a fight affects people in different ways. The Gurkhas halted around us, fell suddenly silent, then a low buzz of talk came from them. Our old subadar-major sighed gently. '*Oho, oho!*' he breathed in a mixture of mild interest and satis-faction. The colonel let his false teeth fall to his lower lip and recovered them with an audible click. For myself, I had moment-arily an uncomfortable cross-channel feeling where my breakfast should have been. Why do battles always start at dawn on an empty stomach?

The transport was now halted and closing up in the shelter of the outcrop that cut off our view. The colonel and I walked for-ward until we could see round it. There, rising from one corner of a large walled enclosure was the tower, a tall, rather graceful structure, tapering to its summit, just below which ran the usual projecting platform.

Through our glasses we could see a company of the Frontier Force trickling forward in workmanlike fashion from cover to cover towards the walls. A Lewis gun was making the dust fly every five seconds round a loophole half-way up the tower, and a couple of machine-guns joined in, steadily traversing along the wall. A platoon in two widely extended lines passed out of sight at the double round an angle of the enclosure, and a few moments later we saw khaki-clad figures on the wall. We heard later that the half-dozen die-hards in the tower had all been accounted for as they attempted to bolt.

'I suppose', I said to the colonel, 'we'll sit here for an hour or two while they burn the place?'

'Ought to burn that in half an hour,' he replied, 'but I expect brigade'll spend two hours writing orders about it!'

But apparently they were not going to, for suddenly the

transport began to stream on again, and rather mystified we followed. After half a mile there was another halt. From ahead came the sounds of what might have been a slow practice on a musketry range—a report, silence for a few seconds, then a couple of shots together, another pause, and a single shot. Once or twice we heard the loud *bang! bang!* of the 2·75-inch mountain guns, followed by the dull *whump! whump!* of bursting shells.

The old signaller, Ranbir, squatting behind me, had seized the opportunity to clean his *kukri* before the rust of its immersions of last night had eaten into it. His young friend, Jaspati, sat beside him, flicking a flag occasionally at a picket in the way signallers have. The desultory shooting ahead went on, sometimes dying away, at others brisking up into a respectable fusillade. After about half an hour we began to wonder what was happening.

'Go and see what they're up to,' ordered the colonel.

I went forward with a couple of runners, past the ambulance with the doctor still sitting on his pony, and found all the transport huddled in the gorge between two outcrops. Here, to my astonishment, the column ended. I hailed the British warrant officer in charge of the transport.

'Where's the rest of the brigade?' I asked blankly.

'Gone on,' he answered simply. 'Told me to halt here.'

'What are they doing?'

'I dunno, sir.'

'Where have they gone?'

'Dunno, sir.'

I sent a runner back to tell the colonel that we seemed to have been left behind and forgotten. In a few minutes he joined me, having wisely brought with him headquarters and one company. He arranged our local protection and then told me to go forward again and get in touch with the brigade.

I collected the two signallers, Ranbir and Jaspati, with my runners and moved along a rough track on the side of the long outcrop on our left. We were thus completely sheltered on that side, but on the right quite open. As I walked along, followed by the four Gurkhas, I heard the vicious whine of a bullet overhead followed by the distant report of a rifle out in the plain to the right.

'Somebody is shooting at us!' announced Jaspati in a rather awe-struck voice.

'They are,' agreed Ranbir, 'and when that happens, *sati*, do not go near white stones or sahibs!'

Out of the tail of my eye I saw him hold the others back until there was a twenty-yard gap between us. It made me feel rather lonely. I looked back, and there were our headquarters and the best part of a company all comfortably seated under cover, faces turned expectantly towards us. They must have felt like people in the stalls watching a show; I felt rather like one of those tin animals that are dragged slowly across shooting ranges at country fairs for yokels to bang at. However, it was up to the adjutant, whatever he felt like, to give an example of indifference under fire. I comforted myself with the thought that the bullet had been a long way from me . . . perhaps it was not aimed at me at all, just a stray shot. . . .

A bullet hit the track about five yards ahead of me. No, not a stray!

I stepped out a little more briskly. Another crack, behind me this time, and a horrid thud as the bullet found a soft spot in the hillside. One in front, one behind—a bracket! The adjutant must set an example, the adjutant must . . . I was not running, but I was walking fast, very fast. I began to count my steps, one, two, three, four. . . . A giant clapped his hands in my ear, splinters of rock showered over me, and I was running, running as hard as Providence and a good pair of legs would let me. From below came the full-throated roar of a hundred–odd men laughing fit to burst at their fleeing and discomfited adjutant.

We were soon in the lee of another low bump on top of which I saw a Gurkha picket. I scrambled up and found it was one placed by the advance-guard. The havildar in charge received me with a broad grin.

'Why didn't you give me covering fire?' I demanded angrily.

The grin spread all over his flat face.

'Sahib,' he said simply, 'I forgot. We were watching you run!'

I changed the subject.

'Where's the brigade?' I asked.

He pointed over my shoulder.

'Burning the village,' he said.

'What village?'

'Panch Pir,' he answered as one surprised at a foolish question.

'Panch Pir! But that's——' I looked. There sure enough below us, on the far edge of the plateau, was a village. The usual collection of mud hovels, hardly distinguishable from the brown earth around them, a mean village, but the veritable Panch Pir. As I looked, thin wisps of white began to rise from one end of it; gradually the line of smoke moved through the village as the demolition parties lit up the houses. The separate smoke columns rose straight into the almost windless air, blended into one another, changed colour to a dull brown, and towered up hundreds of feet, a great, dirty smudge across the sky.

'Where's brigade headquarters?'

The havildar pointed to a mound with a group of figures on it, half-way between us and the village.

'Call up,' I ordered.

Ranbir obeyed. No answer. Jaspati came to his assistance and waved vigorously. A couple of semaphorists from the picket supplemented their efforts, and finally the havildar himself contributed a masterly display with two Gurkha hats. Just as the performance was working up to a crescendo of effort, a voice said: 'Hullo! What's this? Classification of signallers? I always say you Gurkhas would train at your grandmother's funeral! I give the old boy with the hats a "distinguished".'

Beany Harkness rode slowly up to us.

'No use training signallers', I growled, 'with a brigade headquarters that's blind, deaf, and in blinkers.'

Beany laughed.

'And we had a peach of a paragraph in orders about *Intercommunication* too! Anyway, what's the excitement?'

I told him.

'Tut-tut!' he said. 'Did I forget you? Sorry, digger. Never mind, everything's lovely. We're for 'ome, 'Orace! You're rear-guard!'

'Thanks!' I said drily.

He pointed out the line we were to hold to let the column through, and went cheerily back to the mound.

Before I left, the havildar proudly showed me a dead tribesman, lying just below the picket. It is difficult to estimate a man's height when he lies sprawling on the ground, but that fellow must have been within an inch or two of seven feet. The Gurkha took off one of the dead man's *chuplis* and gleefully drew my attention to its colossal size. I had certainly never seen bigger footwear on a human being. We heard afterwards that he was the local giant and rather famous in those parts.

'Where's his rifle?' I asked.

'His friends got that,' said the little havildar regretfully, and then, cheering up again, 'but we got *him*!'

The colonel came along and we soon had two companies deployed as rear-guard. Nor had we long to wait. Half a dozen stretchers, four bearers to each, passed through, two of the figures lying on them with covered faces—the giant was not unavenged. Then a flock of goats, chivied along by militiamen, who had slung their rifles and taken to sticks. A couple of mountain guns, the British machine-gun section, and an officer of the Frontier Force with a list of pickets joined us. Behind them came the rest of the force, and as soon as they were well clear we raised the red flag and the retirement began.

The red flag was familiar on the Frontier, I believe, long before it achieved a wider notoriety elsewhere. Here it had no political significance and only indicated rear-guard headquarters to anxious pickets, being used to signal their permission to withdraw.

Everything went steadily until we drew level with the isolated tower that we had at first thought was Panch Pir itself; then we were told to hold on while it was destroyed. A few shots came our way, and everybody got under cover, the colonel and I sitting with our backs against a big rock, while he cursed the delay.

'They'll be on top of us properly if we hang about now,' he complained. A bullet smacked into our rock and went shrilly ricochetting off into the blue. 'And to think', he groaned, 'I've only six months to go for pension!'

We sat mournfully contemplating the distant tower. It stood straight and defiant, dominating the drab landscape, one side in full sunlight, the other dark in shadow. Suddenly a puff of white smoke shot out from its base, the great square tower rose bodily, and for a second hovered in the air. Then it sank gently back again and, as a dull boom came to us, dissolved completely. A swelling bronze beehive of smoke and dust bellied up, looking as solid as the tower it had replaced.

'As many pounds of gun-cotton as the diameter of the tower in feet plus five,' murmured the colonel.

Then we got really busy.

The Frontier Force company that had covered the demolition came sprinting back, reported to us, and went on to join its battalion. By this time the tribesmen had recovered from the surprise of our visit, and all the lads of the village and of a good many other villages were after us. While we were waiting, a picket on our left had reported that the enemy were creeping in on them. We had heard a good deal of firing from it, and had made our arrangements to cover it, but it was an anxious moment —a casualty up there now would be very awkward.

The red flag gave the signal and for a moment nothing happened. Then, up on the hill-top, little black blobs like beetles appeared, crawling slowly over a stretch of smooth rock. Suddenly with one accord the beetles stood up, revealing themselves as Gurkhas, turned, and were running in short zigzags towards us. The last man waved a semaphore flag, the recognized invitation to us to deal faithfully with anyone who appeared behind him. But no one did. Our machine-guns had the summit taped to an inch and the mountain guns, experienced in these matters, landed a shell neatly each side of it just where a rush might be expected. The N.C.O. in charge of the picket reported all complete at the red flag and showed me his *kukri*, its wooden handle neatly removed by a bullet.

The retirement went as such retirements usually do. The main body plodded steadily on, seemingly heartlessly indifferent to the tribulations of the rear-guard. There was the awful moment when we thought we had missed a picket, and the relief when we found we had not; the nerve-racking delay while a wounded man was brought in; the constant anxiety about covering fire; and the maddening habit that all headquarters have of standing about in bunches.

We held the edge of the plateau to cover the column across the river, and then ran for it. As we were splashing through one of the streams I saw a Gurkha ahead of me stop, bend down, and carefully put his hand into the water. I shouted to him to get on. He took no notice, but gave a sudden flick of his wrist. There was a flash of silver and a sizeable fish was jerking on the stones. He picked it up, shoved it into his haversack, grinned cheerfully at me, and doubled on. I have never known a Gurkha miss a chance to fish, but I have never seen a chance taken so quickly.

We had another delay after crossing. The transport had, for both speed and safety, forded the river on a wide front, and some time was taken in sorting it out while the advance-guard was putting up pickets again. We seized the chance to eat a hurried meal from our haversacks, and the tribesmen took that opportunity to get over the river downstream of us, as we soon discovered.

When we moved again, it was evident that there were a good many hanging on to our left as we retired. Then a picket mistook its signal and came in too soon. There they were, tearing down the hill, and we had no covering fire ready for them. Worst of all, a picket further out was still up.

'That picket's come in too soon!' I yelled to the colonel. 'The enemy'll be there in a minute!'

'They are there, my dear chap,' he answered quite cheerfully. 'I can see 'em!'

Luckily someone else had seen them too—the havildar-major of 'B' Company, a fellow of energy and initiative. He seized a couple of passing Lewis-gun sections, and in a flash had them spluttering away at the vacated picket site. Lewis guns are not designed for overhead covering fire, but they did it that day all right. We soon had machine-guns and the mountain battery on the job, called in a couple of pickets in rapid succession, and ran hard for five minutes, thus, like the wise soldiers we were, avoiding the danger by running away from it.

After that, things steadied up. One line of the rear-guard would retire while another covered it, but this leap-frogging is at the best a gruelling process. The rear party, if pressed, flings dignity to the winds and frankly bolts until it is behind its support, but at headquarters we could afford to be rather more deliberate, and we moved at a walk from one stand of the red flag to another. Once, as we trudged along at the head of our little procession, we found a group at the side of the track. A stretcher lay in the dust, and on it a six-foot Sikh havildar of the Frontier Force; a bullet had got him an inch from his belt buckle, as grim a wound as a man could have. He had already been carried some miles, and his only hope was to survive the agony of another ten. The four bearers from the ambulance were obviously almost exhausted, and there was nothing for it but to detail some of our men who could ill be spared. They raised the stretcher and staggered off, but although they kept moving and we got more bearers from the ambulance, they could not catch up with the main body, and our pace for the next five miles or so had to be regulated by that stretcher. The more I saw of that Sikh, the more I admired him for his uncomplaining fortitude on that ghastly journey.

Still, we got on quite well. The ground was much more open, and guns and machine-guns, well handled, were keeping the tribesmen at a reasonable distance. We had done between four and five miles after crossing the river, and our rear parties were leap-frogging steadily through one another, when a hitch occurred.

Headquarters was safely behind the second echelon of the rear-guard and we were waiting for the line nearest to the enemy to fall back through us. We saw it rise, turn, and begin to double back. Then one platoon, on the left, stopped and got down again. I could see some of our men dodging about, and a Gurkha officer whom I recognized as old Subadar Bombahadur, a dear, bone-headed old fellow, prancing up and down among them. Broderick, the British officer commanding that company, halted the rest of his people about half-way towards us and seemed as puzzled as we were. Pickets on each flank had been called in, and if we hung about much longer we might have the enemy between us and the main body.

'Get that damned old fool back at once!' ordered the colonel.

I blew my whistle till I was bursting, signalled the retire, and waved the red flag, all to no purpose.

'Go and tell him!' roared the colonel. 'Take your horse!'

I did not altogether relish the idea—the dilatory platoon was attracting other attention besides our own—but there was nothing for it. I called up my *syce*, and mounted Nigger. With some vague notion of signalling with it, I still grasped the big red flag by its six-foot pole. I had an idea that the faster I went, the safer I should be, and so I kicked the old horse heartily in the ribs, and off we went. And very ridiculous we must have looked; for Nigger, revelling in a gallop at last, went all out. I became involved in that beastly red flag, which wrapped itself round my head, and for a time I thought we should end up back in Panch Pir again. However, I managed, rather flustered, to pull up at Broderick, dismount and get Nigger taken under cover. Broderick, a young subaltern, under fire for the first time, struck me as having a very good grip of himself and of the situation. He had just sent back a platoon under another subadar, Ratanbahadur, to help extricate old Bombahadur, and kneeling behind a friendly rock he told me what had happened.

A machine-gun section had been in action and, when the time came for it to up-sticks and leap-frog back, the guns had been duly loaded on to the mules. Then the trouble started. One of the mules had been wounded, broken loose and bolted, unfortunately towards the enemy. As it went, it bucked, burst a girth, dragged its saddle until it could kick it free, and vanished. The result was that as old Bombahadur came doubling back, he found himself passing through an area littered with bits of machine-gun, spare parts, and saddlery. At once the old man halted his platoon, and set it to work methodically to collect the pieces. At last almost every man in the platoon had retrieved something, but Bombahadur, running his eye over the spoil, saw an essential was missing.

'Tirpal?' he asked, but no one had the tripod.

Bombahadur stood upright and peered round. Several interested spectators behind rocks had shots at him, but he remained standing till he saw the precious tirpal. He pointed. A young lance-naik rose, slung his rifle, and ran forward. The gentlemen behind the rocks were roused to an increasing interest. Spurts of dust sprang up round the running Gurkha, but after about fifty yards he stopped, and in a moment he was running back with the tripod, still pursued by those ominous puffs of dust. Bombahadur, satisfied, gave the word, and his laden platoon sprinted back.

Meanwhile the other subadar, Ratanbahadur, had got his platoon up on Bombahadur's right. We could see him walking about unconcernedly, searching the ground in his turn. Ratanbahadur is worth a word. He was the biggest, blackest, and most powerful Gurkha I have met. Rumour had it that he was an escaped slave, though I never heard of anyone brave enough to ask him. He had risen by sheer strength, courage, and personality, in spite of the very real handicap of his origin. Although an officer, he was not quite a gentleman; he was noisy, boastful, and in his cups distinctly hairy-heeled, but he was generous, cheerful, and feared positively nothing, animal or human, natural or supernatural.

Ratanbahadur walked up and down; then he saw something that Bombahadur had missed. It was the machine-gun pack-saddle lying where the mule's last frantic kick had left it. A pack-saddle is no mean weight, and a more awkward thing to carry it would be hard to devise; but Ratanbahadur picked it up with an easy swing and gave the order to retire. They came at the double, the subadar with the saddle resting on his hip. After a hundred yards he slowed to a walk, and himself halting, faced towards the enemy, raised the saddle high above his head, the broken girth streaming loose, and roared: '*M'lai her!* Look at me, Subadar Ratanbahadur Rana, I.-D.-S.-M.', and he fairly rolled the initials of his decoration, the Indian Distinguished Service Medal, off his tongue.

He then did a couple of press-ups with the saddle and resumed his retirement. As a bit of bravado it was worse than foolish—but there was something magnificent about it. It pleased the men tremendously; the Gurkha is a simple soul who likes people to behave in character. So do I, when it is Ratanbahadur's sort of character.

After this delay, the tribesmen pressed more boldly, and for the first time we caught an occasional glimpse of a grey figure scurrying from cover to cover. Our battery had always a couple of guns in action, and they helped us as only well-handled mountain artillery can. We speeded up. Our bounds, as one party leap-frogged through another, became shorter, but had to be faster. The afternoon was drawing out, the men had covered a lot of ground in the last twenty hours, a good deal of it at the double, and they were tiring. There was, too, a marked increase in the tribesmen's fire. They were particularly concentrating on the two British officers with the rear parties; puffs of dust followed them wherever they moved. They changed their topis for less conspicuous Gurkha hats, but, whatever he wears, a British officer is somehow always identifiable, whether in Piccadilly or on a battlefield.

It looked as if we were in for a run of bad casualties. The only thing that was saving us was the tribesmen's extraordinarily bad shooting. At the time we could not understand it and only hoped it would continue. But we could not expect it to, and we got back from the ambulance some riding ponies, fitted with special saddles that not-too-badly wounded men could cling to. These ponies we managed collect at rear headquarters, but it was not so easy to keep them there. The *syces* were only unarmed followers, hurriedly enrolled; they were very conspicuous, and one had been killed already, so it was trying them rather high. It was something else to watch, and by this time we had more than enough to keep our eyes on.

At last we reached the big village, Fakir Kot, that we had rounded up the night before. For the moment things had eased up a bit, as we had rapped rather smartly the knuckles of some sportsmen who had been too bold in following us, and they were now hanging back a little. The Sikh battalion we had left yesterday in the village had gone on, leaving the inhabitants to their own devices, and we looked rather nervously at the long wall and the towers only a couple of hundred yards on our flank. We could see heads bobbing on the ramparts and what looked like a crowd at the gate.

As we drew level, a drum began suddenly to beat. I was riding with the battery commander; we looked at one another and our lips formed the same words, 'The *Chiga Dol!*'—the call to arms. The crowd at the gate, about fifty of them, all with rifles, streamed towards us, the drum still beating. The gunner was just getting his section into action at point-blank range when we saw a khaki-clad figure in a topi running with the mob and recognized it as the political officer.

His achievement was remarkable. He had persuaded the Fakir Kot *chiga*, the village pursuit party, or at any rate some of it, to turn out to help us. What eloquence, what promises, what threats he had used, I do not know, but there they were, looking none too friendly and far from eager to fling themselves into the fray. The political officer shepherded them into a rough line along a small *nullah* and took his stand behind them, ready to nip in the bud any idea of premature retirement.

He asked me to stay with him to see that there was no mis-understanding between our fellows and their new allies, and I called to our subadar-major to join me. It was well we stayed, as we were just in time to catch our old friend Subadar Ratan-bahadur Rana—'I.–D.–S.–M.'—stalking the line from a flank with a Lewis gun. I explained, and regretfully he passed on.

Our rear party doubled through and left the three of us with nothing but that thin and shabby line of 'friendlies' between us and whatever might be following. Frankly, I did not like it a bit. I quite expected that *chiga* to start the proceedings by bolting and/or, as we say in military documents, shooting us. However, exhorted by the political officer, they remained, crouching along the shallow *nullah*, while we fixed our eyes on a low rise about three hundred yards away. Suddenly, a ragged bunch of figures came swarming over the crest, and I liked the position still less.

'Fire!' yelled the political officer in perfectly good English.

The *chiga* obeyed, but I noted that every rifle was pointed sky-wards—they were not going to risk any unpleasantness or blood-feuds with their neighbours. At the ragged volley, the three of us turned and ran. The political officer had, not so long before, been one of the best sprinters at his Varsity, but he told me after-wards that he had never done the 220 in better time. Be that as it may, I was never more than five yards behind him, and the fat, bow-legged old subadar-major was a close third. It only shows that how fast you run depends on what is after you.

But now our troubles were nearly over. The *chiga* certainly had not shot anyone, but they had, at least, rather flabbergasted the pursuit. Dusk was coming down as we approached the final crossing of the river, and to our immense relief we found our old friends, the Sikh battalion, in position waiting to cover us across.

I stood with Broderick, whose company was rear party, waiting to give the word to an officer of the Sikhs that we were all through his line. Among the last to pass was the wounded Sikh havildar, carried by a mixed party of Gurkhas and ambulance men, all so exhausted that they had dropped right back to the rear-guard again. He was still conscious and spoke to me, but it seemed impossible that he could survive the appalling journey. Nevertheless, he did, and eventually was invalided on a pension. I hope it was a good one, and that he is still enjoying it in some Punjab village.

The men were whacked. With little rest they had done over

thirty miles since the previous evening. Actually, the length of the
track we had followed was thirty-two miles, but to that must be
added the digressions to pickets and flanks that most of them had
made, and the constant doubling of the rear parties. Now that
they were almost in safety, they staggered and shuffled past in the
fading light, tired and more than tired, but still cheerful.

I turned to the officer of Sikhs.

'That's the lot, I think.'

'Right-o! We take over,' he agreed cheerfully.

Then we saw creeping towards us through the deepening gloom
a bowed, hump-backed little figure. Slowly and unsteadily it
drew near, a very small Gurkha, bearing on his shoulders a leather
two-gallon container that held water for a machine-gun. It was
his share of the rescued equipment. He had been told to bring it in,
and bring it in he would. He was in the last stages of exhaustion,
and no wonder, for the poor little mutt had not had the sense
to empty out the water. We relieved him of his burden and went
down to the river.

Almost my last memory of a full day is the doctor's bulky
figure, still perched on his wretched pony, planted fairly in the
middle of the river. The patient beast had struck at last; its head
was buried in the water. It was almost dark, but the doctor's ample
silhouette showed black against silver, and some sportsman out
beyond the Sikhs was having a farewell shot or two. *Plonk!* A
bullet splashed into the water, and the doctor's fat legs jerked
frantically, drumming his heels on the horse's ribs, but it only
sank its nose deeper. *Plonk!* The doctor removed his topi and
belaboured his mount with it, but to no avail: that horse meant
to drink his fill. Luckily for them both, the light was gone and the
tribesmen were still shooting atrociously.

Later on we found out why. In the informal way things are
done on the Frontier, we sent a message to the enemy, telling
them, among other things, that we did not think much of their
shooting. We received an answer which complimented us on our
raid. It had been, they said, a thoroughly good show, and they
regretfully admitted that for the first time on record we had
killed more of them than they had of us. In fact, the training of
the troops had shown much improvement on any they had so far
met, and reflected great credit on the brigadier. Touching the

matter of their shooting they were rather ashamed, but there was a reason. Their rifles were all Short Lee-Enfields, acquired in previous fights with our troops—a shrewd cut that—while their ammunition, which had been generously provided by the Amir of Kabul, was British also, but it was unfortunately the old pattern Mark VI, and the rifles were sighted for the new Mark VII. They had not realized this at the time, but had now calculated the adjustment necessary, and they would be delighted, should we give them an opportunity, to demonstrate what a difference it made to their shooting! One cannot help feeling that the fellows who wrote that ought to be on our side.

An hour after we reached camp, having collected the dozens of reports that everybody wants to give an adjutant when he is most tired, I crept to my tent. I was dead beat. I lifted the flap, switched on my torch, and the first thing I saw in the circle of light was that beastly Hindustani book, lying where I had tossed it two days ago. I thought of Rahman Buksh and of examinations—and I groaned.

Student's interlude was ended.

VI

COUNSEL OF FEARS

The hard fact remains that the operation at Gallabat, carried out early in November, failed of its object.

British Official History: Mediterranean and Middle East,
Vol. I

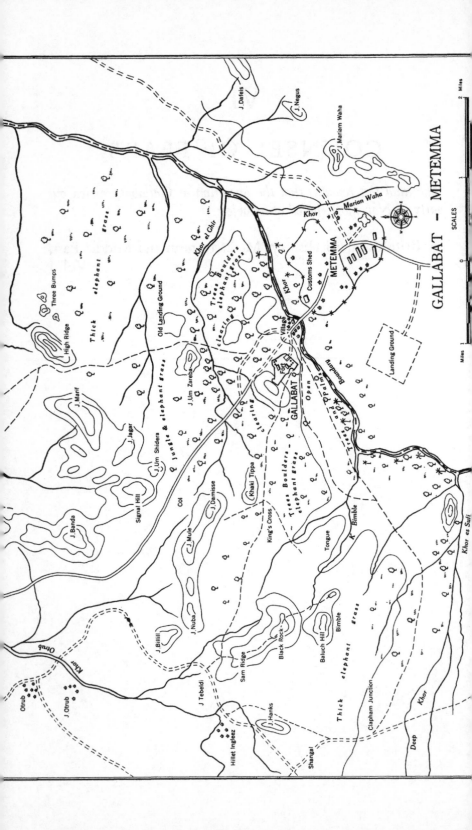

GALLABAT – METEMMA

COUNSEL OF FEARS

THE Secretary of State for War held out his hand: 'Well, good-bye, Brigadier. Thanks for your hospitality and for showing me round, and'—with an amused twinkle in his eye—'and the best of luck on Wednesday!'

As we shook hands I felt rather foolish. I had enjoyed this visit from a man for whom I had always had a great deal of admiration and who, on actual acquaintance, had proved so interesting and so knowledgeably interested. But I had not said anything to him about Wednesday. I had been grimly determined to mention Wednesday to no one unless he simply *had* to be told—not even to the Secretary of State for War! Now it was plain, as of course it always ought to have been to me, that he had known all about Wednesday. He must have thought my clumsy secrecy quite ridiculous.

Yet Wednesday *was* a secret: a secret on whose strict keeping the winning of a battle and men's lives would depend. For Wednesday, the 6th of November, 1940, was the day on which the first British offensive of the second World War was to be launched. True, a very little offensive, only a single brigade group with a few old-fashioned aeroplanes, but in 1940 a land offensive by British forces, however small, would be an event. It certainly would be to me, for I was to command it.

Like all commanders on the eve of a battle, much as I might try to appear calm and confident, I was inwardly anxious and restless. I was angry too. A few days before, one of my three Indian infantry units, a tough, quick-moving, well-commanded Punjabi battalion had, in accordance with some policy decision made in far-off Whitehall, been suddenly taken from me and replaced by a British battalion. The Punjabis had been part of my brigade since its formation and with my other two battalions, a Baluchi and a Garhwali, they had gone through our hard training in India and shared in the at times frustrating but always hilarious, conversion from animal to mechanical transport. I knew them, officers and men, and I think they had got used to me. Now, just before our first serious fight, a completely unknown element had been inserted in my command in their place. The new-comers might, for all I knew, be the finest battalion in the British Army, but whatever they were I hated losing my Punjabis.

At this time, before Wavell's great victories in North Africa, opinions as to Italian fighting capacity varied, but I did not think it could be high, or we should not have been where we were—still on the border between the Sudan and Abyssinia. For months on this front the Italians had held an overwhelming superiority on land and in the air, in numbers and in equipment. Even now, when an Indian division had arrived to reinforce the Sudan Defence Force and the three British battalions which up to then had been all we could muster, it seemed to me that the Italian commander-in-chief need not be a Napoleon to hustle us out pretty briskly. A sergeant-major would do. All he had to say was, 'Fall in! By the centre, quick march!' and we should be hard put to it to stop him. But neither general nor sergeant-major gave the order. Instead, after a few early nibbles that had bitten off one or two of our meagrely garrisoned frontier posts, the enemy appeared content to relapse into an inglorious defensive.

One of the posts lost to us had been Gallabat, a mud and stone fort built on the eastern slope of a rocky hill overlooking a deep *khor*, or dry stream bed, which here marked the boundary between the Sudan and Abyssinia. Since their occupation the Italians had greatly strengthened Gallabat and the fort was now surrounded by a ham-shaped outer defensive area about six hundred yards long and four hundred wide. The perimeter of this enclosure was a stout wall of stones and logs, mud cemented, with a barbed wire entanglement in front of it and, beyond again, a most awkward thorn *zariba*. In addition, the slopes of the hill for several hundred yards had been cleared of scrub and bushes to give an all-round field of fire.

Opposite Gallabat, the other bank of the *khor* rose gradually to a larger and more imposing collection of dwellings, the native village and Italian frontier station of Metemma. Here the whole area was heavily defended by several strong field works and fortified buildings, all enclosed by two separate and deep wire entanglements of a most formidable kind. The boundary *khor* itself and a tributary also presented serious obstacles on three sides to any approach to Metemma; even the road that ran across the *khor* from Gallabat was heavily wired on both sides.

This rather forbidding fortress area of Gallabat–Metemma was defended by an Italian force, which Mark Ash, my very efficient intelligence officer, calculated with all the accuracy of his accountant's training to be numerically about the equal of mine, that is, three native colonial battalions, an Italian Blackshirt machine-gun unit, an artillery detachment of six 65-mm. guns, two anti-tank platoons, some engineers and a few hundred native levies. Of these one colonial battalion with machine and anti-tank gunners was believed to be in Gallabat.

In the air the Italians held a definite local superiority. We could raise only nineteen Gladiator biplane fighters and a few ancient Vincent and Hardy Army Co-operation machines, slow and easy meat for any enemy fighter. A hundred miles away at Gondar the enemy had at call some forty fighters of a type the equal or superior of ours and a number of bombers. There were also in that area, ready if necessary to reinforce Metemma, considerable numbers of troops of all arms.

My orders were to capture Gallabat–Metemma with the object of opening one of the main routes into Abyssinia, and thus rousing the whole province of Gojam to active rebellion against the hated Italians. With the preponderance of force probably on the side of the well-entrenched enemy, my only hope of success rested on surprise and speed. I guessed that the arrival of Indian infantry before Gallabat must have been observed, but I did not think the Italians would expect us to be so rash as to attack through their obstacles and wire without the support of at least artillery. It was therefore above all essential that I should hide from them the fact that I had a regiment of field artillery and, still more, the presence of what I hoped would be my secret weapon—a squadron of armour, six light and six cruiser tanks. So guns and tanks were held far back while, night after night, we dug gun-pits hidden in the bush, and load by load dumped ammunition beside them. Before they made their reconnaissances for start lines and routes of advance, the tankmen were careful to remove every sign of the Tank Corps from their uniforms and to change their conspicuous black berets for the ordinary Wolseley cork helmet.

Briefly I planned to fight the battle in two phases. In the first,

after a night deployment, to seize Gallabat by a surprise assault at
dawn or soon after, using the Garhwali battalion and the tanks
under the heaviest artillery cover we could give them. Detachments of Sudanese and Baluchis were to take post forward on the
flanks to threaten the Italians and prevent any attempt they might
make to encircle our attacking troops. In the second phase, which
was to follow as soon as possible after the first, the British battalion
with the tanks to lead them through the wire was to break into
Metemma. We proposed to open the battle with the whole of our
air strength in an attempt to disrupt the enemy's communication
with Gondar and to create confusion and delay in his ranks. After
that all our aircraft were to withdraw before the Italian airmen
could arrive on the scene, as they undoubtedly would, in great
numerical superiority. We abandoned any idea of having continuous air cover over our troops as likely to be too costly, and
intended that our air force should reappear only at intervals and
then in its maximum available numbers.

As darkness fell on the Tuesday night, I made for my command
post on a small hill just above the track that ran gently up hill
straight towards Gallabat about a mile and a half away. Standing
there, I listened to the muffled sounds of troops and guns moving
up and the last loads of ammunition being dumped. The tramp of
the Garhwalis, as company by company they passed up the road
to their deploying positions, came up to me muted by the thick
dust. I could even hear a faint swishing murmur away out on the
right where some of the Baluchis were pushing through scrub and
long grass towards a hill overlooking Gallabat to secure our flank.
Then all other sound was blotted out by the roar of an aircraft
flying low to drown the engines of the tanks as they rumbled
forward. By ten o'clock all was silent; our outposts gave no sign.
Once or twice a white Very light had soared up from Gallabat
as some nervous Italian peering over his ramparts thought he
heard a stealthy move in the darkness beyond, but no burst of fire
followed and all sank to quiet again. Our plans were made, the
attacking troops had reached their start lines, and guns and tanks
were ready with their crews sleeping beside them. I felt as I lay
down and pulled a blanket over me that while like other mortals
we could not command success, we had done all we could to
deserve it.

I awoke, still in darkness, to find my Garhwali orderly shaking my shoulder with one hand while in the other he held out an enamelled mug of tea. I sat up, tried the tea and found it too hot to drink. Around me my staff was beginning to move about. They talked, quite unnecessarily, in whispers, while signallers under shaded lights called up units in turn on the field telephones. I threw off my blanket and stood up, shivering a little; I was chillier than the cold before dawn justified. As I began to sip my tea a shapeless lump of blackness loomed up beside me, and Ripley, my imperturbable brigade major, his shoulders draped in a blanket, reported that all units, including the Baluchis, were in place. The tea warmed me but not, I think, as much as the presence of this tough cavalryman, with his strong face and deep-set steady eyes.

To the east, the hills behind Gallabat, Jebel Negus and Jebel Mariam Waha, began to show up as dark and distant silhouettes against the first pale lemon wash of sunrise. Gently, the lemon deepened to gold and changed to soft luminous blue, but the hill of Gallabat remained invisible, sunk in blackness at the base of the further hills. As the light slowly strengthened and spread, in place of Ripley who had returned to some dug-out where he had established his office, I saw the slighter figure of 'Welcher'. In the quarter light a lock of hair drooping across his forehead made his resemblance to Hitler almost startling. Welcher commanded my regiment of artillery and in addition doubled two important appointments, those of my second-in-command and of my principal morale sustainer. He was, I saw, prepared for the day's work, for his distinguishing badges, known to every man in the force, were in place—a great telescope hanging from one shoulder and a six-foot spear grasped in his hand. Energy and cheerfulness exuded from him even at this hour.

Alongside him was the R.A.F. squadron commander, my air adviser, with whom I had meticulously worked out how we would dovetail, minute by minute, the air action into the progress of the land assault. He was a quiet, competent, professional airman, who knew what his people could do, how they should do it, and could be relied on to see they did do it. I was lucky to have three such men with me. The squadron-leader tilted his wrist-watch to catch the pale light: 'They ought to be over in eight minutes from now,' he said.

We were silent and I became conscious of a growing movement outside the command post. A rustling in the bush below us
as camouflage nets were pulled away from gun muzzles, the voices
of men as they finished their breakfasts and somewhere, the
unexpected thud of an axe on wood. Standing, we ate our breakfasts from cracked enamelled plates. There was little conversation;
what was there to say? We were ready and we waited. The light
grew brighter; the hill of Gallabat stabbed its shadow towards us.
It was day.

Behind us far off to the west we heard the faint hum of
approaching aircraft. As we turned and looked up, the sunlight
caught their wings and they were overhead. They droned on, it
seemed so slowly, but in a minute there came back to us the dull
thump of bombs and the stutter of machine-guns as the fighters
dived to the attack and our few bombers came in low to blast the
Metemma wireless station and to plaster Gallabat.

The battle had begun.

A moment later, for the first time on that front, British guns
opened fire. Carefully and deliberately they registered their
targets and then came down with a sudden crash of rapid fire
that caught the Italians dashing to man their defences. The smoke
and dust on Gallabat hill thickened and rolled up in great brown
clouds, pierced continually by flashes of bursting shells. The
crack of 18-pounders and the duller thud of 4·5-inch howitzers
firing hard to our right rear beat on our ear drums, whisps of
cordite fumes drifted across our nostrils, and all the time the sibilant
rustle of shells slipping away from us filled the air. There was no
enemy retaliation; it really looked as if we had indeed surprised
them.

Our aircraft were now flying back overhead to their base.
Anxiously the squadron-leader counted them and gleefully
announced, 'All present and correct!' A moment later, a signal
from the air told us that direct hits had been scored on the wireless
station, which we hoped would at least delay the appeals for help
that the Italian commander was now no doubt trying to send out.

Our eyes quickly returned to the rough, undulating ground,
scrub and tree scattered, which stretched away from us, rising
gently towards the foot of Gallabat hill. It was light enough to see,
about a thousand yards from the fort, the tanks lumbering and

rocking forward astride the track. As if by magic out of the ground rose lines of little slouch-hatted figures that pressed on behind them—the Garhwalis moving to the assault. A few moments later, first the tanks and then the infantry began to breast the steeper slope of the hill itself. As machines and men vanished into the curtain of smoke and flame that blotted out Gallabat, our guns lifted on to Metemma beyond. The din changed its note as machine-gun and rifle fire rose to a sustained crescendo, punctuated by the sharp bangs of the tanks' 2-pounders. From the command post we could see nothing; a pall of smoke hung heavily over the battlefield, but we knew that now the Garhwalis, scrambling through gaps in the wire blasted by artillery or ripped by tanks, were going over the wall with the bayonet.

The clamour around Gallabat died down, yet through the steady beat of our guns still shelling Metemma, we could hear sudden abrupt bursts of machine-gun fire and, occasionally, the bark of a tank. The smoke drifted heavily away to the left uncovering, yard by yard, the forward slopes of Gallabat hill. We swept them with our field-glasses, but from where we stood, they seemed, except for two or three ominously motionless tanks, quite deserted. Then from the summit whooshed high into the sky the smoky trails of Véry lights curving gracefully over to burst into red and green stars—the success signal! We had taken Gallabat.

The command post sprang to instant activity. Ripley, squatting beside a field telephone, ordered the British battalion up to Gallabat and a field battery forward at once to a position of closer support. In a couple of minutes the first of the guns, drawn by its high, clumsy, but powerful 'spider', bounced dustily past at speed on the track below us.

It was time I got forward too; so calling to Welcher and my Garhwali orderly, I scrambled into an infantry carrier. The carrier is a beastly vehicle, most uncomfortable as it lurches and jerks on its tracks and, as it has no overhead cover, extremely unsafe. We found ourselves too, in the midst of the battery going forward. The gunners might not be as picturesque as they had been in the days of glossy horses straining at the traces, their drivers urging them on with whip and voice, but they had not lost the eagerness with which they have always greeted the order to move up. Gun after gun bounced past us and, sitting beside my Baluchi driver, I breathed and ate their dust, but I was feeling happy. All had gone well; those signals from Gallabat had sent our spirits soaring too. I ought to have known that in a battle nothing is ever as good or as bad as the first reports of excited men would have it.

Soon the last of the guns had passed and we began to overtake the British battalion, its lines extended across the road, pressing on towards Gallabat. An N.C.O. of Indian Sappers and Miners waved us to a stop and told us that the road ahead was mined; his section was at the moment clearing it. He pointed out a roughly marked diversion to the left which he said was safe, but being anxious to get forward as soon as possible and believing Italian mining had been confined to the road, I told my driver to turn off to the right and take a direct line to the fort. This, alas, was not at all clever of me, for as we drew level with the leading line of British soldiers we and they discovered simultaneously that we were all well and truly in the midst of a minefield. Another carrier some distance ahead blew up in a cloud of brown smoke and dust, while two or three unfortunate soldiers set off small Italian anti-personnel mines around us.

Everything that is shot or thrown at you or dropped on you in war is most unpleasant but, of all horrible devices, the most terrifying—at least to me—is the land mine. A man ought to be able to plant his feet on his Mother Earth with some confidence; when instead, on his footfall she erupts into flame, blast and hurtling steel, it is unnatural and very, very frightening.

We stopped our carrier and looked rather forlornly at one another. At that moment an officer of the battalion who was coming towards us trod on a mine and lost most of his foot. Welcher and I dismounted and, having done our best for him with his and our field dressings, looked around us. The lines of infantry, after a pause, were moving cautiously forward again, heads bowed like men looking intently for something extremely valuable that they had dropped—rarely do men strain their eyes more than when walking through a minefield. We followed their example for a couple of hundred yards, the carrier moving closely in our footsteps. There were no more explosions; the field seemed to have been only a small one. We decided to make a dash for it, climbed on board again and rattled on. We met no more mines but came up against increasingly large stones hidden in the coarse, tufty grass, a great threat to the carrier's tracks. At last we reached the slope of the hill and roared up it, passed through gaps in the *zareba* and the wire where a tank had obviously torn through, and cruised along the wall looking for a breach.

The first people we saw were half-a-dozen unarmed and frightened Italian native soldiers scuttling along, hands up and bodies bent under cover of the wall, with the obvious intention of surrendering at the first opportunity. We shoo'd them on, down the hill. Behind them appeared a figure moving with rather more dignity—an Italian officer, his khaki uniform resplendent with red and gold.

'A Wop general!' cried Welcher.

This was a fish worth pulling in. Revolvers in hand, we both leapt from the carrier to grab him. He at once—and rather wisely —stopped, raised his hands above his head and awaited the two excited British officers who so threateningly advanced on him. He evidently recognized my red tabs, insignificant as they must have appeared beside his own adornments, for he lowered one hand to the salute, keeping the other stretched high. He looked a nice fresh-faced young man; indeed I could not help thinking rather youthful for a general.

'I surrender,' he said in good English. 'I am Capitano in the colonial battalion.'

From general to captain was a bit of a comedown. However, I did not despair of higher game. With my revolver pointing at the buckle of his belt, I asked him where his commanding officer was.

'In Metemma by now,' he answered, bitterly. 'As soon as your bombardment started he rushed out crying, "To the walls, to the walls", and disappeared towards the boundary *khor*. He has not been seen since!'

I gathered that our capitano had somewhat lost confidence in his senior and would, if he could have met him, have delighted to tell him so. We stood there, the British brigadier and the Italian captain, until someone from inside the enclosure fired a few bursts from a light automatic just over our heads. At each burst the Italian with his hands still above his head and I with my revolver still pointing at his belt buckle, in perfect unison, flexed our knees

and sank below the wall to rise again just in time to duck once
more. We must have looked remarkably silly.

The firing ceased and four native prisoners appeared carrying
on their shoulders a stretcher on which lay a British officer whom
I knew, shot through the throat. Behind them followed a few
more prisoners and a couple of Garhwalis with fixed bayonets as
escort. Handing over to them our captain, who still looked like a
general, we once more got back into our carrier, and skirting the
wall continued towards a gap some way ahead.

We rattled merrily along towards a party of Garhwali soldiers
among an outcrop of rocks to our right front. They greeted our
arrival by waving their hats and shouting. What with the din of
our carrier and the noise of shooting that still continued I could
not hear what they were saying but I was gratified by their welcome. My heart warmed towards them; here were my gallant
troops cheering their commander at the moment of victory.
Precariously I stood up in the lurching carrier to acknowledge
their ovation. How precariously I did not realize until suddenly
it was borne in upon me by their emphatic gestures and a yell of
'*Khabadar, dushman hain!*' that, far from cheering their commander, they were trying to tell him not to be such a fool as to
drive slap into the enemy. Their warning was emphasized by a
prolonged burst of machine-gun fire from straight ahead,
directed luckily not at us, but at the Garhwalis. Bullets smacked
into the rocks behind which they crouched and ricochets whirred
in all directions.

I sat down abruptly and became at once shatteringly aware that
immediately in front of my stomach was not a nice piece of
armour plate but a gaping oblong hole through which we should
have had a machine-gun projecting. Unfortunately, we had no
machine-gun. My driver appreciated the situation and swung the
carrier at full speed into a tight turn which presented our armoured
side to the enemy and quickly carried us behind the rocks. Here
we sheltered ignominiously while the Garhwalis methodically
wiped out the Italian machine-gunners with hand grenades.
Meanwhile, I began to wonder if the officer who had fired the
success signal had not been a trifle premature.

Through the noise of the local dog-fight we could hear from
the eastern side of Gallabat a great racket of rifle and machine-gun

fire in which artillery soon joined. It was still going on when, the machine-gun finally silenced, we drove through a gap in the wall into the fort enclosure. There were everywhere signs of our bombardment and some—not as many as I had expected—enemy dead and wounded lying about. Leaving the carrier, Welcher and I walked towards the wall on the Metemma side, and as we passed the fort itself all firing except for a few rifle shots died away.

Coming to meet us was a younger edition of Mr. Pickwick—chubby figure, cherubic face, gleaming spectacles, genial smile and all, surmounted by a slouch hat. 'Snap' Taylor, the colonel of the Garhwalis, was easily recognizable not only because of his Dickensian appearance but because, whatever the circumstances, he always looked fresh, cheerful, alert and completely unruffled. Battalions are as good as their commanding officers; he was a very good one indeed.

As if he were a preparatory school headmaster who had just watched his boys win a football match, Snap told us the firing we had heard was his fellows smashing a counter-attack, delivered, we afterwards discovered, by two colonial battalions. This was a remarkably good effort by the Garhwalis still in the inevitable confusion after an assault and, to be honest, not a bad one on the Italians' part to put in their counter-attack so quickly. Snap beamed through his glasses as he ended, 'I don't think those Wops will try it again in a hurry!' 'I bet they don't,' I agreed. 'Now while they're all shaken up, the sooner we get on to the next stage and have a crack at Metemma the better. From where can we see it best?'

He led us over to an embrasure in the eastern wall which gave us a view across the boundary *khor* down into Metemma, sloping gently up from us like a model on an inclined table. While Snap told me that his casualties had been lighter than he had feared they might be, I studied our next objective through my glasses. The buildings, even the wireless station, looked intact, some round native huts in one corner were burning fiercely but the formidable belts of wire seemed untouched—our tanks would have to see to that. I turned to speak and found myself face to face with the tank squadron commander who had just joined us; his face told me he did not bring good news. Nor did he.

He reported that in the assault five out of his six cruiser tanks and four of his six light tanks had been disabled. Most of the damage took the form of tracks broken by mines or from striking boulders hidden in the grass. The lorry with spares was now on the way up and he thought that when it arrived he could in four or five hours repair all but two or three of the tanks. In the meantime, only one cruiser and two lights were runners.

There had also been one most unfortunate effect of our successful concealment of the arrival of tanks before Gallabat. On going into action the crews had naturally resumed their black berets. As a result, when their tanks were disabled and they emerged, either to attempt repairs or to continue the advance on foot, they were in their unexpected headgear more than once mistaken for Italians and fired on by our own men. The squadron sergeant-major, a splendid fellow who had become a great favourite with us all, was killed in this tragic way as he moved in the open from tank to tank.

I looked again glumly at the Metemma wire; it was no use trying to rush that without tanks or prolonged artillery preparation. Any chance of storming the place before the enemy could recover his balance had vanished; the next phase must be delayed until at least late afternoon. The British battalion was now arriving in Gallabat and I went through its orders for its attack on Metemma, arranging for all possible artillery and tank support we could give it. Zero hour I should have to fix later.

Leaving Welcher to lay on a bombardment of Metemma, I started off to return to my command post where the postponement of the attack had made my presence necessary. On the way to my carrier I walked through the fort itself and paused for a moment in what had been the ante-room of the Italian officers' mess. I was amused to see traces of former British occupation in months' old numbers of glossy English illustrated weeklies. A lot of plaster had been shaken down and dust was thick on everything, but the place was still habitable and I picked up a couple of unbroken Chianti flasks to compensate for my disappointment over the tanks.

Everything was strangely quiet; both sides were evidently sorting themselves out after the first round. Back in the command post I had sent Ripley up to Gallabat to help in the preparations for the next phase. I was looking at a map and talking over the telephone at the same time to one of the Sudanese companies out on the flank when a distant drone of aircraft approaching from the east grew louder. The noise betokened a considerable number of aeroplanes and the east was the direction of Gondar, the enemy's main airfield. So the Italian commander *had* managed to call for help from the air and was about to get it. I stepped out, looked towards Metemma and saw a sight, none the less disturbing because we had been expecting it. Approaching was a formation of Caproni bombers—at least ten I thought—with about double that number of fighters weaving high over them. They came on steadily, the bombers shook out into line ahead and flew unhurriedly across Gallabat. At once, machine by machine, they began to drop their heavy bombs. As each stick fell, separate explosions were distinguishable but they followed one another so quickly that the general effect became a tremendous rumble. The whole of Gallabat hill spouted with great gouts of smoke and flame. No wonder there was no answer to our attempts to call up Snap Taylor's headquarters.

Somebody pointed directly overhead. Two lone British Gladiators were flying high straight towards Gallabat. The squadron-leader and I exchanged startled glances. This was contrary to our air plan which had been based on our fighters, whenever they appeared, doing so in the greatest strength we could muster and never singly or in pairs. To come in ones and twos when the Italians were out in these numbers was suicide, but the Gladiators sailed on, dipped their noses and plunged towards the bombers. Half-way through their dive there were Italians already on their tails, and against such odds there could be little hope. They did not fly back over us. The squadron-leader was by now on the phone to our landing strip but he was apparently unable to stop further small driblets of our aeroplanes arriving to suffer much the same fate. During the morning we watched most of our fighters shot down in these unequal combats, while all we could do was to send out patrols to try and pick up the pilots we had seen parachuting to earth. Among the few we thus rescued was the very gallant commander of the South African squadron, but to our great grief he died of his injuries.

At last the bombing stopped and in a very short time no aircraft were to be seen. After the pasting we had had in Gallabat, if the enemy were to put in a quick counter-attack now it might be awkward. But we had two battalions up there and I doubted if the Italians, remembering their experience of the morning, would be eager or indeed able to stage another attack. The bombing must have been extremely nasty but, by the time it came, I hoped both battalions would have shaken out and at least partially dug in, so I was not unduly alarmed. I hung my field-glasses on a bush beside my equipment and awaited the reports that Ripley would send as soon as the wires were mended.

Just where the track from Gallabat passed below us, was a traffic control post manned by Baluchis. I was surprised a few minutes later to see the Indian officer in charge hurrying up the hill. He arrived excited and breathless from running.

'British soldiers from Gallabat,' he panted, 'are driving through my post, shouting that the enemy are coming and that the order is to retire. We cannot stop them; they drive fast at anybody who tries!'

'Nonsense,' I said, 'they must be just empties coming back to refill. You have misunderstood what they are saying.'

The jemadar shook his head.

'Look, sahib.'

I walked to the shoulder of the hill. Two trucks about a hundred yards apart were coming very fast down the track; a couple of sepoys stood waving their arms to them to stop. The trucks filled with gesticulating soldiers crashed on, the sepoys leapt for their lives, and both vehicles surged by in clouds of dust. It looked bad.

With the jemadar and the staff captain, I ran down the hill and reached the post just as another vehicle, with its load of shouting soldiers, slammed past, driving as if the devil were after them. I told the Indian officer to cut bushes and make the best obstacle he could across the road and sent the staff captain back to telephone all posts behind us to block the road with vehicles at once.

Very alarmed and without thinking very clearly what I was doing, I began to walk rapidly up the road towards Gallabat. I had not gone far when I had to jump for it as another truck-load of soldiers, ignoring my frantic signals, swept past yelling, 'The enemy are coming!' I had seen panic before and I recognized it.

I had covered another quarter-mile of deserted road when it began to be borne in on me with increasing urgency that I was rather lonely. Lonely and naked too, for I had left my revolver in my equipment hanging on that bush; if the enemy were coming I had nothing more lethal than a walking-stick. Indeed, someone *was* coming; a straggling group of men on foot was advancing towards me. I was saved from making a dive into the bushes by recognizing their pith helmets as British, and I moved on more confidently. There were half-a-dozen of them, all but one with rifles; I stopped them and asked what they were doing. Interrupting one another they poured out a rambling story that the Italians had retaken the fort. There had been great slaughter, they had resisted desperately and were probably the sole survivors of their battalion. Their colonel, they assured me, was dead and one of them, to make the tale complete, rashly announced, 'The brigadier's killed too!' I noticed he added no expression of regret. I think I convinced them that this item of news at least was incorrect, and with some difficulty forced them to retrace their steps. We soon met other stragglers, one party with an officer who angered me very much. Our little group began to swell, although I noticed that before I decided to walk behind them, some men had already disappeared into the bush.

Vehicles rushing at me from the front I had come to expect, but I was not prepared to have them coming at me from the rear. Yet this happened. A column of artillery spiders roared up the road. At my signal the leader stopped and told me they had got orders a few minutes beforehand to come at once and get the forward guns out of action. That did not sound too good, and when they had passed, still herding my reluctant party, I followed with some misgivings.

We were now at the minefield that had so embarrassed us earlier in the day. Here I found the section of Indian Sappers and Miners had taken up three or four small defensive positions covering the road, and with fingers on triggers were awaiting the promised arrival of the enemy. The sight of these handfuls of well-disciplined and determined troops did something to steady my party. We next encountered another group of stragglers, this time with a few Garhwalis intermingled. The Indians said they had no idea why they were coming back but that British troops had told them the order was to retire and they had done so. They were quite ready to go back and, forming up, did so cheerfully.

A few hundred yards from Gallabat on the left of the road we found the spiders which had passed us hidden among trees and bushes. Ahead of them the guns were still in position and on the track, revolver in hand, stood the battery commander. He told me that, after the bombing, the first he knew that anything extraordinary was happening was vehicles roaring past, filled with soldiers yelling to his men that the enemy were coming. He had got his men out to cover the guns, collected all the fugitives he could, and as a precaution ordered up the spiders. The major was very angry, and interrupted his narrative to assure the frightened-looking bunch standing awkwardly under the rifles of his men that he would shoot with his own hand the first adjectival so-and-so who tried to bolt. He looked quite capable of it; in fact rather anxious to do it. Reverting to me he said his forward observation officer in the fort had told him there had been no attack, only bombing—and a lot of it.

With a very jumpy collection of fugitives, I entered the enclosure. It was not a pretty sight; there were many wounded and terribly mutilated men being attended to or awaiting evacuation. Everyone looked very shaken. As a first experience of war, as it was for most of them, it was a pretty beastly test—no wonder some failed.

At Snap Taylor's headquarters, which were not in too good a shape from a near miss, I found him imperturbable as ever, Ripley grim and angry, and the tank commander obviously very worried about something.

Their story was not a pleasant one. Snap and Ripley had just been round the whole position. Casualties had been fairly heavy, especially in the British battalion which had not had time to make itself much cover. The ground, almost solid rock, had doubled the lethal effect of the bombs, and they were lucky to have suffered no more. But they were in no shape for a repetition. There had been no attack but at the height of the bombing an ammunition truck had exploded near the reserve company. This was too much for some men, already demoralized by the bombing, and they fled shouting to others to get out as the enemy were coming. The panic spread and was not checked until a number of men had broken away, seized first-line vehicles at the foot of the hill and fled in them. Snap said his own battalion was all right; their casualties had been much less than in the other.

Worse was to come. The tank commander had got his lorry of spares into the enclosure and had already organized and started the repair of his disabled tanks before the bombing began. By a stroke of the grossest ill-luck a heavy bomb had scored a direct hit on this precious and irreplaceable lorry. It had completely disintegrated and its spares, broken and mangled, were strewn over acres of ground. He did not think it would be possible now to repair the tanks for days. It was a gloomy party that moved to the wall and once more stood with me gazing dejectedly at Metemma.

Three things were obvious. First, it would be madness to attempt to storm through those dense wire entanglements without tanks or at least prolonged artillery preparation; any idea of an attack tomorrow was definitely off. Secondly, added to that, the present state of the battalion detailed for the assault was such that it would be unwise to use it; that meant more delay while the Baluchis were collected and brought up to relieve it. Thirdly, the longer we delayed the more likely was it that enemy reinforcements would arrive from Gondar. There was nothing for it but to postpone the second phase of our operation and see how things looked tomorrow. I had a walk round the troops and was alarmed by the state to which the bombing had reduced some of them; I feared the effect of further doses of the same medicine.

Bringing Ripley with me I returned to my command post where I did some hard and not pleasant thinking. I felt in my bones that the tanks could not now be repaired for days and that it was likely to be longer before the battalion so shaken by the bombing would be fit for anything but defensive work. Our fighters had nearly all gone down gallantly against overwhelming odds; an occasional quick reconnaissance was all we could hope for from the air. The Italians would be very slow if, by the time we were ready to resume our attack, they had not reorganized themselves and probably been heavily reinforced. Direct assault on Metemma thus seemed to be off. Was there any other way by which Metemma might be taken? I cudgelled my brains but, with only two reliable battalions and the Sudanese available, all the schemes I thought of were plainly impracticable.

Then I changed my approach to the problem. Up to then had I not allowed myself to be obsessed by my own difficulties? What about the enemy's? What was he feeling like? Not too happy, I began to think. He had lost Gallabat; the sudden appearance of our artillery and tanks must have shaken him and he must be wondering what other surprises we had up our sleeve. I doubted if he realized we had only three battalions; he might think we were the whole Indian division of whose arrival in the Sudan he must by now have heard. It was most unlikely that he knew of this afternoon's panic and its effects or that we had no more tanks. He too had had *his* losses. According to native informers the colonial battalion that had garrisoned Gallabat had disintegrated, the survivors fleeing into the countryside; neither of the other battalions that had taken part in the counter-attack could be in very good shape—we had already had deserters from both of them. On the ground he had shown, since that counter-attack, no inclination at all to anything but a passive defensive; I had the idea that the enemy was sitting behind his barbed-wire in no very happy frame of mind. Could I play on that, gamble on it? Even if I could not fight him out of Metemma, could I not frighten him out? The more I thought about it, the more I thought I might.

About a thousand yards to the east of Metemma, running north to south, stood the long, bare ridge of Jebel Mariam Waha, which completely overlooked the whole Italian position from the rear. If I collected my one remaining battalion, the Baluchis, and with them all available Sudanese, and marched by night wide round the left flank of Gallabat and Metemma, I could seize Jebel Mariam Waha at dawn. It is true I could no more attack through the wire from there than I could from Gallabat, but how would the enemy commander feel when he saw us there? If he was already as nervous as I thought, might he not, finding himself threatened with attack from two sides, lose his nerve and make for Gondar? A gamble, of course; but the more I thought of it, the more I was tempted to try it. By heck, I *would* try it!

There was yet another bombing of Gallabat that evening; the enemy was even generous enough to spare a stick or two for our area. It was unpleasant but did little damage, and I went to sleep hugging my new plan to my bosom, but tormented by the spectres of its risks that rose menacingly round me all night.

We breakfasted next morning soon after dawn, and with the meal the sinister Capronis and their fighter escort appeared again over sorely battered Gallabat. Once more we watched the clouds of dust and smoke spurt into the air, saw the flash of bombs and heard that fearsome crumping rumble. The attack seemed as accurate and even more intense than any of its predecessors. Our own fighters were no longer able to intervene and the enemy bombed at leisure.

When the bombers had gone and the smoke was beginning to drift away, with some trepidation I called up Snap Taylor. Rather to my surprise the line was working and I was immensely relieved to hear his cheerful voice reply, 'Well, it wasn't exactly what we'd have ordered for breakfast, but we're still here!'

Reassured on that point, I confided to Welcher and Ripley an outline of my new plan. The more I thought about it, the more I liked it, gamble as it was. After all, had I been the Italian commander in Metemma, what would I have liked least?—the British appearing behind me. My plan was received somewhat doubtfully but, before objection could be put, I asked the two of them not to give me their reactions until we had all had another good look at Metemma.

Later, when we went up to Gallabat, I had not been there long before I realized that stout-hearted as Snap and his Garhwalis were, if the enemy continued his incessant bombing—and there was no reason why he should not—even they could not endure indefinitely. By spreading out the British troops beyond the fort enclosure, Snap had greatly lessened the casualties of the last raids, but too many of the men seemed listless or jumpy. None of us was happy about them.

We found Snap at his headquarters, alert, cheerful and unruffled as ever, sitting at a camp table across which was spread the Italian flag that yesterday had waved so bravely over Gallabat. He was confident that his Garhwalis could hold the place against bombing, ground attack or anything else, but he admitted that unless we were going to take Metemma in the very near future there seemed few prospects in just sitting under these heavy air attacks.

We moved to our old stance at the wall and looked down on Metemma. Welcher's guns were methodically hammering at enemy positions and buildings, but no retaliation came from the Italians; they seemed to be sitting tight, awaiting the next attack. As we watched, a shell fell on what was evidently a petrol store and a great fire-ball of yellow flame shot up into the air. For a few seconds it hovered, a complete sphere, writhing on itself in a turbulence of black smoke shadows and gleams of internal explosions. Then it swelled into a huge black smudge billowing up, high in the air, and the sound of the explosion, a sharp *whump!* like the flap of an immense wet cloth, struck us. The store, belching flame as drum after drum of petrol burst in the heat, burnt on merrily.

But it was a time to consider more serious things than fireworks. There, on the wall, I put my plan for seizing Jebel Mariam Waha to Welcher, Ripley and Snap and asked their views. They pointed out the whole thing was a gamble and made it clear that they thought the odds were decidedly against it. I had now, they argued, for all practicable purposes, only two battalions and the Sudanese, with two or three tanks. The Italians, even if we wrote off their battalion from Gallabat, still had two and their levies. We had already had reports that at least two more colonial battalions and some white troops were on their way from Gondar. With motor transport we might expect them in Metemma tonight or tomorrow. When they came, even if it were not as soon as that, our small force on Mariam Waha would be caught between two fires and would be hard put to it to fight its way out.

As to Mariam Waha itself, it was just a hill. We had no certainty that there would be any water there; in fact it was most probable there was not. What then? If we had no answer to bombing in Gallabat we should have even less on Mariam Waha; we could be blasted off it in a couple of hours. Supposing, too, that my idea that the enemy would run away if they found us behind them did not work, and they just went on sitting behind their wire? We could no more attack Metemma without tanks from that side than we could from here. The best we could hope then would be to scramble out—if the Italian reinforcements did not catch us. It was too much of a gamble.

Was it, I wondered? I still had a hunch my idea would work, but these three men were each of them braver than I was. Would they hesitate if the risk were a reasonable one? If indeed it were such a gamble, was I justified in taking other men's lives on what I had to admit was a hunch? I was wobbling. And yet, even if my battle had gone wrong, did I have to accept there was nothing I could do to retrieve it?

Then Ripley produced a last argument. My overriding directive from above, he pointed out, had been that I must prevent any Italian advance into the Sudan by the Gallabat route. That had been given me before the present battle but it still held good. If I attempted my plan, a dozen things beyond my control could easily wreck it; my brigade would be scattered, perhaps destroyed and left with nothing but its disorganized remnants to hold one of the main entrances to the Sudan against superior forces. That must not be risked.

I had by then let the catalogue of dangers make me question my own judgment, and this last argument shook me further. What would be my responsibility if, contrary to all advice, I gambled with the ultimate stakes—the security of the Sudan? Surely the chance of capturing Metemma was not worth that throw of the dice! I weakened; I gave way. Yet I was unhappy, not because I had allowed myself to be persuaded—I have little use for the what-I-have-said-I-have-said school of commander— but because somewhere at the back of my mind was still the insistent, nagging thought, 'But I *was* right!'

As we were thus abandoning any immediate attempt against Metemma, to cling to Gallabat under constant heavy air attack was only to incur purposeless casualties and what was perhaps worse to wear down morale. Gallabat without Metemma was of little tactical and no strategic value. Sadly, I decided to withdraw from Gallabat. If we were to do it, the sooner the better; I ordered the withdrawal for that night.

In the dark I stood beside the track just below Gallabat and saw the guns go past back to their original positions; then the infantry, silent and depressed, followed them, so different from the men who had hopefully moved up two nights ago. And all the time beating in my brain was that some torturing thought, 'You ought to have tried it!'

Unhappy days followed. We asserted our superiority over the Italians in patrol and minor harrassing actions. Gallabat became a no-man's-land where we nightly re-entered the fort and clashed with the enemy along the boundary *khor*, while by day the Italian Air Force retaliated by bombing us. But Metemma still blocked the way into Abyssinia. The British battalion was withdrawn from the front and given a chance to recover its true form. This it did in no mean fashion; when next I met it in another theatre of war, it had gained and deserved a splendid fighting reputation.

The best antidote to disappointment is action. We redoubled our efforts to annoy the enemy and if we did not do him any serious harm we at least got plenty of exercise and some excitement. I remained unhappy and still reproached myself. My bitterest pill, however, came about ten days after our withdrawal when I saw for the first time some intercepted and deciphered signals, sent from Metemma just after our capture of Gallabat, which showed that the enemy was—or thought he was—at his last gasp. These messages, reinforced by reports we were getting from numerous deserters, convinced me that had we occupied Mariam Waha the enemy's nerve would have given way. If only I had followed my hunch!

But I did not. Like so many generals whose plans have gone wrong, I could find plenty of excuses for failure, but only one *reason*—myself. When two courses of action were open to me I had not chosen, as a good commander should, the bolder. I had taken counsel of my fears.

VII

IT PAYS TO BE BOLD

By the evening of the 1st July the foremost troops were under shell fire from Deir-ez-zor. General Slim insisted on two combined attacks—one frontal, one very wide round the left flank. These were made on the morning of the 3rd July and succeeded at once. Nine guns and about one hundred prisoners were taken which suggests that many of the garrison had melted away.

British Official History: Mediterranean and Middle East,
Vol. II

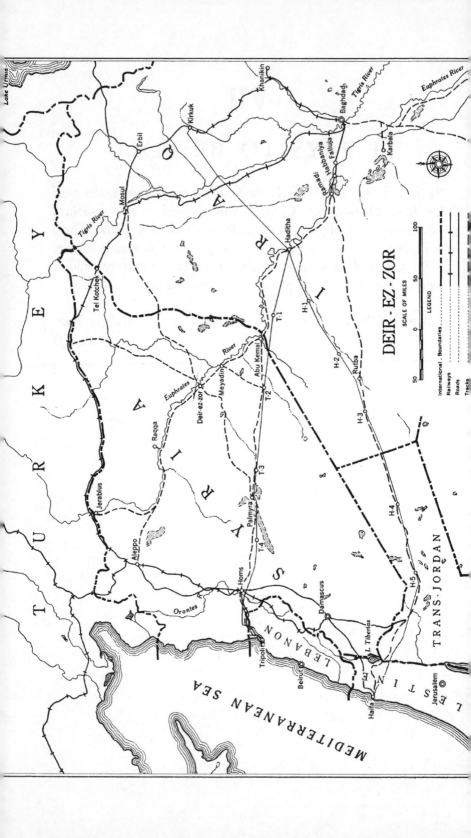

IT PAYS TO BE BOLD

I BUMPED my head as I ducked clumsily out of the last armoured car of the line, stepped back a little, and had a look at it. It was clumsy, too. A high, ugly machine with, perched on top of it, a turret like an old fashioned bee-hive from which poked a Vickers machine-gun, its sole armament. I noted that it did not carry any anti-aircraft weapon—a deficiency about which, for personal reasons, I held strong views—and that its large wheels had tyres of a size used by no modern vehicle. The body of the car was twenty years old; its engine five. Both had led hard lives. Now, in the hot early summer in 1941 in Iraq, an armoured car regiment, equipped with these museum pieces, had joined my Indian division. I had clamoured for armour and here it was—of a sort.

Not over-impressed by the vehicle, I shifted my gaze to the crew, drawn up beside it. They were better worth looking at. Lean, hawk-nosed Pathan cavalrymen, in their khaki overalls, web pistol-belts and black berets; even stiffly at attention, they gave an impression of lithe energy. As I walked down the short line I was conscious that their keen eyes were inspecting their new general at least as thoroughly as he was inspecting them. When I turned to the British officer commanding the regiment, a stocky major who looked—and as I later discovered was—cheerfully efficient, I could, whatever I might think of his cars, compliment him on his men.

Beside him stood his risaldar-major, the senior Indian officer of the regiment, a man in his middle forties, of about the same height as the major but slighter. His face, little darker than the sunburnt Englishman's, was rosy-tinged through the brown, like a good russet apple. Except for his darker eyes and neat, grizzled beard, he might have been one of the West Country farmers of my youth. He looked as fit and as competent as his commanding officer, but not nearly as cheerful. Indeed, he exuded gloom. I asked him how he liked Iraq.

'A bad country, sahib,' he answered. 'Bad country, bad people and a bad war—no fighting!'

The major laughed.

'The risaldar-major,' he explained, 'thought we were bound for the Western Desert. He feels that here we are in a back-water. He's rather a blood-for-breakfast sort of chap.'

'Well, risaldar-major sahib,' I said. 'We haven't had much fighting up to now, but I promise you a proper fight one day.'

'If it is the will of God,' he answered politely enough, but he sounded as if he doubted both the Almighty's interest and my ability.

As in the succeeding weeks we sweated north over sand and splashed through Iraqi-made inundations to the relief of the besieged Royal Air Force station at Habbaniya, it looked as if this lack of faith were justified. We had occasional flurries with Iraqi machine-gunners, swooping in and out of the desert in their Ford cars, wide on our flank, at speeds which our armoured cars could not rival. There were a few long-range exchanges with the enemy artillery and we chased his elusive infantry. Then a small British column from Palestine beat us to Habbaniya and there was nothing left for us to do but go on and occupy the Mosul airfields from which the German Messerschmitts had already vanished. The Iraq rebellion had collapsed; the country was now nervously on our side.

To disgruntle us further, a force of British, Australians, Indians and Free French had meanwhile invaded Syria to the west of us to forestall its use, with Vichy connivance, as a base for Axis air squadrons. The French were resisting the Allies stoutly, and here were we, a good fighting division, left to kick our heels in Iraq. No wonder the risaldar-major's gloom deepened.

Then, about the middle of June, my division was suddenly transferred from the Iraq to the Syrian Command, and I was told to advance as speedily as possible up the Euphrates into Syria. My objective, a hundred miles inside the French frontier, was the town of Deir-ez-zor, the capital of eastern Syria, where desert routes from all directions converged on the only bridge spanning the river for the five hundred miles between Habbaniya and the Turkish frontier. Once there, I should outflank the French line across Syria and might menace Aleppo, far in their rear. At the moment the British and Australian forces were fighting slowly northward against strong opposition in a two-pronged drive on Damascus and on Palmyra. My division would make a third prong a hundred miles to the east. Or at least it would when I could get started, and there was some doubt about that.

As usual it was a question of transport and supply. Distances were considerable. At Habbaniya, I was three hundred miles from Deir-ez-zor, five hundred from Aleppo; the only road the rough track along the river bank. Worst of all, apart from the first-line vehicles of fighting units needed to carry their immediate supplies and ammunition, the only transport I had was a company and a half of three-ton lorries with which to maintain and move my force. Even Deir-ez-zor looked a long way off.

But I was lucky. In charge of the administrative side of my division was Lieutenant-Colonel 'Alf' Snelling. At the start of the Iraq operations I had stolen him from a Lines of Communication Area and introduced him, much to my own advantage, to what I think he would agree was a fuller life. His great faculty was conjuring—producing rabbits out of hats, making bricks without straw. When I told him what I wanted to do he replied, in words I was to hear him repeat more than once later, 'What you ask is, of course, impossible with the resources we have—but I will arrange!' However, it was soon clear that, in spite of using native boats on the Euphrates, hiring all available civilian lorries from Baghdad and even the village donkeys, we should have to jerk ourselves along like those hump-backed caterpillars who draw up their tails behind them before the next step forward. It was also obvious that only part of my division would be able to advance and that the further we went the smaller would be the striking force, the more vulnerable its line of communication.

I chose Haditha, a crumbling mud village on the river bank about midway between Habbaniya and the French frontier, as my next base, and Snelling began, using every form of regular and irregular transport he could scrape up, to stock it with fifteen days' supplies for two brigade groups. Meanwhile, under cover of outposts, I moved my tactical headquarters to T.1, a pumping station on the now idle pipe-line from the Iraq oil-fields to Tripoli. Here I was only about twenty miles from Abu Kemal, the first French post on their frontier. In the comfortable bungalow the oil company had wisely provided for its employees in such a wilderness, I prepared my plans and from it made my reconnaissances.

The Euphrates, at this time of the year from two hundred to two hundred and fifty yards wide, flowed through undulating desert, formed by successive low stone-covered ridges interspersed with large areas of soft sand with now and then patches of good going. On the right bank, up which we proposed to move, there were two routes from the west across the desert, both from Palmyra, one to Abu Kemal and the other to Deir-ez-zor. In addition there was the Euphrates track which we were to take, the best of the three, but of course unmetalled, very rough, inches deep in dust, and often hard to follow where drivers had struck out to avoid the worst stretches and built up strange meandering routes of their own. The desert was completely bare; even along the river bank the only vegetation was the sparse patches of cultivation near the villages, twenty or thirty miles apart. The only water for a hundred miles to east and west was the river to which any movement, unless it could carry its own water, was thus tied. The country was, as twenty-five years before I had heard a disgruntled British soldier describe Mesopotamia, 'Miles and miles of sweet Fanny Adams, with a river runnin' through it!' A cruel, hard, desolate land.

While we were stocking up at Haditha, Damascus fell. In spite of this, the French continued stubbornly to resist, as well they might, for their forces, numerically superior to ours, were intact and still held four-fifths of Syria.

Our stock-piling at Haditha had gone well and, on the night of the 27th–28th June, I sent forward two companies of Gurkhas and some armoured cars to surprise Abu Kemal. The French post was a high-walled fort on the outskirts of a fair-sized village, near the river. Its garrison was reported to be a detachment of Syrian gendarmes with French officers and it was said to be visited occasionally by a mobile column from Deir-ez-zor, but of this we had seen nothing. Our reconnoitring parties in the past few days had been fired on and had encountered enemy mounted patrols. We had hoped to introduce ourselves into the Syrian campaign by surprising and capturing the whole garrison, but I fear our security arrangements were not as good as they should have been. At dawn when the Gurkhas closed in on the fort and the armoured cars swung wide behind it to intercept any fleeing enemy, they found the garrison already gone. A few shots were exchanged at long range and a couple of straggling gendarmes picked up as prisoners.

During that day, the 28th June, and the two succeeding, most of the brigade group was concentrated about Abu Kemal, while Snelling feverishly poured in supplies in every vehicle he could raise. The Iraq Command, by depriving all its formations except one brigade of second-line transport, had greatly increased our regular mechanical transport, so that we were able, after unloading them, to keep some three hundred lorries for troop movement and to supplement our supply capacity. This would enable me to move the whole brigade group in a dash on Deir-ez-zor. We all worked tirelessly to this end.

It was difficult to get reliable estimates of the French strength and of their defences around Deir-ez-zor. Our air force, four Gladiators and four Hurricanes in all, brought us some information gained at great risk in the face of the more numerous and more modern enemy aircraft. As far as we could judge from this, the town and airfield were most strongly protected in the south and west, where well dug-in positions, with concrete machine-gun posts and gun emplacements, covered the tracks from Abu Kemal and Palmyra. On the north a fortified arsenal, said to mount heavy guns, and a walled barracks looked threatening, but there seemed little in the way of earthworks. The garrison strength, as given by local informers and our two prisoners, varied between two and four thousand, including at least one battalion of Levant infantry with French officers, an artillery group of three or four batteries, a desert company, some European Foreign Legion, and a number of armoured cars. Several aircraft had been seen on the landing-ground and we should, of course, have to reckon with many more, both fighters and bombers, within easy reach on the airfields to the north. I regarded the estimates of enemy troops as almost certainly exaggerated, but dug-in as they were, supported by artillery and a greatly superior air force, formidable enough.

If I could have attacked with my whole division it would have been plain sailing, but it was by now evident that a brigade group would be the most that could be maintained as far forward as Deir-ez-zor—and that not for long. A quick attack with an element of surprise was our best hope—not so easy to attain in the face of the enemy command of the air. Together, the brigade commander, Weld, an old friend trained in that nursery of good soldiers, the Indian Frontier, and I hammered out our plan. He was to advance up the river with the bulk of his brigade group to within striking distance of Deir-ez-zor. Meanwhile, from T.1 behind him, under cover of darkness, a motorized force of the armoured car regiment, a section of field guns and an Indian Frontier Force battalion in lorries would move far out into the desert, cross the Palmyra track wide to the west of the enemy position, and attack Deir-ez-zor down the Aleppo road from the north. As soon as this mobile force began to close in on the town, the main part of Weld's brigade, two Gurkha battalions supported by the field regiment, was to assault from the south.

The plan had certain obvious risks. To begin with, it was impossible to conceal the eighty-mile approach of the main body over country completely innocent of cover. For three or four days at least we must be exposed to heavy air attack. If, in spite of that, we got safely within striking distance and launched our flanking column, we would then have split our small force in the face of an enemy probably at least our equal, and thus invited the classical defeat in detail. It would not be easy for our flanking column to drive over a hundred miles across the desert in darkness, to keep direction and be in position to attack by dawn. Only those who have attempted to guide such a column can imagine all the catastrophes that might befall it; yet I did not think we would carry the enemy's carefully prepared positions by frontal assault unless there was some distraction in his rear. So refusing to be overwhelmed by possible disaster, I told Weld to carry out our plan.

One of the most valuable qualities of a commander is a flair for putting himself in the right place at the vital time. It is not always easy to decide where and when these are—at least I have not found it so. I had every confidence in Weld, and in his place I should not have wanted my divisional commander breathing down my neck during the preliminary moves, but I felt I ought to be on hand when the actual battle was joined and fresh situations might arise. I decided, therefore, to remain at my present headquarters during the approach march and to join Weld early on the morning of the 2nd July for the actual assault.

I had another reason to keep me back at T.1. We were losing lorries on our L. of C. and we could not afford that. It threatened everything. To save fuel by avoiding the windings of the river track we had laid out more direct routes, marked by empty petrol tins across the desert. Even in daylight, the glare, dust, sand-storms and heat made the strain on the Indian drivers severe enough, but by night—and the French aircraft forced us to move mainly in darkness—their journey became perilous indeed. It was so easy for a lorry to wander from the ill-marked track, to bog itself in soft sand or to damage itself on rough ground. A lost lorry was hard to find; its crew might die of thirst wandering in the desert. Now I discovered, as the number of missing lorries in-creased, that to all these perils had been added a worse one.

After the disaster of Dunkirk, India had shipped to Great Britain so much of her reserves of rifles and other weapons that when new Indian divisions were raised later there were grave shortages in their equipment. Thus when my division went to war in 1941, some five hundred of its soldiers in the transport com-panies were virtually unarmed. They were combatants and should have carried rifles, but alas, there were no rifles for them. Second-line transport would not normally be called upon to fight, so, as somebody had to go without arms, it had better be these drivers. Unfortunately, as from the dawn of history, in the Iraq and Syrian deserts there prowled marauding Arabs who, soon realizing that our lorry drivers were unarmed, increasingly stalked, ambushed and murdered them for the loot in their vehicles. This looting was so thorough that all that was left of a lorry after the Arabs had dealt with it and its contents were the main members of the chassis lying, like the bones of some pre-historic monster, on the sand. Some of these murderous gangs came from the villages en route; others, the most formidable, were organized by one Fawzi Qawukji, who before the war had been a thorn in our side in Palestine, and was now giving good value to our enemies for the hire they paid him. I spent the follow-ing days trying, by tightening our convoy discipline, arranging escorts and raiding villages, often successfully, for loot, to lessen our losses.

Another serious loss we failed to lessen. Petrol, on which our life and movement depended, was at this time carried in the flimsy four gallon kerosene tins of peaceful commerce. However carefully we loaded them, a few hours' bumping and banging over the abominable tracks burst their seams, and a vehicle would arrive looking like a watering cart with our invaluable petrol pouring through the floor boards. Failure, during the first years of the war, to provide an efficient petrol container cost millions in money, weeks in delay, and jeopardized many an operation.

Having satisfied myself that all was well at Abu Kemal and the build-up there under way, I spent the 29th June visiting by air my L. of C. back to Baghdad, inspecting staging posts, concerting means of protecting our convoys, and trying to extract more transport from Iraq Command. In this latter I failed; they had already stripped themselves to help me. On the 1st July, the day on which Weld was due to start his march on Deir-ez-zor, I got back to my tactical headquarters at T.1. The news from Weld throughout the day had been good. His long column of vehicles had been bombed two or three times from the air during daylight but actual losses had been light, thanks mainly to a dust-storm. In spite of delay he had made reasonable progress. The flanking column would be launched as soon as it was dark and his main force would, he hoped, be within striking distance of Deir-ez-Zor at dawn.

Well content, I lay down for a couple of hours before setting out as soon as it was dark to join Weld in time for the expected battle. I had just been roused and was dressing by electric light—a luxury provided by the hospitable oil company—when my G.1, Colonel Roberts, put his face round the door. His expression shattered my complacency. Obviously something had gone wrong. It had indeed! Weld had recalled the flank column; it was expected in a few hours to rejoin the rest of his brigade, already halted on the river bank. Wireless was being badly interfered with by atmospherics and signals were hard to decipher; but that much was clear.

I seemed fated, once again, just when I thought my plans were developing so nicely, to be brought up with a jolt. Something must have gone very wrong to make Weld recall the flank column and halt his main advance. If the column had been discovered in the desert, or if it were seen coming back after daylight, it would not take a very clever Frenchman to guess what our plan had been. Nor did I like the idea of the whole brigade group huddled on the river bank all day waiting to be bombed. I kicked myself for not having joined Weld yesterday—evidently I was not one of those commanders who had the flair for putting himself in the right place! The only thing now was to get there as fast as I could, and that, leaving Roberts to attend to the thousand and one things at my headquarters, I proceeded to do.

Through the night my A.D.C. and I bumped and bounced and rocked in my station-wagon over the rough track. It was an unpleasant drive from any point of view. At Meyadin, about twenty miles from Deir-ez-zor, we passed through a confused mob of vehicles, endeavouring in the dust and darkness to disperse themselves before the dawn, already appearing, brought perils. We were told here that Weld's headquarters were further ahead, and about ten miles on, just as a lovely sunrise spread over the desert, we found him.

There on the river bank, we shared Weld's frugal breakfast, while all around us men purposefully dug slit trenches. A few yards away in a *nullah* an exasperated signals officer twiddled the knobs of a wireless set and monotonously appealed to some code name to answer him—obviously without result. An Indian signaller, the displaced operator, looked on in unhopeful resignation.

Weld, whose sturdy common-sense and unshakeable calm in a crisis I had always admired, ate with good appetite. I tried to follow his example; my A.D.C. had no difficulty—in my experience As.D.C. *always* have good appetites. As we ate, Weld told us what had happened. The day before, his brigade group had made reasonable progress along the river track. Although they had travelled at wide intervals between lorries, they were, of course, very conspicuous from the air and when Vichy bombers, escorted by fighters, came over as they did more than once, there was very little they could do about it. However, our tiny air force had most gallantly taken the skies and attacked to such effect that the bombers had at least been forced to be a little less deliberate in their aim. During the day, our four Gladiators had been shot down by the more modern French fighters and Weld believed a couple of Hurricanes were missing. A vicious dust-storm had raged most of the day which, while it made life hell, put a stop to the bombing before it had done much damage. In spite of these delays, by evening Weld's leading Gurkhas had debussed some ten miles from Deir-ez-zor—about where we were now—and had pushed on another mile or two. There they had taken up positions covered by our artillery, and preparations to assault early this morning had been put in hand.

At this stage we were interrupted by the drone of bombers approaching. We looked sourly at them as they made straight for us, growing bigger with unpleasant rapidity. We rose and made for our trenches, standing beside them with a rather silly bravado until a sinister *Whoosh!* made us jump hurriedly in. There was a great deal of noise and vast quantities of dust for a few minutes, but no one near us was hurt although a couple of trucks some distance away began to burn with a heavy black smoke. We emerged, brushed ourselves and ordered the dust-covered but still unbroken tea-cups to be removed. Weld took up his tale.

As soon as it was dark, he told us, the flanking column had set out to sweep wide round the enemy's right to the Aleppo road. The first part of the route had been reconnoitred by armoured cars and all went well. But as the darkness deepened, the dust-storm sprang up again, not as severely as during the previous day but more than enough to multiply the difficulties of guiding and keeping the column together. Some of the lorries strayed from the route and lost their way. The resulting gaps broke up the column and led to more wandering; the armoured cars ahead and on the flanks got out of touch. The going was worse than expected so that many vehicles, travelling continuously in low gear, used an alarming amount of petrol. Then, owing to the number of sets jarred out of action by the rough journey and to atmospherics caused by sand-storms, wireless communication between the column and brigade headquarters failed. Later, when it was inter- mittently resumed and the state of the column became known, Weld had to decide whether to persist in the operation or to call it off.

Obviously, the column could not be in position to attack by morning, and he rightly decided that to assault Deir-ez-zor frontally with his two remaining battalions alone would have little hope of success. Even if the column could collect again somewhere in the desert, it could not move until its petrol and water had been replenished, and he had neither the petrol nor the transport to do this. He had thus no option but to order the column to return to the river as best it could. Our first attempt on Deir-ez-zor had been abortive.

By the time they got back, the troops of the flanking column were weary, thirsty and disappointed, and they had used up almost all their petrol. Undismayed by this, Weld decided to try again that night. A small consignment of petrol had just reached him and, using this with every tin he could scrape up from his main force, he replenished the flanking column. But this would not allow the wide turning movement on the enemy's rear originally planned. He therefore modified the column's role and ordered it to get astride the Palmyra, not the Aleppo, road and to attack from the west, not the north.

Unavoidable as it seemed, I was not happy about this change. Our ground superiority over the French—if it existed at all— would not be great and if indeed the last of our air force had been shot out of the sky, our meagre defence against their complete mastery in the air had vanished. One battalion with little artillery support attacking the strong western defences would not, I thought, cause the dismay that an assault on its comparatively open rear would bring to the French command. Without that confusion our frontal attack from the south seemed to me to have a poor chance of success. I was therefore most reluctant to alter our original plan and almost equally averse from sitting under a pounding from the Vichy bombers while we laboriously built up for another attempt. But unless I could get more petrol, and get it quickly, one of these two things we should have to do.

The chances of raising the petrol in time seemed slender. There would be little on the L. of C.; all available from Abu Kemal had come in last night and was already with the flanking column. Haditha should have a small convoy arriving that day with some petrol but it could not be got here in time this evening. However, I determined to have a last try before facing the unpleasant alternatives—besides, I had great faith in Snelling and the impossibilities he might arrange.

I sent him the most urgent signal I could compose, ordering him to collect the last drop of petrol to be found anywhere, even if it meant that every vehicle and formation behind us was rendered immobile. I ended by saying that the petrol '*must*, repeat *must*, repeat *must*' reach Weld's brigade by not later than 1800 hours that evening. This order sent, there was little we could do beyond one final inquisition round the brigade which, amid groans of protest, extracted a few more tins, but left us, except for the flanking column, almost completely immobile. I paid a visit to the Frontier Force infantry and the armoured cars; they had sorted themselves out and were well dispersed against air attack. The men I saw seemed to be little shaken by what must have been an exhausting night, and when I told them to get all the sleep they could because I hoped to put them at it again tonight, they took it very well. I then joined Weld who was up with the forward troops, and found the leading Gurkha battalion spread out in depth astride the road.

As he was pointing out their dispositions there came a distant *Crack!* followed almost simultaneously by a much nearer *Whump!* A smudge of dirty brown smoke and dust drifted between us and the low hills to the north.

'That's the Frogs at it again,' the brigadier explained cheerfully. 'Seventy-fives! The shell comes so fast you hear its burst and the report of the gun at the same time.'

After that, at long intervals, French guns from behind the ridge south-west of Deir-ez-Zor fired a few rounds, concentrating almost entirely on the road itself where some wrecked vehicles slumped at strange angles. Our own ancient 18-pounders were too far back to return this rather harmless fire, and to bring them forward to within their range would have exposed them in the open to the full view of the French observation posts. Weld had ordered our guns to move up after dark and dig in within range. At the same time the leading Gurkha battalion would edge forward to a starting point for the attack and the other Gurkha battalion take its place in support. We had just got all this under way when enemy bombers arrived overhead again. This time they were equally noisy but even less effective. Like their artillery, they concentrated on the road, which by now was notably devoid of traffic. It was surprising what attraction wrecked and burnt-out vehicles seemed to have for the French. After this noisy interlude the battlefield lapsed into bored silence, and we went back to the flanking column to see if there were any news of petrol.

None had as yet arrived but, to my relief and I must confess not a little to my surprise, there was a signal saying it was on the way. Later in the afternoon, one by one, a motley collection of vehicles began to straggle in—signal trucks, engineer, baggage and ammunition lorries, all having dumped their normal loads, carrying petrol. Snelling had not failed us. He had milked everything within his reach of every drop, even to emptying the tanks of division headquarters's vehicles. Until more petrol arrived from Baghdad every unit behind us was now immobile. By seven o'clock the last lame ducks of this ill-assorted convey had limped in and the petrol had been issued. The commander of the flanking column declared he was ready to start.

But was he? Sitting on a heap of hard-baked earth, in the midst of the bustle of preparation, with the indefinable smell of desert dust in my nostrils, I wondered. A careful check had shown that the column was still not refilled up to the quantity of petrol it had started out with last night—and that had not got it very far! Yet by our calculations if all went well, that is, if there were no duststorm this time, if the new route reconnoitred today almost as far as the Palmyra track proved easier than the old, if there were not too much low-gear work, if nobody got lost, and if the enemy were not met on the way, the column *could* reach the Aleppo road, north of Deir-ez-zor. But if it did, it would have only enough petrol still left in its tanks to take it perhaps another ten miles.

A lot of 'ifs'! And should any of them not work out right, our precious column would be in a perilous state. Even supposing it did arrive north of the town, then would come the biggest 'if' of all. If the column's attack failed from lack of surprise or for any of a dozen other reasons, it could not get back; immobile, it must be destroyed either from the air or the ground at the enemy's leisure.

In the fading light I squinted at the crossed sword and baton on my shoulder. If that happened I wouldn't be a major-general very long! What about playing for safety? Try Weld's plan; if that failed, the column could at least get back. Wouldn't it be wiser even to wait here until, in a day or two, more petrol might arrive? So far the bombing hadn't done all that damage. There was still time to change my mind. Fears and doubts began to creep in on me.

Then I remembered Gallabat, eight months before, when I had

taken counsel of my fears, and missed my chance. This time I would not. I would listen to my hopes rather than to my fears. I would take the risk. I felt in my bones that if we got that column coming in from the unexpected and ill-defended north just as we attacked in the south, we should catch the French off balance and topple them. I got up feeling much better and joined Weld.

As soon as the men had finished a hot meal from well-screened cooking places, the marshalling of the column began. Brief dusk turned to darkness as it moved slowly off into the desert—the clumsy cars, the troop of artillery, and the lorries packed with Frontier Force riflemen. Thick dust billowed up, shrouding them and deadening the bump of wheels on uneven ground, but the sound of engines carried far. At last even that noise died away and we were left standing in almost oppressive silence. For a moment, I had once more that hollow feeling of doubt in the pit of my stomach. But the die was cast—it was no use worrying now.

Although it meant using more petrol, the column had been ordered to keep well out to the west to avoid enemy patrols and to cross the Palmyra track at least fifteen miles from Deir-ez-zor. Regardless of all obstacles, natural or human, it was to push on to the Aleppo road, and until that was reached wireless silence was to be broken only in the gravest emergency. There was, therefore, little use in our sitting up waiting for news. With my A.D.C's help I got my camp-bed from the station-wagon, set it up, and turned in under the stars.

While I slept, others were busy. The foremost Gurkhas pushed cautiously up the road and dug in on their starting lines. Behind them in silence, gunners sweated at their gun-pits and before dawn brought up their 18-pounders. They knew what to expect as soon as it grew light, but that was a risk our gunners have always cheerfully taken to support their infantry. The French, hearing movement, let off a few rounds of harassing fire, but if they sent out patrols they were too cautious to approach closely, and the night passed quietly enough.

At brigade headquarters we were up before dawn when Weld and I moved forward to a few humps and *nullahs* on the river bank which gave us observation and cover. We were having an early breakfast there when, with the sun, came the Vichy bombers who this time had no need to bother about a fighter escort. They

flew very low, just out of rifle shot, and unloaded at leisure with
more than their usual accuracy. However, by this time it had
become second nature for every man to have his slit-trench ready
and practice had made us quick at getting into them.

As the bombers droned away we crawled out just in time for
the next display of French bad temper—the shelling of our
artillery positions by their seventy-fives. Their shooting was
accurate and at first rapid. Our reply was immediate, and in a few
minutes a brisk little artillery duel was raging. To us it seemed,
from the shell-bursts and spouting columns of dust and smoke
around our gun-pits, that the crews must suffer heavily, but they
were well dug in and, although there was one direct hit on an
18-pounder, there were not many casualties. After a while the
shelling on both sides died down to an occasional petulant salvo.
We were not anxious to expend ammunition as it would be
almost impossible to bring up more in daylight, and the French,
who had not taken the advantage of their superior observation
that I had expected, were probably waiting for us to come out in
the open, as we must, to attack. Both armies appeared for the
moment content to lie low and watch one another. Weld and I
on our mound were free to look around.

Towards us flowed the winding Euphrates, broad, placid and
now beginning to reflect the sun. East and west on either side
stretched, mile after mile, the desert, flat and featureless, a muddy
brown. To the north, a low *café-au-lait* ridge ran obliquely away
from us to the north-west. We saw only its rounded end, coming
down in a steep but even slope to within a few hundred yards of
the river bank. Through the gap between ridge and river the
white thread of the road ran on past the airfield into Deir-ez-zor.
The ridge screened a large part of the town and all but a corner
of the aerodrome from our view. Judging by the size and height
of the flat-topped houses we could see, the town promised to be
bigger and more imposing than I had expected. If we got our
small force involved in fighting through those streets, it would be
soaked up like water in a sponge—not a very comforting thought.

It was now full daylight. Weld and I walked slowly up and
down, waiting. I looked surreptitiously at my watch: *six-thirty*—
surely the column *must* be there! Soon it would break silence and
call up! The hands of my watch crawled on. *Seven.* The French

could not have failed to locate the column by now. Still no signal came. *Seven-thirty—eight*. If the column was ever going to reach the Aleppo road it must have done so already and, wherever it was, the enemy must have seen it! I told the signals officer to call it up. No answer; obviously something had gone wrong—very wrong.

We resumed our measured pacing, stopping every now and then to gaze through field-glasses at the enemy positions. No visible movement there and a silence broken only once by the French guns firing again at their first love, the wrecked trucks on the road. As we walked, to conceal our mounting anxiety we spoke of old days in India, of our friends, of casual things, yet our minds were elsewhere. What had gone wrong? Where *was* that blasted column? If only I had an aeroplane, just one aeroplane, to send out to look for it! A couple of armoured cars? No, they would take too long. I glanced sideways at Weld; I hoped I appeared as unperturbed as he did.

A messenger stumbled hurriedly up the mound. Our hearts rose; news at last! But it was only from the armoured car squadron we had held back from the column; patrolling early this morning towards the Palmyra track, they had encountered eight enemy armoured vehicles and driven them back on Deir-ez-zor. The squadron had no news of the flanking column except that it had crossed the Palmyra track. The armoured cars would remain in observation. Through our field-glasses we could see, to the west of the ridge, three cars of the squadron cheekily trailing their coats in front of the enemy positions. As we watched, one of the cars moved daringly closer in. Immediately the French gunners retaliated with half-a-dozen shells, one of which knocked off its back wheel. After that our cars were considerably less venturesome.

Nine—conversation languished; we walked in silence. *Nine-thirty!* As at a signal, we stopped and faced one another. I was quite sure my plan had failed. I had pushed Weld and his brigade into a far worse position than they had been at the end of their first attempt. Then he could reunite his force; now the flank column could not possibly get back—it would have no petrol left. Should I order a frontal attack with what we had in hand or call the whole thing off and concentrate on an attempt to rescue the column—how, I had no idea? It is always a nasty moment when one faces a disaster knowing it has been caused by one's own obstinacy in persisting in a plan against advice. I was having such a moment now.

Weld's common sense came to my rescue. 'We haven't heard any firing north of the town', he pointed out. 'If the French had spotted the column there would have been din enough. Better hang on a bit. All the chaps down there have their orders—we can start an attack in a matter of minutes if we want to.'

'All right!' I agreed, grateful to him for this excuse to put off decision. 'We'll wait another half-hour.'

We resumed our silent promenade.

No gun fired, no aeroplane flew, no bomb crumped—all was quiet. Quiet, except that it required an increasing effort of will to continue this steady march up and down, up and down. . . .

Footsteps behind us. We turned and there charging towards us, waving a signal form in his hand, was the brigade signals officer.

'The column's come through,' he gasped. 'They're on the Aleppo road, a couple of miles north of Deir-ez-zor and advancing. Leading troops nearing town. No opposition so far!'

Ten years and a ton of weight dropped off my shoulders. I turned to Weld to say 'Let battle begin' or words to that effect, but he and the signals officer were already sliding down the mound to the signals truck.

A quarter of an hour later, our guns started with a grand and simultaneous crash. I dare say there have been bigger and better bombardments, before and since, but no general ever listened to one with more relief than I did on that mound. The upper part of the ridge vanished in rolling clouds of fawn dust. The racket grew as rifles and automatics joined in and the French guns thumped away at ours.

The bombardment of the ridge was at its height when uneven lines of Gurkhas began to move forward across the flat ground at its foot. Luckily for them the billowing curtain of dust half-way up the slope blinded the French earthworks. The distant lines of little figures pushed on up the steep incline at a real hillman's pace and disappeared into the smoke and dust. Our guns had by now lifted and were firing over the ridge; I could see some of their shells bursting beyond the aerodrome.

The cloud on the ridge thinned rapidly and drifted away. The Gurkhas were half-way up, some of them shooting from the hip. Suddenly, on the top of the ridge, silhouetted against the smoke and sky, appeared an agitated figure or two, arms waving, bodies bent. Then more, then a crowd of them, scrambling wildly over the crest and vanishing down the other side. The French native troops were abandoning their entrenchments. A few moments later the Gurkhas reached the top of the ridge and plunged out of sight after them.

The noise of gun and rifle fire died away except for the chattering of light automatics from the aerodrome. I turned my glasses in that direction and could see our men advancing each side of the road, some already at the corner of the airfield. As the din wavered towards silence, I heard for the first time a strange confused murmur from the town itself, punctuated by bursts of machine-gun fire, rifle shots and the crump of shells—the column! A vehicle, leaving a trail of dust behind it, fled madly down the road from the aerodrome into the town; others followed it and rifle fire started again. Coloured Véry lights—success signals—leapt up from the ridge and from the aerodrome. The enemy was on the run. The double attack had been too much for his nerves. We were into Deir-ez-zor!

Into the town, yes, but had we got the bridge? Or were we being held up by a desperate house-to-house defence? The bridge was the real prize. I left Weld to move up his reserves and control things from his headquarters, and taking my A.D.C. ran to my station-wagon. My Indian driver needed no urging and we were off as hard as we could go up the road to the town.

I have had one or two drives that for various reasons I remember but none that I found at the same time so exciting and so amusing. I stood up with my A.D.C. looking through the open roof of the station-wagon, and almost at once we were passing through the reserve Gurkha battalion, all very cheerful, moving up to support the one ahead. I waved to the C.O. as he disappeared in our dust and he waved back. The next incident in our progress was less reassuring. A large and formidable French lorry being driven at speed away from the town suddenly bore down on us. As we edged to the side of the road to give it room, I saw that towed behind it, swaying dangerously, was a 75-mm. gun. Just as the lorry was drawing level with us the gun lurched sideways, broke its coupling, and came tobogganing viciously, broadside on, across our bows. My driver stood on his brakes and the gun slid past, missing our bonnet by inches. The lorry stopped and its driver climbed down from his cab. I got out too. He was a young British officer of Sappers and Miners, whose section had been detailed to advance with the leading infantry and remove any mines or obstruction found on the road. He had the decency to appear somewhat perturbed when he recognized me. I asked him with soldierly embellishment what exactly he thought he was doing. He replied that he had found lorry and gun abandoned at the road-side, and had thought it best to remove them to a place of safety lest the French re-took them by a counter-attack! Having briefly made clear to him my opinion of young officers who left the job they were supposed to be doing to indulge in nonsense of this kind, I sent him back, minus gun and lorry, to get on with his search for mines.

Somewhat sobered by this episode, we drove on and were soon level with the aerodrome. At the far end were half-a-dozen aircraft outside the hangars, Gurkhas swarming round them. But the sight that attracted us was nearer the road. Scattered over the fields on each side were a number—a large number—of native Syrian troops, soldiers of a Levant infantry battalion, in their khaki jackets and voluminous Zouave trousers. Without exception, as far as the eye could see, they were busily engaged in divesting themselves of their uniforms. My A.D.C., whose refined diction had never been corrupted by the rude language of those with whom war had compelled him to associate, exclaimed, 'Dear me, how very curious!' Indeed it was strange to see one's enemy thus vigorously de-bagging himself on the battlefield, but the explanation was simple. It was only another form of the soldier's historic gesture of flinging down his musket—they would soldier no more! Having discarded their arms and tell-tale uniforms, they proposed, in their somewhat scanty underclothes, to fade gently but rapidly into a civilian background. In this they were most successful; our prisoners except for some wounded were almost entirely French.

We drove on past the Syrians, who were much too busy to take any notice of us and were now beginning a rather straggling cross-country race for home, and entered the town by a wide street with well-spaced houses on either side. As we advanced, the houses grew closer together until they became continuous lines of shops. The road we had to ourselves. It was completely deserted, except that well ahead, Gurkhas, rifles at the ready, were moving forward, close to the houses on each side. Passing a side street, we saw more of them picketing the corners. Suddenly in front of us a great deal of noise broke out—shouts, yells, rifle shots and the stammer of a machine-gun. A platoon of Gurkhas appeared from nowhere and doubled hard towards the tumult. We followed and without warning ran into what at first sight looked like a riot.

The street was full of men milling round, Indian sepoys, native civilians, and, judging by their undress, some of our friends the Syrian soldiers. They were all yelling at the tops of their voices and pressing in on the centre of attraction. This, I could see from my vantage-point in the station-wagon, was composed of two armoured cars, one ours with its beehive top, the other French, looking remarkably like an inverted bath-tub on wheels. They were leaning up against one another like a couple of drunken men. However, their deadly combat—if there had been one—was now over. Four or five unhappy Frenchmen were being hustled out by exulting Pathan cavalrymen, amid the approving shouts of the citizens and the disappointed looks of the Gurkhas who had arrived too late to shoot anybody. Showing high above the crowd on the other side, I caught sight of the Sikh turbans of Frontier Force sepoys. Evidently this was where the flanking column had met the attack from the south, and there was a sort of Wellington meeting Blücher feeling in the air. In fact the bank holiday atmosphere pervading the scene did not fit in at all with my idea of the serious business of capturing a city by assault, and the general lack of dignity would, I was sure, distress my A.D.C. However, the Gurkhas from one side and the Sikhs from the other soon sorted out the crowd which was much too good-humoured to resent a little pushing about.

We were now at the centre of the town where another wide street ran into ours at right angles. I guessed it led to the bridge and we turned the station-wagon down it. This street was completely empty except for a party of Frontier Force Rifles under a

British officer who were about to advance on the bridge and seize it. The officer told us he did not know if the enemy still held it but thought they probably did as it was their only remaining escape route.

On hearing this it struck me that the station-wagon might be a little conspicuous, so out we got. The Frontier Force riflemen moved off briskly in files on each side of the street and, letting them gain something of a start, my A.D.C. and I followed at a more sober pace. A couple of Sikhs, their fluffy attempts at beards betraying their youth, attached themselves to us as escort. Both carried tommy-guns which they were cheerfully anxious to use. I asked them if they had shot anybody yet; with charming smiles they assured me, as Sikhs would, that many enemy had fallen to their marksmanship. I doubted it.

The four of us moved on down the empty street and then a strange, fairy-tale sort of thing began to happen. As we came past, here and there a door opened and, at first nervously and then with increasing confidence, native civilians slipped out and fell in behind us. In no time, we were moving at the head of a large and enthusiastic crowd. A greasy nondescript native shuffling beside me assured me, in some queer brand of French, that the enemy had fled and that the victorious British and magnificent ''Indoo' would find no one but friends in this city. I turned to answer him—but he was not there! At that instant a rapid succession of startling cracks had sounded just above our heads, and I found myself, my A.D.C. and the two Sikhs standing, looking rather foolish, alone in the street. The crowd had melted, heaven knows where, in a flash. It did not take even our slow wits long to realize that the nondescript gentleman had not been quite accurate. The French had not gone; they were in fact at that moment shooting up the street with a light automatic!

We leapt together for an open door and crushed through it, into what seemed to be an office building. Firing sounded pretty general outside but we could see nothing, so I led a dash for the roof. At the head of the stairs we came out on a fair-sized stone-flagged landing. Facing us was a wide arched entrance to another room with a couch against the far wall. As we stood peering through, a figure in khaki, carrying a rifle, leapt across the opening from right to left. The Sikh beside me without raising his tommy-gun fired a burst from his hip and the figure crashed to the floor. It may have been a fluke, but I have never seen a better snapshot and I revised my opinion of Sikh marksmanship. We ran forward. The victim was a native soldier, badly hit in the side and thigh. We left him to more Sikhs who were now appearing, and by another flight of stairs reached the roof.

From there we could see our sepoys working forward over other roofs from house to house. Some were well ahead and should be overlooking the bridge. There was still a little firing but it was dying down and in the street below us, apparently no longer under fire, more Frontier Force were doubling forward. It struck me I was not exercising much control over the battle for the bridge, so we hurried back down the stairs. Someone had put the wounded man on the couch where he lay groaning.

In the street we soon caught up with the Frontier Force as they reached the end of the first bridge spanning a channel of the river to an island in mid-stream. Our men were already on it. I was told they had surprised and driven off a French detachment, thought to be Foreign Legion, before they could blow the demolition charges. The second bridge, from the island to the east bank, was at once rushed regardless of probable mines. I waited to see the whole bridge safely in our hands and a company securely established on the far side.

Willing informers, emerging from their hiding places, told us that a small motorized French column with two field-guns—all that had escaped from Deir-ez-zor—had crossed an hour before and made off north. We whistled up a squadron of the armoured cars to go after them, which they very promptly did, but alas, a few miles out they had to turn back, their petrol almost exhausted. Had we only known it, we had at this time captured considerable quantities of petrol and could have made our victory absolute by adding guns and infantry to the pursuit and rounding up the last remnants of the garrison.

Having assured myself that the whole bridge was intact and safely in our hands, I turned back towards the town. The cessation of firing had been the signal for even bigger crowds than ever to come swarming into the streets. We were at once mobbed by officious and self-appointed guides whose enthusiasm had to be restrained by a platoon of Frontier Force detached to rescue us. We were vociferously urged towards what I understood to be the municipal offices, and after a short walk we found ourselves in the midst of a noisy multitude in front of a more than usually imposing building. At the main door were waiting two or three Syrian functionaries who, with almost overpowering politeness, led us upstairs into a large and airy room.

I was greeted by a distinguished-looking Syrian in European dress who introduced himself as the deputy-governor. The governor, he explained, had been also the French commander, now in flight. The deputy-governor welcomed us, the British, as deliverers, and trusted the French would never return. I made no comment on this nor did I confide in him that I thought General de Gaulle might have different views. He then formally presented a line of city councillors and senior officials. As I moved along, shaking hands with each, out of the corner of my eye I caught sight of a French officer in uniform standing last in the row. I was intrigued to know who he was, because as far as I knew no French, other than prisoners, had remained in the town. When I reached him, it was explained to me that up to a couple of hours ago he had been the Vichy chief of police; he was still chief of police but no longer Vichy—he was now a staunch de Gaullist. I was a little suspicious of so speedy and opportune a conversion and resolved to keep an eye on him.

The deputy-governor in a neat little speech formally and gracefully rendered the town into my keeping. I was sorry there was no key on a velvet cushion to be offered but, apart from that, it was all very properly done. I assured him and his colleagues that as long as they and the citizens kept the peace, gave no help of any sort to the enemy and obeyed all orders of my officers, they need have no fear. I ordered him to start all municipal services again and to encourage the townsfolk to resume their lawful avocations and to surrender all arms. I told the chameleon-like chief of police to get his men on the streets again and to take all his orders from my provost marshal who would arrive that day. After coffee I left amid protestations of esteem, got into my station-wagon, and set out through increasing crowds for the governor's house.

My arrival there coincided with that overhead of ten Vichy

bombers with seven fighters. The crump of the first bomb had a magical effect in clearing the streets once more. I heard later that most of the bombs fell on the northern outskirts. We suffered some casualties in men and vehicles but the French failed in what I imagined to be their main object—to destroy the petrol, ammunition and stores they had abandoned in the arsenal.

The governor's residence was a largish Mediterranean villa-type house right on the main street. As we turned sharp in through a gate in the iron railings, I had a sudden spasm of alarm—the house appeared to be occupied by the Foreign Legion! Their *képis* seemed everywhere. A couple of legionnaires were on the steps of the doorway, others in the courtyard, and an N.C.O. stood at attention beside a very smart black saloon car. On a second glance I was relieved to see they were all unarmed, and that at the corner of the house was a workmanlike picket of Gurkhas.

A short, broad-shouldered sergeant, in Legion uniform, stepped forward, opened the station-wagon door, and saluted. I could not understand his French very well—I think he was a Jugoslav—but I gathered that he was my French predecessor's major-domo, that the men I saw were the house staff and at my service, including the car and its chauffeur. Did I desire any refreshment? A glass of wine? *Déjeuner?* The lunch prepared for the former governor was still available and could be served in no time. There was a touch of romantic fitness in all this that appealed to me; besides, I was devilish hungry! As if it were the most ordinary thing in the world, I ordered lunch.

The sergeant conducted me over the house, indicated that the best suite was mine, and seemed to have no more difficulty in changing his allegiance than had the chief of police. It was obvious that my opponent had had no intention of abandoning his house when he rose that morning. His personal belongings, sword, medals, photographs, were all in place, his correspondence on his desk. The only thing missing was the key of the big safe in his study, and a little gelignite would replace that. The Tricolour had already been hauled down from the tall flagstaff on the roof, and I at once ordered the Union Jack to be hoisted in its place. Alas, the closest search throughout my division failed to unearth a Union Jack! We had to wait until we had taken Aleppo before we could borrow one from our consular service there.

Weld and some of his officers joined us and, as we ate an excellent lunch waited on with something of a flourish by our former enemies, reports began to come in. With the exception of the two that had escaped, we had taken all the French guns. In the arsenal were found large quantities of weapons, including a great many rifles—here I decided was the means of arming our up-to-now defenceless motor-drivers—and much ammunition. Even better, besides petrol we had taken eighty lorries in good running order and—an incredible stroke of luck—a number of tyres that would fit the wheels of our ancient armoured cars. With the petrol and the extra lorries we could, I thought, resume our advance on Aleppo almost at once while the French were still in confusion.

As a matter of fact we did. Two days later we were in Raqqa, seventy miles further up the Euphrates, and soon after our funny old cars—with their new tyres—were shooting up the enemy as they scrambled over the river at Jerablus on the Turkish frontier, fifty miles north of Aleppo—a threat which was not without its effect on the French decision to surrender a few days later.

Glimpses of these possibilities for the future and healthy appetites made our lunch a most satisfactory meal, and it was with a happy sense of repletion I strolled to the gate. Two Gurkha sentries clicked to the present and, endeavouring not quite successfully to emulate them, two Syrian policemen also saluted— evidently the chief of police was out to make an impression. The street was filling again after the bombing and, for the first time, women were promenading in their best as if on a fête day.

Slowly down the road came two of our armoured cars, patrolling the city. They stopped opposite the gate and from the first sprang my old friend, the once gloomy risaldar-major. A broad grin broke through the caked dust on his face as he advanced on me. Not waiting to salute, he seized my hand.

'You said you would give us a proper fight, sahib,' he exclaimed, pump-handling my arm, 'and, name of God, you did!'

VIII

PERSIAN PATTERN

In the north, troops of the 10th Indian Division, released for the purpose from North Eastern Syria, and the 2nd Indian and 9th (British) Armoured Brigades advanced eighty miles into Persia to Shahabad. . . . Seven squadrons of the Royal Air Force under Air Vice-Marshal D'Albiac co-operated by reconnaissance and a show of force; only at one point was it necessary for them to make an attack. On the 28th August all resistance ceased.

British Official History: Mediterranean and Middle East,
Vol. II

PERSIAN PATTERN

IN the summer of 1941, the troops of my Indian division, after a running scuffle with Iraqi rebels from Basra to Mosul and a more serious campaign against the French, were taking things a little easier, some still in Syria and others on the shores of Lake Habbaniya, near Baghdad. The soldiers, enjoying this comparative rest after strenuous operations, were happy. I was happy, too —in an aeroplane on my way to attend a conference in Jerusalem. To be honest, I was not caring very much what this conference was to be about; I was toying with the pleasant vision of a few days in the comfort and civilization of the King David Hotel. Alas, like so many of my visions, it was to remain a vision.

We had hardly been flying half an hour when the pilot handed me an urgent signal telling me to return to Baghdad at once and report to the Army Commander. My mood of pleasant expectation was replaced by a somewhat apprehensive curiosity as to why he wanted to see me in such a hurry. It seemed a little ominous. I liked the Army Commander, but I had an uneasy feeling that at the moment this liking was not mutual. One or two minor incidents had occurred lately and had not, I feared, endeared me or my division to him. There was the unfortunate occasion when the Army Commander returning from Jerusalem had found his aircraft cluttered up with oddly-shaped packages in the charge of a young officer, who when asked what the devil they were, innocently replied, 'Instruments for a jazz band, sir. General Slim sent me to buy them in Jerusalem.' True, Army Headquarters had issued the strictest orders that the utmost economy in all forms of transport must be enforced and only essentials required for operations were to be carried, but how was I to know that our friends, the R.A.F., with whom we normally had a most sympathetic understanding, would be so tactless as to load those beastly instruments into the same aeroplane as the Army Commander?

My head was still bowed under the stinging rebuke this *faux-pas* had earned me and my expressions of contrition were still ringing in my superior's ears when cruel fate intervened again. Bivouacking in the sand under the parching heat of a Mesopotamian mid-summer, the British soldiers of my division desired nothing so much as beer. Yet in Iraq and Syria beer was as scarce as corn to Joseph's brethren in their famine, but, like them, Alf Snelling, my resourceful administrative officer, had heard that there was plenty, not in Egypt, but in Haifa, six hundred miles away. To get it we sent our captured French lorries and, I must admit, some others; to pay for it we heavily overdrew our contingent account. Our organization was brilliant and all worked most smoothly until, within a few miles of my headquarters, the returning convoy loaded to the limit with thousands of bottles of most admirable Australian beer, met the Army Commander in his car proceeding on his lawful occasions in the opposite direction. All would yet have been well had not the leading lorry, blinding happily down the middle of the road, forced the great man's car, flag and all, into the ditch. There ensued some embarrassing questions:

(i) Why was the road discipline of my division so lamentable?

(ii) Why had I disobeyed orders this, that and the other by using transport to carry unauthorized supplies over great distances?

(iii) How was it that my division was holding, undisclosed, a considerable number of captured enemy vehicles?

(iv) Why had I overlooked Financial Instructions, Paragraphs So-and-So, which required higher authority to sanction such an overdraft as I had incurred?

(v) In general terms what did I and my division think we were?

The dissipation of the ensuing cloud of misunderstanding was not hastened by my somewhat ill-judged refusal to sell any of the beer to the Army Headquarters staff.

Such minor contretemps were, I felt, better forgotten, but I was by no means sure they had been. I was aware also that certain activities, innocent and even beneficial in themselves, in which I knew my division was indulging at the time might, if viewed by jaundiced eyes, appear a trifle unorthodox. Indeed, I was haunted by the fear that in spite of the stringent precautions we had taken to avoid giving further pain to the Army Commander, some new incident might have revealed these fresh examples of initiative.

I was, therefore, considerably relieved, even if more than a little surprised, when I was told that I was forthwith to take command of a small force now collecting at Khanaquin and with it in three days time invade Persia. It seemed a fairly tall order. Persia was a big country with a large if not reputedly very efficient army; I had not much time to find out what it was all about or to make plans, and my force, I found, was to be a rather bitty-piecey one. I had always had—and still have—an aversion from breaking up formations, and I was not happy about a scratch force made up of an armoured brigade and a regiment of light tanks from another brigade, even when it was to include a brigade group from my own division. Nor was I greatly reassured when the order transferring the 'armoured' brigade to my command naïvely explained, 'It has no armour'. As a matter of fact, it was made up of dismounted cavalry carried in 30-cwt. trucks, and I was most intrigued as to why it should call itself 'armoured', until I discovered that the staff of an armoured brigade was considerably larger than that of a normal one.

The background to this hurriedly improvized invasion was that Persia was harbouring over three thousand Germans who, thinly disguised as diplomats, technical advisers, engineers and businessmen were, with the full connivance of the Persian authorities, working tirelessly and with some success against us. With so much on her hands and the need not to offend Russia, notoriously sensitive to events in Persia, there was little that Britain could do beyond making unavailing diplomatic protests. When, to our and their own surprise Hitler suddenly turned the Russians into our allies, not only was it easier to take action but it became imperative to do so. The activities of the powerful German fifth column, if allowed to continue, could have made impossible our plans to supply Russia across Persia. In mid-August the British Government and its new ally presented a joint demand that Persia should expel these Germans. The reply was evasive and unsatisfactory, and a combined Anglo-Russian invasion was decided upon.

Not for the first time, the two Great Powers drew a line across the map of Persia, somewhere about its middle, dividing it into spheres of influence or, in this case, of occupation. We were to have the southern half, the Russians the northern. The plan was for a simultaneous crossing of the Persian frontier by my force moving on Kermanshah from the west, by another Indian division directed against Abadan and Ahwaz in the south, and by a Russian corps from the north.

With the brigade from my division I moved to Khanaquin on the Persian border, arriving there on the 24th August and finding the other units of my force already assembled. Khanaquin I remembered from the first World War if only because of a ditty then much in favour, one verse of which ran:

> *The Khaimaqam of Khanaquin,*
> *Is versed in every kind of sin,*
> *For all the grosser forms of lust,*
> *He makes a gorgeous bundobust.*

The dusty town looked much the same as it had then, although its remembered smells had now been overlaid by the all-pervading reek of an oil refinery. We had neither time nor opportunity to discover whether its ancient but dubious delights still remained. I for one was fully occupied going over with Aizlewood, the brigadier of the armoured brigade, the plans he had already prepared for the first phase of our invasion—the forcing of the formidable Pa-i-Tak Pass, which within thirty miles of our crossing the frontier would bar our way. With time so short it was fortunate that I could heartily approve his plans, and I decided to act on them without serious alteration.

Accordingly, before dawn on the 25th August, led by the Hussars in their always gallant but decrepit and slightly ridiculous old Mark VII tanks, whose only armament was a single Vickers machine-gun apiece and whose armour almost anything could pierce, we crossed the frontier. By that time I was becoming accustomed to invasions; this was the fifth frontier I had crossed in the past year. All the same, there was a thrill about it. But very little happened. A few harmless shots from vanishing frontier guards greeted us as we encircled the village of Qasr-i-Shirin, about ten miles inside Persia, but we met no real opposition. As it grew lighter, Aizlewood and I pushed on with the advance-guard, and by mid-morning we were almost at the entrance to the Pa-i-Tak Pass. Here we stopped and, covered by a screen of light tanks, stood on the roof of my station-wagon to study this historic gate through which, over the centuries, so many armies had passed or tried to pass.

Viewed from below it was a most formidable and threatening obstacle. The interminable flat plains of the Tigris and Euphrates which stretched behind us for hundreds of miles here came to an abrupt end at the great boundary wall of a mighty escarpment stretching from north to south across our path. The road to Kermanshah which we must follow rose sharply into the mouth of the pass and, climbing in curves and loops, vanished among cliffs and gorges to emerge, three thousand feet higher, on to the plateau of Gilan. It looked as if a handful of men could hold it against an army many times the size of mine.

At the moment there was no sign of even the proverbial handful in the pass or on the crest of the escarpment. Both appeared completely deserted. Yet our intelligence was quite firm that there was a Persian force, reliably reported to have been reinforced to a strength of five thousand, well dug in on and around the pass. It was so still and deserted that we began to wonder if there really were any enemy at all. Curiously but cautiously we drove on a few hundred yards and again searched the hills and cliffs. Not a sign of movement; not the sound of a shot. Proceeding in this way, growing bolder with continued impunity, we reached the point where the road entered a sinister and narrowing gorge, the jaws of the pass itself. The road, quite empty, ran uphill from us to disappear with surprising suddenness round a sharp corner a couple of hundred yards further on. At this corner stood a white-washed *chai khana*, a tea shop, the Persian equivalent of a tavern, with a few small trees growing at the roadside in front of it; all utterly peaceful, drowsing deserted in the sunlight.

The irresistible urge to look round the corner that comes on every winding road fell upon us. Why not? It looked safe enough! Standing boldly upright, our heads and shoulders through the open roof, we drove slowly to the corner, cautiously poked our bonnet round it and peered up the pass. I had just spotted above the road what I took to be the oil-pumping station marked on our map when a bang, well behind us and off to one side, made me jump.

'What's that?' I asked Aizlewood.

His reply was emphasized by a much louder and nearer *crump!*

and a cloud of dust, smoke and stones level with us but some way off the road. Almost simultaneously with it came the *crack!* of a gun ahead.

'By God, they're shooting at us!' exclaimed the brigadier in an aggrieved voice.

Our driver had already realized this unpleasant fact, and we jerked in reverse back around the corner as a couple more shells from the anti-tank gun smacked into the road at the spot we had just left. The driver needed no orders to turn the car behind the *chai khana*, and we left the Pa-i-Tak Pass a good deal more briskly than we had entered it.

There was an interesting postscript to this incident. Some days later the anti-tank battery fell into our hands and we were told that just as it was ordered to the Pa-i-Tak Pass it had been issued with brand new guns. The first shot its crew had ever fired from one of these was the opening round at us, and, as a Persian gunner wistfully remarked, a little more practice would have made them shoot better!

We could now, at any rate, be sure there were enemy on the pass and that they meant to hold it against us. The idea of a frontal attack up the rugged and in places almost vertical escarpment was not attractive, but the brigadier when studying his map before my arrival had spotted a route by which any position at the Pa-i-Tak itself could be by-passed. This was a track which crossed the escarpment some twenty miles further south and went via the village of Gilan to Shahabad on the main Kermanshah road, about thirty miles south-east of the main pass. It was a long—about ninety miles—and rough track but it was said to be passable by wheels. Although we could hardly expect it not to be blocked by the enemy, all reports agreed that their strength there was small, and, even if we were delayed the threat to the Persian rear would, we could hope, at least divide their force. I therefore decided to send the armoured brigade by this track and, as soon as the enemy began to feel the threat against their rear, to attack on each side of the Pa-i-Tak Pass with the rest of my force.

On the 26th, the R.A.F. located enemy defences in the pass and along the escarpment, and later in the afternoon bombed them. Throughout the day the infantry carried out their reconnaissances and preparations for the attack while the armoured

brigade began its arduous and hazardous march, the first stages
of which were to be completed before daylight. About Gilan the
column was delayed for a time by road blocks and some infantry
and machine-gun fire. An overheard radio conversation when this
skirmish was at its height, while it did not diminish our fear that
the column might be seriously held up, did at least give us a smile:

First Signaller: 'This is getting a bit too hot! I'm going under
my truck. Over.'

Second Signaller: 'I *am* under my truck! Out!'

Before dawn on the 27th, two Gurkha battalions, one each side
of the Pa-i-Tak Pass, began in real mountain warfare style to
scramble up the escarpment. Hardly had they got going when I
was most relieved to receive a signal from the flank column that
it had taken Shahabad. The news of this had proved too much
for the Persians, already shaken by the bombing, and they had
pulled out hurriedly across country north of the road while it was
still dark.

When I drove up to the top of the pass early that morning I
found a very cheerful infantry brigadier, with his headquarters
established beside the road, issuing orders to his first battalion to
arrive to press on hard along the road for Shahabad. About fifty
bedraggled Persian prisoners were squatting in a group near his
headquarters. They were not very impressive as soldiers but
prisoners rarely are. They said their officers had left them in the
night and made off without telling them they were going. During
the morning we gained touch with armoured brigade patrols
coming to look for us and I issued orders for both brigades, the
infantry ferrying in their own transport, to push on hard for
Kermanshah, a good forty miles beyond our present advanced
troops at Shahabad.

Tired as most of them were, especially the armoured brigade,
they responded nobly, and we had reached a point some fifteen
miles east of Shahabad when the discovery of a strong Persian
force barring our way made it imperative for us to close up our
strung-out units. This we did behind a ridge astride the road and
there, covered by outposts, we passed a quiet night.

Next morning, just after a cloudless dawn, I was sitting behind
the best cover I could find on the forward slope of this bare ridge.
Through my field-glasses I scanned the seemingly peaceful valley

spread out below me. In the clear, cool early light it was a charming view, but I was not enjoying it as much as I might. There are few things more exasperating than to have someone hitting you without being able to hit back, and that was what was happening to us. The road to Kermanshah came through a gap in our ridge and ran straight as a ruler into the distance. Half-way across the valley it passed through a tree-studded village, to disappear some miles further on, over a saddle in the line of hills forming the eastern horizon. Concealed among these hills a battery of Persian artillery was firing at us, and I cursed their modern 155-mm. guns which so easily and so far outranged our old 18-pounders.

My meditation on a not altogether favourable situation was interrupted by another salvo of shells which rustled menacingly overhead to burst in clouds of black smoke and brown earth on the road below, not far from a group of sheltering 30-cwt. trucks. No harm was done but the Indian drivers so contentedly eating their morning *chupatti* in the sun were suddenly galvanized into action. In no time, with a roar of engines and some clashing of gears, the trucks were off to seek a safer parking place. It was as well they had, for within half a minute another salvo slid almost lazily over and burst noisily below us.

'Damn cheek!' growled Ouvry, my G.S.O.1. looking up malevolently.

I agreed, but indignation would not help us to solve our problems. At the moment we had three, an administrative one, a political one, and a tactical one. We had or were about to outrun our maintenance which was based on Baghdad. Indeed, a senior staff officer had at dawn arrived to tell us so, but with us that was no unusual thing, and I had little anxiety on that score. Alf Snelling, my redoubtable administrative officer, had it in hand and would, no doubt, as he had done so often before, 'arrange'.

The second problem concerned the safety of the fifty or so British subjects at the oil refinery in the Kermanshah area. I had not been particularly anxious about them but during the night I had received news that, when our troops landed at Abadan in the south, several members of the oil company's staff had been killed. I assumed that they had been murdered by Persians and became increasingly alarmed for the safety of our people in Kermanshah. Actually, the unfortunate civilians at Abadan had rashly exposed themselves while trying to watch the battle and had been shot accidentally by our troops. The Persians were in this blameless. The danger which I believed the British prisoners at Kermanshah to be in made speed essential in the solving of our tactical problem.

This was immediate and formidable. Facing us, in position along a line of hills astride the road about four miles away, was a Persian army corps of two divisions and a cavalry brigade. Our patrols had also reported armoured vehicles, though whether cars or tanks they could not be sure. The enemy were known to be well equipped with modern Czecho-Slovak weapons—at the moment we were having convincing evidence of this from his artillery. In spite of his great numerical superiority the Persian commander had shown little inclination to leave his hills and come down into the valley. It looked as if I was not going to have Cromwell's luck against the Scots at Dunbar; I should have to attack myself. We had no very high opinion of the enemy's military qualities but a couple of brigades was not quite the force with which I would have chosen to attack a full strength corps, even a Persian one. But it was no use waiting. I issued orders for a general advance to begin at ten o'clock, with a view to an attack, if possible, that afternoon.

By 8.30 a.m. the orders had gone out and the last preparations for the advance were being made. I had returned to my observation post on the ridge and had just had my attention drawn to some movement in the village half-way across the valley. It had been visited that morning by our patrols and was at the moment supposedly empty, so I was surprised to see emerging from it a large, black saloon car. At first as it drove slowly along the road towards us I could not make out what was strange about it, but as it drew closer I saw that sticking out from it at odd angles on both sides were large white flags. Evidently the enemy desired a parley.

Two of our light tanks went forward to meet the car and escorted it in. At the foot of the ridge the three vehicles halted. The door of the car almost hidden by a fluttering white flag opened, and there emerged a small and dapper Persian officer, a major I think. From the high heels of his field boots to the top of his smart *képi* he was immaculate, a credit alike to his tailor, his bootmaker and his batman. Flanked by large military policemen he climbed the ridge and approached the two British officers who, dressed in rather scruffy khaki shirts and trousers, awaited him.

I stepped forward to meet him. He seemed to have little English but excellent French. He announced that he had a message from the Persian commander-in-chief to deliver to the British commander. I told him I was commanding the British forces. A flicker of incredulity seemed to pass over his face to be quickly suppressed and, reassured I hope, by the red tabs on my shirt collar, he bowed politely and continued. At first he glanced about him, obviously and understandably not very sure of the reception he would get, but as our attitude showed more curiosity and perhaps at times amusement than brutality, his confidence grew to a cock-sparrow assurance. His complexion was what on an Indian passport is described as wheaten, his dark eyes sparkled intelligently, and his well-shaped hands gesticulated gracefully as we conducted our negotiations, on his part, in a comic mixture of poor English and Parisian French and, on mine, mostly in schoolboy French which had luckily been lately given an airing in Syria. Soldiers looked at us curiously as we talked but the meeting had more the air of a casual conversation than a momentous military conference.

The Shah, our major explained, wishing to avoid further bloodshed, had ordered his commanders in the field to arrange with the Allied forces a cease fire. The terms proposed for this were, as far as I could follow the rather too fluent French, that all hostile action on both sides should cease and the British forces remain in their present positions until the terms of peace were settled between governments.

I had no authority to negotiate but, even if I had, these terms seemed completely unacceptable. In any case, I could feel, behind the veneer of confidence with which the major gallantly attempted to cover his proposals, that whatever the motives the Shah might have, the Persian army was not anxious for a fight. I answered to the effect that in no circumstances could I agree to anything that limited the freedom of movement of my forces and that I had my terms for a cease-fire too. I put them to him as:

    (i) All hostile action on both sides to cease.

    (ii) Persian forces to withdraw from their present position at a time I would state and assemble in areas I would designate.

(iii) Unrestricted passage to Kermanshah for my force and facilities for its maintenance there.

(iv) The delivery to our forces of all British subjects in Persian hands unharmed and well treated.

At first this drew indignant protests from the major. He was not here to negotiate a surrender but to arrange a truce! Rather than accept these terms they would fight. It was not the military situation but pure humanity that had induced their offer. In fact, orders had already been issued that, if we were so foolish as to reject a cease-fire, overwhelming forces would without further delay attack and destroy us. Dramatically he pointed to where, even at that moment, the Persian cavalry were poised to hurl themselves upon us. I replied that I only hoped they would as we had made what I was sure were adequate arrangements to receive them, and I signified the interview might well terminate now.

The major, somewhat crestfallen, made the best of a bad job. It was only, he said, because the Shah himself had ordered it that his commander would even consider such suggestions as I had made. He then very gamely argued against each condition in turn. After some minutes I interrupted him and asked him point blank to accept or refuse. When he began again to hum and haw I told him that, as he seemed to have no power to accept, I would give him an hour to go back and fetch his commander with whom I would deal direct. At this our little major, looking even more uncomfortable, replied a little sadly: 'It is not the custom in the Persian army, as it appears to be in the British, for the general to be in the front line!' He then, with considerable charm, gave way on all points and on behalf of his commander accepted our terms.

He still, however, protested that my demand that the Persian forces should have evacuated their present positions by two o'clock that afternoon was impracticable. It did not give time, he insisted, for the necessary orders to be issued and arrangements to be made.

'*Excellence*,' he cried with heartfelt conviction, '*ce n'est pas possible!*'

'*Néanmoins*,' I countered in my best French, '*il faut que vous le fassiez.*'

The little man, fixing me with his eyes, faced me portentously: '*Mon général, je suis officier de l'Etat Major Iranien et je vous assure que ce n'est pas possible!*'

'*Et moi aussi*,' I retaliated, '*je suis officier de l'Etat Major Britannique, et je vous dis que c'est très possible!*'

At this counter-stroke, he drew himself to his full height, squared his shoulders, and discharged what he evidently was confident would be the final broadside in our encounter.

'*De plus*,' he announced impressively, '*de plus, j'ai été élève de l'Ecole Supérieure de Guerre, et je vous dis, Excellence, que ce que vous voulez est vraiment impossible!*'

But I had not yet used my heaviest guns.

'*Moi aussi*,' I assured him, 'I also am an *élève de l'Ecole Supérieure de Guerre, l'Ecole Supérieure de Guerre Britannique*, and not only am I an *élève* but I was *professeur!*'

He must have held his Staff College instructors in the most commendable awe, for no sooner had I declared that I had been *professeur* than he bowed to my authority and thereafter regarded me with an obviously increased respect.

He made only one more attempt to argue. Alarmed as I was for the safety of the British in Kermanshah, I demanded that every one of them, in accordance with a list I had, should be produced unharmed and unmolested at my headquarters by four o'clock that afternoon. In vain he assured me, almost tearfully, that they were collected at the oil refinery, that they were in no danger whatever but, on the contrary, were enjoying every comfort under the most solicitous care of the Persian army. Mr. Robertson, the manager, was held in the highest esteem by the general and was his personal friend of the closest. When I still insisted he assured me that my action would only cause great inconvenience to my countrymen; indeed, he doubted if they could be persuaded to come without the use of force! He would, however, as I was so insistent, telephone my directions to the headquarters in Kermanshah. We then parted on the best of terms, with a good deal of saluting and bowing on both sides, and we watched him speed back along the road white flags still fluttering. We had grown quite fond of him.

My Army Commander approved the terms I had laid down and also my intention to advance and occupy Kermanshah. During the morning we received reports from the air that the Persian army had begun its withdrawal from its positions and we prepared to occupy them. Our patrols on the ground pushed forward, keeping a close watch on the retreat but were careful not to tread so heavily on the Persians' heels as to provoke a breach of the cease-fire by some trigger-happy soldier.

All was thus proceeding according to plan and we were expecting at any minute to be told our patrols were on the Persian position when, rather to our surprise, we again saw a saloon car, this time rapidly driven, approaching along the Kermanshah road. I thought it was probably our friend the major coming back to re-open the argument but when it reached us, instead of his dapper figure, there got out an Englishman. His linen suit, perfectly pressed, and his solar topi were perhaps the civilian counterpart of our little major's impeccable turnout, but there the resemblance ended. Our new visitor was a well set up man of about my own age, who came briskly towards us, a pair of humorous eyes twinkling through glasses.

He introduced himself as Robertson, the manager of the oil refinery, and explained that as soon as the Persian authorities had given him my message he had thought it best to drive out himself to see me. The fact that he would have to drive without escort through an angry and possibly hostile army in retreat he brushed aside lightly as no risk at all. I thought otherwise and that he was a very brave man. This was not the only time my admiration has been roused by the matter-of-fact way in which British civilians in the East, relying on their knowledge of the country and its people, have undertaken the most hazardous missions.

Robertson assured me that our Persian major had been right. All the British on my list—and a few more—were safe and well at the refinery. There had been no attempt at molestation; even the Persian staff had not been interfered with. In fact he had left some of his people about to arrange an afternoon's golf. When Robertson had protested at the abrupt order to pack all the British into cars and bring them out to me, the Persian officer who had brought it agreed heartily that it was stupid, but it was not *his* order; it came from the mad English general. So they had better pack up and get moving! Eventually Robertson had obtained permission to come himself, explain the real position to me, and thus save everyone a lot of trouble. He had not mentioned to the Persians that he was quite sure, also, that I would like to have reliable first-hand intelligence of affairs in Kermanshah.

He added that everything there was perfectly orderly and peaceful. All Persians, civilians and military, were only too delighted the fighting was over. They were, however, terrified of the Russians, rumours of whose advance from the north had reached them; we should be greeted with relief, as much the lesser of two evils, and treated in the most friendly way. If, in fact, I cared to go back with him to Kermanshah and see for myself he could guarantee my safety and my welcome. This novel and rather comic opera idea appealed to me. I wanted to send an officer ahead to reconnoitre, decide the dispositions of our troops on their arrival and make locally what arrangements were possible for much needed supplies. Why not be that officer myself? On the spur of the moment I decided, rather irresponsibly I fear, that I would. There was a little raising of eyebrows and some protest from my staff when I broke the news to them but, having given the necessary orders to cover my absence and taking a couple of them and a small escort with me, we set out for Kermanshah.

Robertson and I, sitting together in the back of his car, led our small procession. The road, like all the main highways the Shah had caused to be built under his modernization programme, was well graded and surfaced and our Persian driver breezed along at a good forty miles an hour. We swept over the low saddle in the Persian position and careered slap into a column of foot, guns and transport, filling the road. It was not a good entrance and we got some black looks; I was nervous when I saw one or two soldiers unship the rifles they had slung over their shoulders. I hoped someone had told them there was a cease-fire! However, our driver, reduced to a crawl, honking his horn incessantly and yelling what sounded like abuse, waved them aside and ploughed on without actually knocking any down.

These soldiers were a much better looking lot than the miserable specimens we had found at the top of the Pa-i-Tak. Their uniforms looked new, their weapons were modern and their equipment reasonably well-kept, even if their march discipline left something to be desired. Their dusty faces, as they shuffled out of the way, continued to look at us in resentful astonishment but we were only once stopped. Robertson exchanged a few words in Persian with a young officer and we were driving on again, through what seemed a never-ending column. Only in this fantastic Persian war could the commander of one side have thus gone honking and pushing his way through hundreds of the soldiers of the other. It did not seem real to me.

At last we were clear of the retreating army and, picking up speed again, we were soon on the edge of Kermanshah. As we skirted round the city I was surprised at its size and the number of people about. They stood and stared as we went by, not hostile, but more apathetic than friendly. They looked a most depressed lot, dressed most of them in accordance with Shah Reza's decrees in slovenly European dress, the men in abominable cloth caps, the women in head shawls instead of the ancient veil. Modernization, whatever else it had accomplished, had done nothing to improve the look of the citizens. I suppose it is not possible to be both efficient and picturesque; it is certainly possible simultaneously to be neither.

At the refinery, a gleaming collection of the apparatus of a laboratory bench magnified a thousand times, a few indolent Persian infantry loafing at the open gates looked curiously and rather blankly at us. Robertson called out something to them and our cars drove in. We drew up before a most attractive bungalow in a delightful garden and Robertson waved us in. We were received by a Persian butler who, in the most butlerlike fashion, relieved us of our hats, sticks and warlike equipment. We passed through an entrance hall with small glowing Persian pictures on its walls, and entered a cool English drawing-room to find a lady presiding over polished silver and delicate china, about to dispense afternoon tea to three or four young men evidently just in from golf. It seemed hardly true, yet after all this was Persia where anything could be true. This sudden transition from bivouac to boudoir was a little startling, but the kindness of our welcome soon put us at ease, although I could not help, as I looked round me, feeling rather a fool for the way I had tried to force rescue on these people who needed it so little.

Believing that there was nothing like striking while the iron was hot, I demanded an immediate interview with the Persian commander. So after tea, with two or three of my officers and Robertson as interpreter, I went into the city. The general awaited me outside his headquarters where he had drawn up his staff and a guard of honour. I am afraid I met his ceremonious politeness with a certain brusqueness—after all, I had to carry things with a high hand for I had no troops—and I declined his offer to present his officers. Somewhat subdued, the general then led us into his office, where we sat round a walnut table while tea was brought. In this more friendly atmosphere I repeated my terms for the cease-fire, to which he made no demur, and told him he might keep his headquarters in Kermanshah, but must have all his troops clear of the city in forty-eight hours. To this also he agreed.

I had been told that a certain German medical man, a notorious Axis agent, badly wanted by our Intelligence, was still in the city, and I asked the general to seize him and hand him over to me. Although he obviously knew where the doctor was, fear of the Germans was still strong and he hesitated. He showed the greatest relief when I solved his difficulty for him by saying I would make the arrest myself if he would tell us where the German was. There was no trouble about this, and two of my officers with a Persian guide were despatched there and then. In a short time they were back with the doctor, who was taken to the refinery, there to remain under guard until he was sent to internment outside Persia.

That night, before my orders for the withdrawal of the Persian troops could be carried out, local tribesmen saw their opportunity in the demoralization of the garrison and raided the magazine. In the confusion they made away with a large number of modern rifles and considerable stores of ammunition, thus making all the problems of internal security much more difficult for the unfortunate Persians and for us. We knew the raid was in progress but without troops could do nothing to prevent it.

Next morning we marched into Kermanshah in style and formally occupied it. Large crowds clustered along the sides of the streets and although I cannot say anyone cheered, there was no doubt that the bulk of them was friendly and even those, who, I suspected, would have liked to be hostile, were at least resigned. Our troops had smartened themselves up, and as they moved through the city on their way to their bivouac areas they looked, in spite of their not very large numbers, workmanlike and, as I meant them to, formidable enough not to invite liberties.

There was some protest from the Persian corps commander, my opponent of yesterday, who had now appeared, at our occupation of the city, and still more when I insisted on taking over from his troops certain positions and buildings from which it could easily be dominated. However it was a little late now for him to object and very sensibly he yielded. The hand-over between my troops and his was conducted with full military courtesies on both sides and, while co-operation was perhaps not enthusiastic, I had little to grumble at in the way my instructions were accepted and carried out.

At Robertson's house I met many of the Persian officials of the oil company and others of their countrymen from the city with whom I had to do business. They were pleasant people to deal with, for whatever faults Persians may have, they go far to redeem them by the engaging social virtues of politeness, hospitality, humour and love of beauty. All these and more I found in my British host and in his house at the Kermanshah refinery. I would have liked to have lingered there, but the harsh realities of command intruded and next morning we were on the move again; this time to secure Hamadan and to meet our Russian allies.

After some varied days spent in these tasks, I returned to my headquarters in Kermanshah and to the comforts of Robertson's welcoming house. There I found a fresh and disturbing problem awaiting us. The Kurds had risen.

Kurdistan is something of a Middle Eastern Poland. It is inhabited by a warlike race, very conscious of its nationality and of its distinctiveness from the often hostile peoples who surround it. Like Poland too, it has spent much of its history forcibly partitioned among these larger neighbours and, under their yoke, the fierce Kurdish desire for independence has simmered and bubbled. At this time, Iraq, Turkey and Persia each had their share. The collapse of Persian resistance against the Anglo–Russian invasion and the confused state of that country were too good an opportunity for the unruly Kurds to miss. The demand for an independent Kurdish state, fanned possibly by outside interests, flared once more and fed by the hope of loot, never far from the Kurdish heart, took the form of inroads into western Persia.

The last thing we British wanted was to get our forces tied down in Persia. We had quite enough on hand already to wish to be drawn into a campaign of the kind to which we had been accustomed on the Indian Frontier. The considerable Persian force, which we had encountered and which was still centred around Kermanshah, should have been capable of handling these Kurdish incursions and had attempted to do so. Unfortunately, the troops were not in good shape; morale was low even for Persia, there had been many desertions, pay was in arrears and the soldiers had lost what confidence they may have had in their leaders. No army would fight well in these conditions and the Persian was no exception. The columns it sent out were no match for the wild Kurds, who came hurooshing through the hills and swept them aside or drove them to such shelter as the towns might temporarily afford.

Villages had been sacked, the countryside laid waste, and now larger towns were being threatened. The Persian authorities were clearly unlikely to be able to stop an orgy of loot and massacre on an increasing scale. We could not divest ourselves of all responsibility and in common humanity, reluctant as we might be to become embroiled, we had to do something. After some delay orders from Whitehall filtered down to us, and I was instructed to send troops into the area to give moral support to the Persian Army and to restrain the Kurds but—and we thought this part rather funny—not to engage in hostilities against them! We gave our sarcasm some rein. Stop the Kurds without using force! Had the people in Whitehall any idea of what a Kurdish marauding gang, athirst for blood, loot and women, looked like? Did they think that we could send them home again by saying, like fatherly London bobbies, 'Now then, now then! What's all this about? Move along, please, move along there!' But the really funny thing was that Whitehall, if those were Whitehall's ideas, was right. We could. In fact, we did!

The junior officers of the Army are an astonishing lot. Sent out with small detachments ahead of the Persian Army, they met these bands of wild tribesmen, and in some extraordinary way *did* stop them. It was a sobering shock to the Kurds, expecting to find no one, or at the worst only the ramshackle Persian troops, to bar their way, to meet suddenly these cool, good-humoured young men with their steady, disciplined, confident soldiers. Like the London policemen they talked soothingly, but always with a hint of force in the background which could and would be used if needed.

In their negotiations our officers started with at least one advantage. The Kurds had no ill-feeling against us; on the contrary, they hoped to enlist our support in their struggle for freedom. Often their first reaction was naïvely to invite our troops to join with them in despoiling the unhappy Persians. When they found we were not inclined to accept, they shook their heads at our incomprehensible stupidity, but were chary of challenging us.

One leader of a large body of picturesque ruffians, after offering to share with our detachment the loot of a sizeable Persian town, then almost within his grasp, begged rather pathetically to be allowed just another twenty-four hours free from our interference. After that he promised faithfully to be good and to go back to whatever fastness he had emerged from—carrying with him, of course, his booty. But even he was persuaded to withdraw his grumbling followers from the promised land of loot, to the unspeakable delight of the Persian garrison and, if the truth must be told, the intense relief of the British officer who had so stoutly outfaced him.

On one occasion I took a journey into the hills and visited a Kurdish *Aga* or chieftain, in his castle. It really was a castle—a fair-sized fort of sun-baked mud and stone, complete with battlements and a crazy pattern of loopholes sprayed on its massive walls. Perched on a rocky outcrop on the flank of a mountain, approached by a winding track, with hardly a place to plant a scaling ladder against its walls, it was, I should have thought, impregnable to anything except artillery or air bombardment. We reached the main gate through a narrow way, cunningly defended by twists and turns to entrap the attackers and covered throughout by carefully sited loopholes. Evidently in Kurdistan, as in more civilized countries, unwanted callers were not unknown; only here more thorough preparations to receive them seemed to have been made.

The Aga himself was a large, jolly man with a slightly shifty eye. He had a huge moustache, its ends well visible from behind him; the rest of his face where not screened by this growth sported a three-day stubble. In fact, his whole effect was of a hearty shagginess, not decreased by the very untidy turban on his head and the general bagginess of his clothes. Across his chest he carried a cartridge bandolier and in his belt a serviceable automatic pistol was flanked by an old-fashioned but, I should judge, also very serviceable knife. He greeted me cordially and over refreshments treated me, through my interpreter, to an eloquent dissertation on Kurdish independence, a brief summary of his opinion—not flattering—of Persians, and a brisk side-kick at the British who incomprehensibly supported them when they could have had magnificent warriors, like him, as allies instead.

He then took me to a large chamber, almost underground, near the gate, which seemed to be a guard-room of sorts. At any rate, it was rather crowded out by about twenty of the most picturesque villains I have ever set eyes on. I noted that in the Aga's private army standardization of equipment had not progressed far. His retainers sported a most fantastic variety of lethal instruments, five or six to a man—jezails, blunderbusses, modern magazine rifles, pistols of all types, revolvers, assorted cutlery and even a Mills bomb or two peeping coyly from a waistband. A cheerful good-humour pervaded the gathering, which reminded me irresistibly of the chorus of *The Maid of the Mountains*. I fear, however, if these gentlemen had burst into their theme song, it would not have been 'Love will find the way'; they had, I suspected, other methods.

I found the Kurds engaging rogues, not so dour as my old friends and enemies the Pathans of the Indian Frontier, but very like them in many ways. Not, I think, likely to be as tough a proposition on a hillside as Mahsuds or Wazirs, but formidable enough. Be that as it may, we parted on good terms.

Apart from the Kurdish trouble, there was general insecurity throughout Persia. Armed deserters roamed the countryside, and frequently joined forces with more established bandits or formed robber gangs of their own. It was also a favourable time to work off old scores and private grudges and for officials to use the various means of extortion at which many of them were already adepts. Usually we knew little beyond ugly whispers of these villainies, but one instance did come rather dramatically to my direct attention.

On returning to Robertson's house one day, I was told that a Persian lady wished most urgently to see me. Before doing so I took the natural precaution of finding out what it was all about, and I was told that she was the wife of a well-known and respected medical man of good family. Both she and her husband were persons of considerable wealth and position, known for their good works and not involved in politics or intrigue. They had been educated in Europe and had travelled a good deal. In the early days of our invasion the doctor had been arrested by the military and flung into prison. There, according to his wife, certain senior officers were attempting to compel him to pay a ruinous sum to secure his release, and he had so far refused to do so. He had not as yet suffered more than threats and confinements, but she feared that his stubbornness had enraged his captors and that it was their intention to murder him. A fate that, I was assured, had overtaken others in a similar position. His wife was now appealing to the British as her last resort.

On principle we had been interfering as little as possible in purely internal affairs between Persians; we were indeed anxious that they should restore their civil administration and regain local control. Even then, in spite of Robertson, my own intelligence staff and some Persians assuring me that the story I had heard was true and that in their opinion the doctor's life was really in danger, I was reluctant to intervene, but under some pressure I agreed to see the lady.

The interview took place in Robertson's drawing room and I had asked him to be present to act, if necessary, as interpreter. He introduced me to a slight, youngish woman dressed simply and elegantly in European clothes. She spoke English well in a low, cultured voice and was plainly under great emotional stress, striving hard to retain her self-control. She repeated the story I had already heard, adding to it only that, by bribing his jailers, she had been able to speak to her husband and had been permitted to send him food daily. He had not so far been maltreated physically but she now feared he was to be murdered, and she obviously believed this.

I asked her why she now was so convinced that he was about to be murdered? She replied that up to last night the guards on his cell had themselves invariably eaten a large portion of the food she had taken for him, but yesterday evening they had not touched it. This, she said, could have only one meaning in Persia—the food had been poisoned after her handing it in at the prison and the guards had been warned. Her husband, seeing the altered behaviour of his jailers, had refused to eat. The poisoning would continue until he either ate or starved—it was a well-known way of disposing of recalcitrant prisoners—and unless the British intervened her husband was doomed.

I thought it very likely. I had heard these stories before; Persian jails were not healthy at that time. She, poor woman, had no doubt whatever, and to watch a wife struggling to retain her self-control as she pleaded in stark terror for her husband's life was too much for me. I told her I would see what could be done, and Robertson gently led her out. At the door, she turned and gave me a last look of desperate appeal. I decided there and then to act.

An officer was sent to Persian headquarters at once to demand that the doctor should be handed over forthwith and unharmed. In a very short space of time my messenger returned, not with the prisoner but with, in his place, an English-speaking Persian colonel. This officer informed me, somewhat haughtily I felt, that the Persian authorities regretted they were unable to accede to my request. The prisoner was under Persian jurisdiction, was well treated, in no danger to his health, and must remain in their custody.

The colonel's manner, rather than what he said, revived my suspicions. Moreover he angered me. I felt this was a test case.

'Go back to your superiors', I said, 'and tell them that unless you are here again in under one hour with the doctor, unharmed and in good health, I shall come with my troops and fetch him myself. And God help you if anything happens to him in the meantime! Now go!'

He gave me a startled salute and went.

To deal with any sudden emergency we kept a strong detachment continuously at short notice to move. Thinking this might be such an emergency, I sent orders for it to turn out. But it was not needed. Well within the hour, the colonel was back, this time with a pale and somewhat bewildered doctor.

The colonel saluted.

'Sir,' he said, simply, 'here is the prisoner, unharmed as you see!'

'I am taking him into protective custody,' I answered, 'and shall hold him. If you have any charges to bring against him let me have them.'

The colonel nodded, saluted and, turning on his heel, left. I am afraid this was one of the moments when he did not like me. I had expected at least a formal protest, followed by an appeal to my superiors, but I heard no more about it from any source, British or Persian.

Robertson, who showed considerable satisfaction at the outcome of this incident, placed a cottage in the refinery grounds at my disposal as a place of confinement for the good doctor—a confinement he shared with his wife and which, I have reason to suppose, neither found too irksome. No charge was preferred against him and in a short while he was released.

Before they left, the doctor and his wife presented me with a talisman which they told me had long been in the possession of their family. This took the form of a small mirror, set in something like the covers of a book, inscribed in decorative and illuminated Persian script with some of the traditional sayings of Solomon. I have not as yet tested its magical properties, but, if the gratitude of the givers could ensure it, I am sure my talisman would be a very powerful and benevolent one.

All the same, I was ungallant enough after the doctor's rescue to issue an order to my staff that for the future in no circumstances were ladies in distress to be brought to me. They would be dealt with by the staff themselves, who would refer to me, in an atmosphere free of emotion, the results of any interviews.

In spite of preoccupations with Kurdish rebels and Russian allies, I had to tour my extensive area and visit the chief towns to impress on them the reality and effectiveness of our occupation. These cross-country journeys happily gave me a chance to see something of the life and people of the villages.

The weather was clear, sunny and, in the uplands, cool. True, most of Persia is desert, but tucked away are fertile valleys, where sparkling streams run through cultivated fields and, here and there, the old trees of a walnut grove tempt to idleness. There is nothing like a hundred or so miles across grim desert to make a man sing the beauties of spots like these, and I could understand and sympathize with the possibly over-enthusiastic praise that the ancient poets have lavished on them.

The Persian peasant, as are peasants everywhere, was hard-working, suspicious of strangers, and a little on the make but, take him by and large, the best man of his race. Again like all peasants, he had an earthy and essential wisdom in the things of his daily life but a strange ignorance of anything beyond it. He was tragically poor, living too often on the starvation level, even where the soil was reasonably fertile and well-watered. Once these people realized that unlike some armies they had known, we paid for what we took, and even at times fed them instead of demanding that they should feed us, they welcomed our coming and talked freely. They had, everywhere, the same hard-luck story to tell. They were poor, they said, because of rapacious landlords, who claimed the lion's share of their crops, and local governors who oppressed them. We heard tales that, when the crops were ripe, soldiers would march into the village and force the cultivators to reap their own fields at bayonet point, and then, under guard, to load the grain into carts and despairingly watch it driven away to the granaries of Shah or governor. It does not do to believe all the stories tenants tell of their landlords or of tax collectors, but the hand of oppression was heavy over the land.

In one district I was anxious to contact the chief civil administrator and to get his organization working again, but he was not to be found. I ordered a search and at last he was haled before me. I asked him, angrily, why he was hiding from us; we would do him no harm! He replied with a slightly amused air: 'Excellency, I was not hiding from *you*! I was hiding from my tenants; they want to kill me!'

I dare say they had some reason, but we felt compelled to discourage them.

On these trips we saw a little of two of the great traditional arts of Persia—carpet weaving and miniature painting. In one small carpet factory, where ancient methods still prevailed, and a row of small boys sat on a bench before a great loom, weaving a richly coloured rug, I was fascinated by a slightly older lad. He stood apart, in his hand an old book, dog-eared by the dirty fingers of generations, and from it he chanted the pattern all were to follow. He was not just reading out directions; he—or the book—made a song of them, a song with an easily recognizable rhythm and a tune. I asked what he was singing, and was told it was something like this:

> *'First a red and then two blues,*
> *Next three yellow and four green.*
> *Careful now, and watch your knots,*
> *Pull them taut and start again. . . .'*

All the little boys' fingers moved deftly to the song and slowly the carpet grew under our eyes. There perhaps lurked a suspicion of sweated child labour about the place, but the young workers seemed cheerful enough and broke off happily to eat our chocolate.

In the lovely and spacious city of Isfahan, which contains a mosque with one of the most beautiful interiors in the world, we found some of the more famous of the modern miniature painters. I am no real judge of their art, but in their workshop-studios I saw nothing that to my mind equalled the work of the seventeenth and eighteenth century masters and only one artist whose work came within arm's-length of theirs. All the same, it was fascinating to watch him, a jeweller's magnifying glass screwed into his eye, putting expression into a tiny face, little more than an eighth of an inch across, with strokes from a brush made of a single hair from a cat.

Several of the larger towns had Persian garrisons and then our entry took on the glamour of military ceremonial. Indeed, we found that the Persians had a most attractive way of surrendering their cities with dignity. The procedure was so uniform that one suspected a drill laid down in Army Regulations. On my approaching the site outside the city there would be drawn up, looking very smart, a Persian guard of honour, a band and a considerable body of blue-uniformed police holding back a large crowd of chattering spectators. Facing the Persian detachment would be a similar party of our Indian or Gurkha infantry, also very spick and span, and, to their flank in a line, three Persians, one in black coat and striped trousers, the ceremonial dress of civil servants the world over, the next in bemedalled army uniform and the third in the distinctive blue of the police. I would alight from

my, I fear, rather shabby station-wagon and, followed by my
A.D.C., stalk towards them with such dignity as I could muster.

The first of the three Persians would step forward, bow, and
either in French or through an interpreter, inform me that he was
the civil governor, that on behalf of his government and all the
citizens he welcomed the gallant British Army, who were re-
nowned, he would add meaningly and hopefully, for the consideration and generosity they always showed towards civilians and
non-combatants. His local civil government, which was well
known throughout Persia to be a model administration, would
co-operate with me and my officers with the greatest enthusiasm.
We would then bow, shake hands and I would move on to his
military colleague.

This gentleman would, with great feeling, say that as a soldier I
would understand with what grief he had received the order to
cease fire. It had been only the personal order of the Shah which
had prevented him from resisting to the last. Yet he was comforted that he yielded the city to an officer the renown of whose
victories and whose reputation for valour and magnanimity had
preceded him. I found that the fact that he did not know me from
Adam and had never heard my name only enhanced the charm of
this speech.

The third official always seemed to me on these occasions to be
rather more perky than either of his colleagues. He would introduce himself as the chief of police. His police, he would inform
me, were admitted on all sides to be the most efficient in Persia;
he and they were now completely at my disposition. A bow, two
steps backwards, and that part of the ceremony was complete.
The guards of honour would then present arms at one another, the
band would play 'God Save the King'—or as near as it could get
to it—and the Iranian National Anthem. All of us, British and
Persians, congratulating one another on the smartness of our
respective soldiers, would adjourn for coffee, sweetmeats and
what Sir Winston Churchill would term 'agreeable conversation'.
It was all very delightful and civilized.

Moving about Persia was pleasant enough, for the ordinary
people welcomed us and the officials and officers were polite and
co-operative, at least on the surface. But in Teheran, we gathered,
it was rather different. To save the Persian Government from

complete collapse, the Allies had refrained from occupying the capital, but the Cabinet showed little appreciation of our forbearance, and refused to carry out the surrender terms they had accepted. It became increasingly likely that further action on our part would be necessary to enforce compliance.

In these circumstances, as a site for my headquarters, Kermanshah was too far from Teheran, and I moved with the bulk of my force a hundred and fifty miles east to Arak, a considerable town, on the railway from Khorramshahr, at the head of the Persian Gulf, to Teheran. This not only brought me to within a hundred and seventy miles of the capital by road, but gave me a much firmer control of this railway, over which we intended that a stream of supplies from Britain and America would soon be flowing to Russia. It also greatly simplified my own supply problem.

Qum, eighty miles nearer to Teheran, would have suited me better. Unfortunately, with the domes of its Golden Mosque flashing in the sun, it was a very holy city, and the stronghold of Shiah orthodoxy. Its ecclesiastics and citizens remained smoulderingly hostile to us Infidels and this was no time to inflame their fanaticism by our presence.

When the likelihood of the Allies having, after all, to occupy Teheran was becoming a certainty, I was told to make direct contact with our legation. The only really satisfactory way of doing this was to go there and meet the British minister, but as the effect of the arrival of a British general in the city might cause reactions, I was told to go in secret and travel in civilian clothes.

Accordingly, Ouvry Roberts and I betook ourselves to the leading store in Arak and bought complete outfits, including the horrible cloth cap worn almost universally by Persian males since the Shah's decree compulsorily introducing European dress. We emerged a couple of desperate looking thugs, as little like British officers as it is possible to imagine, and congratulated ourselves on our promising entry into the Cloak and Dagger Brigade. Our complacency was dashed when the first Persian post on the road turned out and presented arms to us; it dropped lower as every succeeding one did the same.

However we reached Teheran without adventure. Our journey, even if perhaps not really necessary, was undoubtedly most useful to us, for the minister was able to instruct us in the complicated cross-currents of the situation in a way no one else could. I was greatly impressed, not only by Sir Reader Bullard's knowledge of all things Persian, but by the respect in which he was held and the influence, far beyond that of his diplomatic colleagues of other nations, that he exerted. A quiet, almost mild-mannered man, he never lost even in the most trying circumstances either temper or dignity, and could, when it was needed, show great firmness. He and his staff laughed at us on our arrival much less than we expected and showed us the greatest hospitality and kindness. If, when it eventually came, the occupation of Teheran was carried out so smoothly and its result was so effective, the credit was mainly Sir Reader's. Our mission completed, Ouvry and I again donned our disguise and returned to Arak, punctiliously saluted by every Persian detachment on the way.

One other remembered visit we worked into our Persian pattern. After the occupation of Teheran, with three or four of my staff I set out along the great modern highway built by Shah Reza across the Elburz Mountains to Chalus, a new seaside resort on the south shore of the Caspian. The whole of our journey of about a hundred miles would, of course, be through Russian-held territory, and we were careful to provide ourselves with all the necessary passes that Muscovite vigilance demanded. Nevertheless, we had hardly gone twenty miles before we were stopped at a Russian post and detained.

In vain did we show our passes to the lanky youth of a lieutenant in charge; he seemed quite incapable of understanding what they were. At one time I began seriously to doubt whether he could read, but in this perhaps I wronged him. The truth was, I think, that he had orders to let *no one* pass, and the Russian headquarters had forgotten to send their posts on the road instructions to make an exception of us and let us through. He was quite polite and said he knew who I was, but seemed as if he would be content to keep us sitting indefinitely in his little guard-hut. At last, after a great deal of persuasion, he consented to get on the telephone to Russian headquarters in Teheran and ask if we could go on. Then the laborious business of getting through began, with the lieutenant shouting louder and louder and apparently getting wrong number after wrong number. If we had not been growing so impatient, it would have amused me to see that our Allies' field telephone system was even more exasperating than ours.

Eventually he did get through and even let me speak by the interpreter to the Russian general himself. We received his ample apologies for any inconvenience, and I noticed he asked whether I had met with any discourtesy. I looked at a couple of loosely held tommy-guns pointing in my direction and at the now very worried lieutenant, and assured my friend the general that, apart from being delayed, I had been treated with every consideration. The young officer escorted us back to our cars, and we left the poor chap wondering, I think, whether he was to be commended for strict obedience to orders or hauled over the coals for not using his initiative. I hope he got away with it; his fault was on the right side—but he was rather a chuckle-head.

The road was so good that we could easily and safely make up time. The Elburz is no mean range, its highest peak is just under 19,000 feet, snow-capped and impressive, as are several of its brethren. The road climbs through a true alpine pass—bare, rocky and treeless. Towards the summit it runs under great sheds whose sloping roofs carry the avalanches of winter across it. Once over the top of the pass there was a most sudden and striking change in the scenery. Instead of the bare southern slopes, the road passed almost at once into thick vegetation, tropical in its dense greenness. The contrast was uncanny, until one remembered that winds blowing south across the Caspian bear, especially in the summer, immense quantities of evaporated water. These clouds, meeting the mountains, are suddenly forced almost vertically upward, the water vapour condenses in the cold, and practically all of it falls as heavy rain on the northern slopes; little gets across to the south. Hence the surprising variation in vegetation between the two sides of the range.

Chalus, when we reached it, was a small, quite attractive town with the beginning of a harbour and a big modern hotel—another of Shah Reza's ambitious projects to attract tourist revenue. Now, except for its staff, it was quite deserted, and it was rather an eerie feeling when all its echoing rooms were placed at the disposal of our small handful. But we were certainly well looked after and, by the standards of such places, very moderately charged.

We spent most of our two days on the beach and picnicking in the hills above. Here we regretfully drank the last bottles of the beer we had brought from Haifa, washing down with it the great bowls of caviar which, in this centre of its production and in a disturbed world, was a glut on the market, to be had almost for the asking.

To complete one open-air feast, a member of my staff opened a parcel sent by his mother. In it was a note saying that she had searched London for a special delicacy, and she could picture how he would enjoy it. Then, from the centre of the lovingly packed gift, he extracted a package the size of a shoe-polish tin, proudly labelled 'Caviar'! I am glad his mother could not hear the roar of laughter on those Caspian slopes that greeted love's labour lost.

When the time came for us to leave Persia and make the long trek back to Iraq, we stopped again for a few days with Robertson in Kermanshah. Then I said good-bye to my host, my Persian friends, and to his house with keen regret—with, as a matter of fact, a secret personal regret.

As a junior officer in the first World War, I had been presumptuous enough sometimes to hope that if I survived and were not found out, I might with tremendous luck, by the time the next great war arrived, be a general. Then, I fondly imagined my headquarters would move from château to château, from which I would occasionally emerge, fortified by good wine and French cooking, to wish the troops the best of luck in their next attack. Alas, when the time did come and, by good fortune in the game of military snakes and ladders, I found myself a general, I was so inept in my choice of theatres that no châteaux were available. More often than not, I had to make do with a plot of desert sand, a tree in the African bush, or a patch of jungle, while my cuisine was based on bully beef and the vintages of my imagination were replaced by over-chlorinated water. Once or twice, however, I did get, if not my château with its chef and its cellar, at least an excellent substitute—an oil company bungalow. Once having sampled its comfort I would not have swapped Robertson's house for all the châteaux of the Loire. Dug in there, a delectable future had spread before me in which I achieved my youthful ambition and conducted war from linen-sheeted bed and luxurious long bath. But, like other youthful hopes, the vision faded. I was once more, had I known it, destined to châteaux-less wildernesses.

Still, I had seen and loved Persia. Even now, whenever I happen to come across one of those charming Persian paintings, so full of warriors in heroic attitudes, and of all the colour and movement of battle yet without the noise and fury of war, I am reminded of the pattern of our Persian campaign—a pleasant memory.

IX

CAVIAR TO THE GENERAL

On 28th August, all resistance ceased; the Persian Government fell; the Shah abdicated in favour of his son, who announced the intention of his Government to co-operate with Great Britain and Russia. On 17th September British and Russian forces entered Teheran.

British Official History: Mediterranean and Middle East, Vol. II

CAVIAR TO THE GENERAL

WHEN, after the Persian surrender towards the end of August, 1941, we occupied Kermanshah, my knowledge of our new allies, the Russians, was limited to social contacts with some of their military attachés. On these occasions we had discussed, more often than serious military subjects, caviar—caviar and vodka. To be honest I was not terribly fond of either. I had a belief that if in England caviar were a penny a pound, few people would eat it, and a feeling that vodka was a fuel rather than a drink. My sympathetic understanding went out to the British soldier of my old Warwickshire battalion who, in the bewildering general post at the end of the first World War, found himself on the shores of the Caspian. Asked by the orderly officer inspecting dinners if there were any complaints, he had stoutly replied, 'Yes, sir, this jam tastes of fish!'

His opinion of vodka was not, as far as I know, confided to his officers. The British soldier is not, for several reasons, a great consumer of spirits and whatever else vodka may be it is certainly spirits. The only comment I have heard him make on it was a slight gasp followed by a heartfelt 'Cor!' The fact remained that, whether it was an example of inverted snobbishness on my part or of a healthy palate, I preferred kippers to caviar and gin to vodka. Added to these initial handicaps, I spoke no word of Russian, and I feared I was thus not best fitted to meet our new allies in the field. However, it was clear that I should soon have to—and the sooner the better.

I say the sooner the better because almost the first news that greeted me on the 28th August at Kermanshah, brought by many voluble and agitated Persians, was that the Russians were advancing rapidly towards us in two columns. One of these, I was told, had already reached Sinneh, some seventy miles to the north, and could be expected on our doorstep in a matter of hours. The other, I was assured, had already occupied Kazvin and was making for the large and important city of Hamadan, about a hundred miles north-east of Kermanshah.

Next day, the 29th August, our troops formally occupied Kermanshah, but our Persian informants and their countrymen still retained their paralysing dread of Russians. They were prepared to go to any lengths—short of fighting—to avoid occupation by the Red Army. This was not the only time I have been interested to observe that our bitterest enemies, once they have surrendered and face the cruel fact of occupation, are overwhelmingly anxious that they should be taken over by British troops rather than by those of any of our allies. I was now surrounded by enemies suddenly become friends, all beseeching me to save them from the Muscovite bogey. If I would only stop the Russians as far away as possible, everything would be placed at my disposal; supplies for my troops would be forthcoming, petrol would be poured into my trucks, guides would be sent with me, the whole population would exhaust itself to aid me . . . if only I would start now, at once, and keep those terrible Russians away!

I needed no urging. Hamadan and Sinneh were within our allotted zone of occupation and I was under orders to secure both, but, although the Russians were our allies, I had a perhaps unworthy suspicion that if they once installed themselves in those places it might take more than a little persuasion to get them out. It seemed to me that it would simplify things if I got there first.

At the moment I was rather short of reliable information; I had, in fact, little but panicky rumour to go on. Luckily some of the Persian senior officers, who were as anxious as anyone for us to hold the Russians at a distance, had kept their heads and, what was equally useful, their grip on communications. Notable among these officers was the Persian general's chief of staff, a Colonel Mardivan. In a country where the brave were usually bandits and the good only too often cowards, the colonel was a remarkable man. In appearance he was, like most senior Persian officers whom I met, meticulously turned out but, more fortunate than some, he had retained the slight figure and quick movements of youth. His swarthy, aquiline face, alert and intelligent, was set off by a small, well-brushed military moustache. To all this he added an immediate impression of energy, of readiness to accept responsibility and of determination not universal among his colleagues. I was told his mother had been a northern European. He spoke English well, and it was certainly a relief to do without interpreters and to deal with a man who did not talk as much with his hands as with his voice.

The colonel did not like us. Why should he? He resented our presence, our high-handedness and the way we made him and his general do things against their will, but he accepted us as the lesser of two evils. He hated and feared the Russians so much more than he did us that he became our ally, even if a reluctant one, and like all allies he was at times difficult. This, however, was *not* one of his difficult times.

He explained he was in touch with Teheran and all the chief centres, though he ruefully admitted that his telephone and telegraph lines had little secrecy about them and complained that there were Russian agents everywhere. According to his reports the Russians, having advanced two hundred miles in four days, had concentrated their columns at Kazvin, within easy reach of Hamadan, which he assured me they had every intention of occupying soon. The other Russian force, said to be coming down on Kermanshah from the north and whose reality I had doubted, did indeed exist but had not yet reached Sinneh.

If all this were accurate, things were not too bad. We were nearer to both Sinneh and Hamadan than our allies and, unless they moved that night—which I doubted—we should be able to forestall them. Of course, I might be suspecting our Russian friends unjustly of wanting to seize more than their share; but if they did, their intelligence about our moves was likely to be at least as good as ours of theirs—and we had better start early. Understandably, I had as yet by no means complete confidence in Colonel Mardivan's reliability and very little indeed in that of his staff. So I announced that my force, weary with coming so fast and so far, would rest at Kermanshah, at least for a day or two.

My troops were accustomed to sudden moves. Luckily, the refinery, in and around which most of them were bivouacked, lay a few miles to the north of Kermanshah. We should not have to pass through or near the city to begin our move, and we could replenish our petrol without any undue bustle to betray us.

Our plan was simple; to send a small column of armoured cars and infantry in trucks to occupy Sinneh and a stronger force, under Aizlewood, the armoured brigade commander, to Hamadan. We were careful to impress on our troops that their object was to make the most friendly contacts with our allies, to give them every assistance but to occupy places within our zone, if possible, before their arrival. If Russians were already in possession, we would thank them for awaiting our coming and suggest politely that, in accordance with the agreement between our respective Governments, they should now withdraw to their own area. If misunderstandings or friction of any sort arose, every effort was to be made to restore friendly relations. In any case, I was to be kept closely and continuously informed of the situation.

In the early morning of the 30th August, I saw the columns off and a little later Colonel Mardivan, paying his usual call, asked me when I proposed to move on Hamadan. I found it hard to believe he did not know the columns had already gone, but when I said they had his surprise—and his anger—seemed genuine enough. His resentment at the deception I could well understand, especially if, as I afterwards came to believe, he had been playing straight with us. All the same, although he looked at me bitterly enough, I thought I detected a gleam of respect in his eye. I told him that I proposed to go to Hamadan myself later in the day and suggested he came too, but he replied that I would understand he must consult his general first. I wondered who would be told besides his general and toyed with the idea of detaining the colonel on some pretext, but I decided the Persian staff must know by now, and it was not worth worsening our relations by such an act. He left in an obvious hurry and I was glad I had let him go.

Leaving Ouvry Roberts to watch things at Kermanshah, I started off with my A.D.C. on the road to Hamadan. My station-wagon made good time over the wide and well-graded tarmac road until, after about eighty miles, we began to approach the seven thousand feet high Shah Pass, through which the road runs to curve into Hamadan from the north. We had already noticed two or three light tanks fallen out by the wayside, their disconsolate crews vainly tinkering at them, and when we got into the Pass itself we saw that casualties among them had become more frequent. It was a tribute to their men that any of these ancient chariots had crawled so far, and a wonder that any at all had got over the Pass. Even the more modern trucks could not all compete with the steep gradients; there were breakdowns among them too and stragglers were limping in most of that night.

I reached Hamadan in time to see the admirable way in which Aizlewood took over the city and disposed his small force, and to exchange greetings with a still huffy Colonel Mardivan, whom I found refilling the tank of his staff car at a petrol pump. The townspeople, in a state of great nervousness and full of rumours of the approach of the Russians, welcomed us with evident relief and I was glad to learn that the Russians, except for patrols, were still in Kazvin. Persian intelligence sources reiterated their reports that the Russians intended to occupy Hamadan and, whether that were so or not, I thought we had better meet our allies as far to the north of the city as possible. It was too late to send a column out that night but a detachment of Gurkhas was warned to be ready to move soon after daylight next morning.

Then, having assured myself that everything was going well under the brigadier's capable hands, I drove to the oil company's rest house. There my A.D.C. and I had an admirable dinner served by an equally admirable Persian butler, and we passed the night in great comfort—thanks to the oil company and its châteaux!

At dawn on the 31st August, I was wakened with two items of news. The first that the Russians had met our column at Sinneh at 11.45 p.m. the previous night. The meeting had been cordial, they had made no difficulty about our occupying the town and would withdraw to their own areas. All this was well and of good omen. The second piece of news was slightly disturbing. Our Persian friends reported that the Russians at Kazvin, having learnt yesterday of our arrival, were about to advance in strength on Hamadan. Whether they really had any intention of occupying the city I was not sure but, impressed perhaps unduly by the insistence of my informants, I thought it possible. The Gurkhas had better get moving.

I went along to see them. They had eaten their early morning *chuppatis* and *dhal* and were now packing their gear into a line of trucks along the road. Their English colonel, who was to go with them, leant on a stout walking stick watching them. He looked tough and I knew from experience he was tough. It did me good to see him, quiet, confident, alert but relaxed. He had been my machine-gun officer when, some years before, I had commanded this very battalion. He was exactly the man I would have chosen for the task, a cool, experienced soldier, who would keep his head and, hot though it was, his temper, and display, if needed, a certain rugged diplomacy of a type not always too evident in our foreign relations. At the roadside, as I had often done before, I discussed his instructions with him.

The road to Kazvin, which he would take, ran north-east in long straight stretches through populated and well-cultivated country until, after about sixty miles of this easy going, it turned and twisted its way for twenty miles through a formidable mountain range. This it surmounted by the Aveh Pass, eight thousand feet high, to debouch into the plain south of Kazvin. The idea was to get the Gurkhas over this pass as quickly as possible, take up a position on the far side blocking the road, and there await the Russians. When they arrived all was to be friendliness; if a few officers with an escort wished to come on to Hamadan they would be welcome, but larger forces were to be discouraged and if necessary prevented from crossing the pass. I impressed on the colonel that speed was the essence of the operation, and added that I didn't mind how many trucks turned over or how many Gurkhas were laid out, provided only that he got there in time with enough men to do his job.

The colonel called up his officers, briefly gave them their instructions and sent them at the double back to their companies, to issue in turn their orders to their subordinates. At a signal the men climbed aboard the trucks in a disciplined silence that I approved, and in another moment the small advance-guard of the column moved off. I watched them go and after them the main body, gathering speed. Nothing looks as uniform as a Gurkha battalion, nothing looks more workmanlike and few things look so formidable.

I had to attend to some messages and deal with one or two minor problems so that it was about an hour later when I started off in my hard-worked station-wagon after the Gurkhas. The drive was a repetition of that of the day before over a very similar road, but this had much more the thrill of a race with not a few of its hazards. Although along the straight stretches with their occasional well-graded curves my driver kept at a steady fifty or more miles an hour, it was not until we were almost at the foot of the Pass that we began to catch up with the rear of the column, spinning along for all it was worth. At some risk we overtook three or four vehicles and found ourselves close behind a 30-cwt. truck which, swaying dangerously, clung to the centre of the tarmac at what the trembling needle of our speedometer assured us was nearer fifty than forty-five. Its load of Gurkha soldiers, sitting bolt upright in two rows facing each other, looked, poker-faced, to their fronts, every man's rifle held straight up beside his right knee. Evidently my friend the colonel permitted no loung-ing in his transport and only Gurkhas seem able to *sit* at attention. There they were as solid, immovable and expressionless as a couple of brick walls.

We were now entering the first sweeping bend that rose into the mouth of the Aveh Pass. On the inner side of the curve the hill towered steeply; on the outer, the banked-up road ran poised four or five feet above fields of stubble. We slowed down to take the turn, but the Gurkha driver ahead of us had obviously no intention of lifting a foot jammed down hard on the accelerator; equally obviously at his present speed he could not hold the road. We watched fascinated for the inevitable.

The truck swept on.

At last centrifugal force could no longer be denied. The vehicle launched itself sideways into space. For a moment it was air-borne, soaring over the ploughed field below, its Gurkha pass-engers all sitting rigidly at attention, apparently quite unmoved by their novel and precarious situation. With a thud and a cloud of dust the truck landed aeroplanelike on all four wheels. As one man the Gurkhas bounced a couple of feet into the air and remained for a split second poised, their ranks unbroken, their attitude unchanged, still sitting at attention—on nothing. Then, with a crash that we could hear, their posteriors in unison recon-tacted the benches. The truck rushed on without pause, bumping across the furrows, the driver's foot never relaxing on the accelera-tor as he put his vehicle at a steep earth bank. With hardly any loss of speed it bounded up and in one final leap regained the road. In spite of his detour he had not lost his place in the column and, as if it were the most normal thing in the world, he continued his journey at the same break-neck pace. His passengers still sat stiffly at attention. Neither their posture nor their expression had changed throughout; they appeared quite oblivious to the whole incident.

As we wound higher, the pass began to take its toll. We overtook three or four trucks stopped at the side of the road to cool off, steam hissing from their radiators, and one with its wings crushed against the low but solid stone wall that here fortunately guarded the precipice edge. Beside the wreck three or four Gurkhas lay on the ground, being attended to by their more fortunate fellow passengers, and I wondered whether my insistence on speed had not perhaps been a little overdone. However, thanks to the wall, no one seemed to have gone right over into the abyss. As the column, radiators sizzling, engines roaring, gears clashing, swooped and looped round bend after bend, we abandoned as too dangerous any attempts at overtaking, and remained modestly at its tail. Even so, when we reached the summit of the pass we had to call a halt while our driver gingerly unscrewed the radiator cap to release a noisy fountain of boiling water. We refilled from the tin of water which experience had taught us to carry, and, giving the column time to get well ahead of us, we coasted down hill after it at a more sober pace.

It was still fairly early in the morning when, some miles further on, we reached a narrowing gorge where the Gurkha colonel had halted. Already his men were on the hillsides, building sangars covering all approaches from the north; machine-guns were being sited, a control post had just been established on the road itself, and all vehicles were tucking themselves away out of sight round the last bend. A patrol with wireless had already gone forward to give early warning of any movement towards us. We were ready. It only remained for our allies to present themselves—but they didn't! The patrol had no news of them, not a soul appeared on the road.

I waited until after midday. It seemed that our friends were not going to turn up at all and, feeling guilty that I had been away from my Kermanshah headquarters so long, I decided I must return. Rather reluctantly—for the air in these mountains was crisp and bracing, the sky blue with little white clouds chasing one another across it, and the views superb—I called up the station-wagon. Leaving the Gurkhas to put the finishing touches to what was by now a formidable road-block, we climbed back over the pass on the way to Hamadan.

It was not, I heard later, until well into the afternoon that the

Russians did appear. A squadron of their armoured cars, escorting a force of lorried infantry, drove slowly up and halted before our position. Officers emerged from the cars and were greeted by ours. The visitors seemed a little nonplussed to find our troops so far ahead of Hamadan. From the account I had, I gathered that the meeting was punctiliously polite if not noticeably cordial, and it was only when the Russian commander, through his interpreter, announced that he was taking his whole force on to Hamadan that a slight element of strain was introduced. The Gurkha colonel replied that he would be delighted to furnish a guide to the city for the officer himself with a small escort, but as we were in full occupation and had ample forces there to deal with any eventuality, he could not think of allowing our friends to put themselves to the trouble of sending reinforcements. The Russian, equally polite, insisted that it would be no trouble at all. But the Englishman remained firm and after some discussion among themselves our allies went back to their cars and withdrew the way they had come.

Whether they ever seriously intended to occupy Hamadan, especially after they learned we were there, I was never able to discover, but I had a feeling that they would have very much liked to have done so.

Within the next few days we had several opportunities to meet our allies. Commanders and staff officers of both nations exchanged visits and I paid a formal call on my opposite number, Lieutenant-General Novikov. On my arrival, I was conscious of my rather worn slacks and shirt when I was met by three immaculate Russian officers, very smart in their uniforms of dark khaki blouses, breeches and soft black leather field-boots. I was particularly impressed when I noticed, peeping above the hooked-up necks of their blouses, narrow margins of starched white collar!

Nothing could have been more courteous and indeed cordial than my reception by General Novikov; I felt myself becoming ashamed of the suspicions I had nurtured. His uniform was possibly not quite so smart as that of his staff officers; he looked rather the rugged old soldier, lean, weather-beaten, with humorous glinting eyes under shaggy brows, a chest of medals, and a great flow of hearty talk. Never have I regretted more that I had no word of Russian, for he spoke no other language and I felt we could have had a lot to say to one another, even if it were only to exchange the sort of stories current in all armies. However, with the aid of an interpreter, vodka, champagne and caviar, we got on well enough.

This was the first of many meetings I had with the general. It was a little difficult to discover much of the background of any Russian officer, but I was told he had been an N.C.O. in the Czar's Army. He had fought on the Bolshevik side in the civil wars, when by his courage he had earned rapid promotion and, unscathed by purges, here he was a lieutenant-general. Socially, whether as host or guest, he was warm-hearted and amusing, and militarily I always found him, as far as the Red Army, or rather the Soviet system, would allow him, co-operative and understanding. This was true of almost all the Russians we had to deal with; not only were they willing to co-operate but they would even go out of their way to be helpful, provided always that what we asked of them was within their own very limited powers. When there was any doubt of this in their minds—and as often as not there was—they would invariably play for safety, indulging in infuriating delays while they made up their minds whether to risk approaching higher authority. This meant that nothing happened for weeks even if eventually consent were given. None the less, as allies in the field at our level they gave us surprisingly little to complain about.

At this time I doubt if even their senior officers knew the full extent of the disasters the Germans were inflicting on the Red Army, of the hordes of prisoners and deserters it had lost, or of the wide areas of its homeland it had been forced to abandon. Yet even with the imperfect knowledge they had, the Russians in Persia were unhappy and uneasy; they wanted desperately to feel they had friends. The arrogance of success and the effects of their alone-we-did-it propaganda were to come later; they were at this time much more forthcoming than I ever found them again.

All the same, it was not easy for the Russians really to be friends with us. There was first of all the language difficulty; practically none of us spoke Russian and, apart from a few civilian interpreters, I met only one or two Russians who knew any English at all. At this stage of Soviet development, I think, any Russian officer who could speak a Western European language would keep quiet about it—such an accomplishment would smack too much of a bourgeois upbringing. We were accustomed to meeting foreigners of all kinds and colours, but the vast majority of Red Army men had never been outside their own country or even seen a foreigner. All they knew of us British was what they had heard from their propaganda department, and that, up to a couple of months before when Hitler had invaded Russia, was of the decadent-capitalist-robbers type and far from flattering. They believed, quite firmly, that in our own country we lived in a mixture of the feudal system and the worst elements of the Industrial Revolution and that in our Dominions and Empire we were extortioners and slave drivers. In conversation they drew contrasts between Britain where, they averred, women and children worked in coal mines, and the Soviet Union where such things were not permitted; between the privileges and tyranny of our aristocrats and the rule of the proletariat. Several of their officers had read translations of Dickens, who they thought was a contemporary writer, and quoted him to convict us out of our own mouths. Their ideas were very Alice-in-Wonderland but extremely firmly fixed.

I was once walking with some Russian officers, one of whom did speak a little English. We passed a line of 30-cwt. trucks belonging to a regiment of my allegedly armoured brigade, halted at the roadside. Suddenly the Russian touched my arm and pointed. I looked and there, seated on the running-board of a truck, sharing a bully beef lunch with a trooper, was an officer.

'Isn't that an officer?' the Russian asked.

'Yes, a major.'

'And isn't that a private soldier?' he went on.

'Yes,' I agreed, mystified.

The Russian looked bewildered.

'But', he exclaimed, 'they are feeding together.'

'Why not?' I asked. 'You can't run an officers' mess in every vehicle; on the move the crew, officers and men, must feed together.'

He shook his head.

'But British officers never eat with their men in any circumstances; they are aristocrats!'

'Not all of us,' I grinned. 'Although the one you are looking at happens to be—he's a cousin of the Queen!'

The Russian shook his head again and walked on in meditative and puzzled silence.

But the greatest obstacle to any real intimacy was neither language nor mutual misconceptions; it was the Soviet system, which however thoroughly one cast out prejudice and made allowances for something totally different from one's own experience, was so plainly based on fear and on fear's offspring, suspicion. It was understandable that the Russians should be suspicious of us—after all they had been taught to be—but, even more, they suspected one another. No Russian officer, whatever his rank, would dare to be seen speaking to us alone even on purely military business; he would always be accompanied by at least one other. When, as we were occasionally able to persuade them, a group came to lunch or dine and spend the night with us, they were invariably accompanied by a military commissar.

These commissars were officers peculiar to the Red Army. They were combatants and had a high reputation for personal bravery and toughness. They held the same ranks and wore the same uniform as other officers, but were distinguishable by a large red star on the lower part of the right sleeve and, it seemed to me, by some of the toughest faces I have ever seen. As far as I could discover, every Russian officer commanding a unit from company commander to commander-in-chief had a commissar as his *alter ego* or twin, equal in rank and sharing the command with him. This divided responsibility was always something of a mystery to us. One of the commissars told me that, while he did not interfere with the commander's tactical decisions, they had jointly to sign all orders. From what he said and from other sources, I gathered that a commissar was a sort of Pooh-Bah, who combined many of the functions of the staffs of our adjutant-general in responsibility for discipline, of our judge advocate in legal matters, of our civil affairs officers in dealings with occupied populations, and of our chaplains in spiritual welfare—in this case, the party line.

The commissar could thus relieve his twin of a great deal of distracting responsibility and leave him to concentrate on more purely tactical and strategic tasks. There have even been times when

I might have liked to have had a commissar myself, but I doubt it! A grim-faced red-star man breathing down one's neck would not make for peace of mind, especially when one realized that his secret reports on one's political reliability were on their way, through his own channels, to some sinister department in Whitehall.

There were varying views on which was the more powerful in these combinations, the commissar or the commander. A very senior commissar once demonstrated his view on this most graphically. Accompanied by his own interpreter and one other red-star man, he had dined well and cheerfully in our mess and as the evening wore on he mellowed. We ventured, so affable had he become, to ask him who was really the boss, he or his general. For a reply he placed the index finger of his left hand on the edge of the table, projecting about an inch over the surface.

'The general!' he explained, nodding at the finger.

Then he did the same with the index finger of his right hand.

'Me!' he announced.

The two fingers lay side by side, perfectly level, neither in advance of the other.

'The general! Me!' he repeated, lifting and replacing each in turn. 'Equal, just the same.'

He paused for a moment while we stared at the fingers.

'But me . . .' he said gently, 'but me. . . .' And slowly he slid the right hand finger half-an-inch ahead of the left. Then he turned and smiled at us. There was a lot in that smile.

When we first met, I had expected to find the Russians eager to fraternize with us on the largest scale. I had pictured hordes of their soldiers swarming through our camps, and I confess I had been a little apprehensive of a concerted ideological offensive against us. In the event, it was the Red Army which seemed much more nervous of the effect our men might have on theirs. They issued stringent orders against their soldiers having any contact with ours except under the strictest supervision, and they were equally averse from our troops, British or Indian, mingling with theirs. Our attempts to arrange for Red Army soldiers to be entertained by our units received little encouragement, and it was some time before General Novikov yielded so far as to invite a large detachment of our men to a party with his inside the Russian zone.

The general had, however, proved less unbending in allowing visits between officers, although even in this, whether from kind-heartedness or for other reasons, he preferred that the Russians should be hosts rather than guests. Much as I enjoyed Russian hospitality, I must confess I found it, once or twice, if anything a shade over-generous. This was, perhaps, because I never found a really effective way of dealing with the happy Russian custom of drinking innumerable toasts on every occasion, especially when, as sometimes happened, four or five of their officers combined against one solitary Englishman to make quite sure his glass was never empty for longer than it took to refill it. Their heads were hard and, while careful on our ground, on their own they had no inhibitions about getting drunk. Like Jorrocks, too, where they dined they slept!

Our first experience of real Russian hospitality came when a party of about thirty of us was invited to Kazvin to spend the night at their headquarters. We arrived soon after midday to be welcomed by General Novikov and many of his officers, who at once took up their duties as hosts and performed them with unflagging zest for the rest of the day.

We began in a fair-sized room into which the general led both his and my more senior officers. We were offered trays of the usual small glasses filled with vodka and dishes loaded with a wonderful assortment of rather substantial savouries of all kinds—ham, smoked fish, intriguing delicacies of to us unknown origin and, of course, caviar. In good appetite we fell to and began a hearty meal which I innocently thought was to be our lunch. It was not long before the genial Novikov began to propose toasts to which, in common politeness, I had to find responses. It became something of a litany; to the incomparable British Army, to the invincible Red Army; to the confusion of the Fascist beasts, to the victory of the Allies; to the courageous people of England, to the gallant Russian people; to me, to him, and so on until I prayed that our lunch would come to an end and allow a pause for recovery in the fresh air.

It did come to an end! General Novikov, beaming hospitably, turned to me and asked, through the interpreter, whether I was now ready for lunch. Lunch! Rarely have I felt less like lunch. We moved into another room—very large this time—where

long tables were laid for what, judging by the number and
variety of glasses and cutlery, was to be, not a lunch, but a
banquet.

Our officers were distributed at the various tables among our
hosts with Novikov sitting at the centre of the top table between
Aizlewood from Hamadan and me. On my right was a handsome,
greying colonel from whose air of distinction, elegant manners,
and knowledge of French, I deduced a non-proletarian origin; he
was most helpful in the advice he gave me on the Caucasian
wines. Among the Russians, one occasionally came across officers
of this type who, something of a contrast to their colleagues,
looked as if they would be more at home in, say, the French
Army.

Our table at the top of the room, raised on a low dais, overlooked the others and we sat on one side of it only. To make conversation possible, the chief interpreter had been seated opposite
me in solitary state—a strange figure among these robust soldiers.

He was dressed in a blue suit, made either for someone else or
for him when he had been more prosperously ample. He wore
with it a white shirt and a not too white collar, also a size or so too
large for him, which betrayed a palpitating Adam's apple in his
scraggy throat. His sallow skin glistened unhealthily, his pale eyes
protruded anxiously, while his whole face seemed in some strange
way to be projecting itself forward into its most prominent feature
—a large, sharp-pointed nose. His hair, sparse and straggling,
although carefully brushed across his skull, failed to conceal his
baldness. He was not, poor fellow, attractive to look at, but I felt
a sympathy for him; I would have liked to help him, for never,
except in a newly captured prisoner of war, have I seen a man so
obviously terrified.

Fear was written across his face, lurked in his nervous glances,
sat on his rounded shoulders; if he had had a tail it would have
been tight between his legs. We kept him busy at his interpreting
and he spoke English well in a cultivated voice, but in every pause
he wolfed ravenously at the rich food piled on his plate as if he
had not eaten decent food for a week. Perhaps he had not—and for
much longer than a week! Maybe it was only imagination, but I
cast him in the role of a bourgeois university professor, plucked
suddenly from some concentration camp for his knowledge of

English and now in stark terror lest some slip on his part would fling him back behind the barbed wire. Truly, a skeleton at the feast, poor devil!

Skeletons or no, the feast was jolly enough. Course followed course in rich profusion. I was already reduced to the expedient of leaving my flock of glasses full to the brim, because the instant I took a sip a bottle came over my shoulder and the glass was inexorably refilled. At that moment General Novikov rose to his feet.

'We will now have some toasts!' he announced.

Toasts! I thought we had exhausted all possible toasts in the other room but here we were off again. This time we worked conscientiously through the fighting arms of our respective forces: the gallant British Tank Corps, the valorous Red Army Tankists; the indomitable British Infantry, the heroic Russian Infantry . . . until, both our Army lists exhausted, we drank with acclamation to the lovely ladies of Britain and the charming ladies of the Soviet Union.

Late afternoon saw the end of our lunch but not the end of our entertainment. In a corner of the room was a grand piano and a Russian officer played ballet music for us. He was followed by a soldier chorus, who were so obviously professionals of a very high standard, that I asked how such talent had been gathered together. Simple, I was told: you collected all the male performers from the Tiflis Opera House and turned them into General Novikov's Headquarters Defence Company. After them came one of those rousing, semi-acrobatic Russian dances with a balalaika accompaniment and, when they had given us several encores, the general asked me if there were any particular Russian song I would like. Being an Englishman, of course I knew the name of only one, the inevitable Volga Boatmen, and I asked for that. At once a Russian lieutenant with a magnificent bass voice sang it with the chorus coming in on the refrain. He sang it again and as the applause died down, Novikov leant towards me and said: 'Now the British officers will sing!'

In vain I protested we were not like the Russians a musical race, that I had no opera company at *my* headquarters, and that, after the music we had heard, it would be ridiculous for us to attempt to sing. But by now all the Russians were shouting for us and in desperation, like so many British generals before me, I was compelled to call upon my troops to perform a task for which they were neither trained nor equipped and, as on many a stricken field, they rallied—I must confess a somewhat part worn band—to attempt the impossible. We dare not be ambitious in our choice of a song; after a hurried consultation, I announced we would sing a traditional English folk-song, '*Daisy, Daisy!*' We knew only the chorus, which we repeated several times, accompanied in dashing style on the second effort by the officer at the piano who had picked up the tune. The applause of our indulgent hosts was deafening; the honour, if not the musical reputation, of the British Army was saved!

Even then, although certain officers of both armies appeared to be approaching their limits of enjoyment, the party was by no means over and showed little sign of flagging. I looked enviously at my colleague, the brigadier, who, cool, calm and collected, was engaging manfully, glass for glass, a group of Russians and earning their plainly expressed admiration. On myself I feared the ravages of hospitality would soon show. Luckily, I had a legitimate excuse to take my leave; I had, before I realized the thoroughness with which we should be entertained, arranged to meet some senior Persian officials and the time of my appointment had almost arrived.

When General Novikov and I emerged, the sun was low but it was still full daylight, and the contrast from the murky smoke-filled atmosphere we had just left was for the moment dazzling. I noticed, drawn up in two ranks on an open space about fifty yards to our right, a party of soldiers; but it was not until the interpreter said, 'The General asks you to inspect the guard', that I paid much attention to them. Then with something of a shock, I realized that these soldiers were women.

The drab, greenish khaki of the Red Army uniform was not, I should imagine, the most becoming colour for ladies, yet they looked undeniably smart. They wore the Russian blouse, short skirts—much better cut than those I saw later on our own A.T.S. —and the usual black, low-heeled field boots. They were, I judged, mostly peasant girls from European Russia, not very tall but sturdy and buxom, a characteristic somewhat emphasized by the tightness with which they had drawn the leather belts round

their waists. Approaching obliquely from a flank, I had momentarily a fantastic impression that I was looking at a row of old-
fashioned quartern loaves lining some imaginary baker's counter.

I walked down their lines inspecting them. They were very well
turned out and looked efficient and well disciplined; they were
obviously healthy, wholesome girls, proud of serving their
country and, although they never allowed it to show on faces
attuned to a proper military seriousness, they were, I suspected,
highly amused at having such a close look at the British general.
I particularly noted the clear freshness of their complexions, completely innocent of make-up, and the tidiness of their hair, usually
fair, under their rather cheeky forage caps. I was struck, too, by
how well they had kept their hands. And if you tell me that was a
lot to note in a quick inspection, I would remind you I was for
three years an adjutant and I had inspected a great many guards—
although I admit that this was the first female one, and I may have
given it a little more concentrated attention than some. Another
detail that caught my eye was the small pistol in its leather holster
that some of the girls had on their belts. I asked if the women ever
undertook combatant duties, and I was assured they never did.
'What, then,' I asked, 'are the pistols for?' I received no very
definite reply.

Later, moving about the Soviet zone, we often saw these girls,
travelling in lorries, working in offices, directing traffic—which
they did excellently. They always appeared neat, cheerful and,
while on frank, comradely terms with the soldiers, their behaviour
was, as far as we could see, on all occasions above reproach. To the
great regret of our soldiers, however, they never appeared at any
of our inter-allied functions.

After inspecting the women's company, I moved on to the
local Persian notabilities. Among them was at least one who spoke
very good English, so I told the Russian officer and the interpreter
who accompanied me that I would not trouble them. Rather to
my surprise they made no objection and waited outside the room.
If other arrangements had been made to follow the course of my
interview with the Persians, I saw nothing of them.

The deputation, with oriental good manners, expressed delight
at meeting me. Their chief object seemed to be to discover when
the Russians would leave—from their point of view it could not

be too soon—or if there were any chance of our replacing them in Kazvin. They may not have been as fond of the British as they would have had me believe, but they were certainly terrified of the Russians. When I asked them why, what had the Russians done, they shivered, but could not produce any actual instances of horrors to lay at their doors.

A couple of the deputation assured me they had supported the British in the 1919 operations on the Caspian and one, a frail old man, produced for my inspection some carefully preserved letters from British officers of those days and a book, written by one of them, in which a photograph of himself appeared. It was recognizable, but the contrast between the vigorous, upright warrior in the picture hung about with a small arsenal of weapons and the old gentleman who held it out to me, was pathetic and moving. I could only hope he was not another of our friends who had suffered for his loyalty to us. There was, I fear, little I could do for the deputation beyond telling them to urge their people to obey all orders of the Russian commander. I assured them that, if they did this, they would come to no harm. We bade one another polite farewells but I left some disappointed men behind me.

Having picked up my Russian guides again, we walked to the hotel where my senior officers and I were to pass the night. It proved to be a long, two-storey building in a main street. It was quite dark by now and I noticed a guard of about platoon strength standing near the entrance. The officer in command was presented to me, and I was told that he was responsible for my security and comfort. I could only hope the comfort would be as well attended to as the security.

Passing the double sentry at the door, we entered the hall and at once ran into two more steel-helmeted, tommy-gunned guards at the foot of the stairs. Outside my bedroom two more crashed to attention and I was proudly told there were more on the roof above me. Before bidding my guides and guardian good-night, I did suggest that the large guard watching over me might be dismissed or at least substantially reduced. The young officer in charge appeared shocked by this idea. He had personal responsibility for my safety. Reduce the guard? Impossible! I then mildly asked whom he was guarding me against? He replied at once and very firmly, 'The Persians!' So I left it at that.

My bedroom exceeded my expectations. It was large and, even if sparsely furnished with bed, Victorian wash-stand complete with ewer and basin and a wardrobe of the sort we used to call in Indian an *almirah*, it was clean. I opened the windows, undressed and, feeling that it had been a pretty full day, got into bed. My last thought, before deep sleep overcame me, was that it was nice at last to be alone.

It was not very long before through my unconsciousness there penetrated a faint alarm of stealthy movement. Suddenly I was awake and listening . . . a board creaked, a foot slurred the carpet. Good Lord, there *was* somebody there! Had that Russian been right? Was a Persian, long knife in hand, creeping towards me? Without moving, I opened my eyes. The room was still dark, but faint light filtered in through the half-open door. Black against this glow, two figures bent over the side of my bed towards me. I could just distinguish the outline of Russian steel helmets and of a tommy gun slung over a shoulder. Having regarded me intently for some seconds, my two visitors, still in complete silence, tiptoed out and quietly closed the door. I shut my eyes and in a moment was asleep again.

Two hours later this macabre shadow-show was repeated. Again I awoke to see two dim and sinister figures bending over me; again without a word they silently withdrew. Now, I realized what this visitation meant. Every two hours the sentry on my door was being changed and, when that happened, the new sentry was brought in to make sure that I was still there and alive. I suppose this went on at two-hourly intervals throughout the night, but I was inured to it by then and it woke me no more.

Next morning I was regarding my breakfast tray with intense revulsion when my A.D.C., whom I had left the previous night to continue the allied revels, made his haggard appearance. He gazed at me with concern.

'Are you all right, sir? How do you feel?' he asked, anxiously.

I regarded him with a baleful and bloodshot eye.

'I feel,' I said, 'I feel like you *look*!'

Fresh air and exercise—and we soon had plenty of both—restored us and enabled us to take a less jaundiced view of life. For the next week or two I was kept on the move round our part of Persia, where the usual problems of occupation were complicated by a Kurdish rising against the Teheran government. I did, however, return for the first inter-allied party for troops, as distinct from officers.

At this the Russians had again asked to be hosts and it was held in their zone on a large open space, well away from any town or military camp. Marquees had been set up, camp kettles were bubbling, and on long wooden tables piles of food were spread for both British and Indian troops. The whole scene had something of the air of a country fair, the same cheerful bustle, noise and movement. Instead of hoarse voices shouting the wonders of the Bearded Lady or inviting us to step up and earn five pounds by surviving a three-minute round with some human gorilla, we had equally brass-lunged gentlemen with red stars on their sleeves making speeches of welcome. As they all spoke in Russian and, as far as I could observe, their oratory was not translated into English or Hindustani, they must have had more effect on their own men than on ours.

Two speeches, however, were translated. Russians and British, we all collected before one of the senior Red Army commissars, who, standing in the back of a lorry with its tail board let down, delivered an harangue with the emphasis and gestures of a Hitler and with a machine-gun rapidity. Throughout, lurking miserably behind him and looking more lugubrious than ever in a homburg hat, was our old friend the chief interpreter. The commissar ended in a magnificent burst of roaring eloquence and the interpreter stepped unhappily forward. From a paper in his hand he read quickly in an expressionless voice an English translation of the speech. It was mostly about what the invincible Red Army and the indomitable British Army would together do to the Fascist Beasts. The original, although none of us had understood it, had sounded much more convincing than the translation, perhaps because the commissar looked the sort of chap who could do the things he threatened.

Standing with General Novikov in the front row of the audience, I led the applause and was most embarrassed to find myself being almost forcibly hoisted from the stalls to the stage. I was expected to reply! There I stood alongside the interpreter, a couple of aristocrats in a tumbril. We exchanged glances of mutual misery and he announced sepulchrally: 'I will translate.'

My trouble was I had not got anything for him to translate. He came to my help.

'Will you make your whole speech, and I will translate at the end,' he asked, 'or would you like me to translate sentence by sentence?'

I clutched at this straw.

'Sentence by sentence,' I said.

At least that would give me a second or two to think before I spoke. We started off on this verbal leap-frogging, and both of us gained confidence as we went on, until, emulating the commissar, I closed with a blood-thisty exhortation to the slaughter of all Fascist Beasts. The interpreter put this bit over like a man; I suspect he even gilded my tiger-lily a little. Anyway, whether he said what I said or something better, our joint effort was well received, and in a happy mood we all got down to the business of fraternizing.

The Russian soldiers were friendly enough and curious to see what we were like, but they were shy and, I think, very conscious of the watchful eyes of the ubiquitous red-star men. Our Indians were politely interested but a bit suspicious of the food; the Gurkhas frankly amused by everything and especially by their hosts. It was as usual the British soldiers with their traditional, uninhibited friendliness, who most rapidly overcame any stiffness in the party. How often have I seen them, unconscious ambassadors, showing their identity discs or photos of their wives and families, asking questions by signs, swapping cigarettes, buttons and, I am afraid, at times cap-badges; dispelling in allies and in former enemies shyness, suspicion and hostility. With their help to start us off, we all got on very well together, and the party was definitely a success.

Remembering the generosity of Russian hospitality to our officers, I had been a little apprehensive of its possible effects on our men. I need have had no qualms; vodka was not provided. An interpreter told me that while officers were permitted to drink alcohol it was strictly forbidden to lower ranks. I found it hard to credit that, even in the Red Army with its harsh discipline, such an order could have been issued, but I was assured it had. I am afraid such class distinction would not have been taken so docilely in my army.

Looking back over a varied experience, I find I have liked all the soldiers of different races who have fought with me and most of those who have fought against me. This is not strange, for there is a freemasonry among fighting soldiers that helps them to understand one another even if they are enemies and, when peace comes, prevents them from hating too long. It is not surprising then that I quickly got to like our allies, the Russian soldiers. They appealed to me both as soldiers and as men. There was no doubt that they were fine military material, tough, brave, well-disciplined in the essentials and, if often lacking smartness in turn-out, they avoided the last slovenliness of the soldier—ill-kept weapons. While some of the senior officers were not professionally well-educated, there were many among the middle ranks, the majors and colonels, who had attended the post-war staff colleges and were extremely competent and highly trained.

I took all the opportunities I openly could to see something of the Russian troops, on and off parade. I was invited to inspect units and one of the first was a tank battalion. Its commander, a magnificent giant of a man, marched up to me and towering above me, his hand at the salute, reported his unit present. This took some time as he went through the numbers of officers and men by ranks, the numbers and kinds of tanks and vehicles and a great deal of other information which, if I could have understood it, would have been most informative. I found this ritual, however, something of an ordeal, as he stood about a yard from me and, as if I were a brigade a quarter of a mile away, bellowed at me in a voice that matched his frame. He proved, however, to be a most forthcoming man, let me clamber all over his tanks, gave me a ride in one of them, and was obviously, as he had every right to be, very proud of his battalion and of his men.

Off parade when I met the Russian soldier, he proved to be a cheerful, friendly soul who, unless afraid that he might get into trouble by being seen with a foreigner, would always respond to a smile with a good honest grin. He could, too, laugh at himself—a very endearing trait in anybody.

I myself had served most of my military life in an Asiatic army —the Indian Army—and I came to feel more and more strongly that the Red Army was an Asiatic rather than a European one. This was not so much because many of its men were Asians, drawn from the vast areas of Asia that Russia had absorbed in her relentless, centuries-long march of conquest to the east. It went deeper than that. The Russian soldier, wherever he came from, in behaviour, living conditions, lack of outside contacts, recreations and general outlook, approximated more to the Asian than to the European. He was none the worse soldier for that; I was inclined to think he was the better. His nature inclined him to courage and patriotism, the climate of much of his homeland inured him to hardship, and his normal standard of living left him content to be without many things Western soldiers regarded as indispensable necessities—a great military advantage.

Yet the most Asiatic element in the Red Army was not its soldiers; it was the atmosphere that pervaded it from top to bottom. The severity of its discipline, the rule of fear and suspicion, the barbarity of its frequent purges, the low value it set on human life and the fanaticism it inculcated, all had a remarkable similarity to the methods of the Asiatic hordes of history—and they were formidable enough. So, with all its faults and weaknesses, was the Red Army as I saw it.

Between us, the Russians and ourselves had now occupied all Persia with the exception of Teheran and the district round it. Our Governments had left the capital alone as evidence that they had no permanent design against the independence of the country and to encourage stability in the new Government. The Persian prime minister had promised to close the German, Italian and Axis satellite legations, send home all their diplomats and hand over to the Allies all other Germans and Italians in Persia. But, as time went on, he showed little sign of honouring his undertaking. Eventually, after much argument, he did officially close the legations, but made no attempt to stop the activities of the numerous enemy subjects who remained. A joint Russo-British ultimatum, demanding the surrender of all Germans and Italians within forty-eight hours, was delivered on the 10th September.

It was not until a day after the expiration of this time limit that about one-third of the Germans were sent by train into the British zone, but there was no indication that the rest would follow. Needless to say, too, the more dangerous enemy agents remained behind and increased their activities. Stung into action, the British and Russian Governments ordered Teheran to be occupied by their joint forces on the 17th September. Realizing that the game was up, Shah Riza, the tough old man who, by courage, cunning and character, had risen from the stable to the throne, on the 16th abdicated. He chose to be handed over to the British rather than to the Russians and was exiled to Mauritius. He was succeeded by his elder son, the present Shah.

On the day of the Shah's abdication, my force for the occupation of Teheran halted a few miles south of the city, while the Russians approached from Kazvin. A number of Italians, packed into motor-cars with their families and innumerable suitcases, arrived in our lines and announced that they wanted to make sure they were our prisoners before the Russians arrived. No doubt they were wise. No Germans, however, appeared and we were told that they were collecting in the German Legation, claiming diplomatic privilege and refusing to surrender. The Persians appeared unwilling or frightened to turn them out and there were all sorts of rumours that the Germans would resist us.

One of the Russian liaison officers attached to me said that he supposed, as there were many women and children in the Legation, the British would hesitate to fire on it. I told him that, as the Germans had bombed my mother, aged ninety, and my children at school, I should, if they refused to come out, have few scruples about returning the compliment. In earnest of which, I trundled up my old but still very effective 6-inch howitzers. This bloodthirstiness cheered up my Russian friend considerably.

As I expected, there was no need for such drastic measures; the Germans, like the Italians, at the last minute decided it was better to surrender quietly to us than to wait for the Russians, and a large number, men, women and children came over. Owing to Persian inefficiency or more likely connivance, some of the most dangerous Nazi agents were allowed to escape, and they gave us a lot of trouble before they were rounded up.

Among the Germans who had surrendered to us were some particularly wanted by the Russians and we handed them over. An officer of General Novikov's staff, after checking his list of these prisoners, thanked me for our help and added most politely: 'If there is anything you wish to know about these Germans, where they have been, what they have been doing, their contacts, or anything at all, just let us know and we will tell you.'

'That's very kind of you,' I answered, 'but how will you get them to tell you all these things?'

He smiled pleasantly and replied: 'We shall interrogate them *severely*!'

I felt a little chilled. War is war, but a *severe* interrogation by our allies was quite another thing; though, I dare say, these Nazis would only be getting a dose of the medicine they had administered often enough to others.

The entry into Teheran was not a particularly triumphant or spectacular affair. We just marched quietly to the areas allotted to us, through undemonstrative crowds of depressed-looking citizens in shabby, down-at-heel European clothes. What with their own political excitements, the comings and goings of innumerable politicians, their attempts to glimpse the new Shah, and the Axis legations being packed up, Teheran was very like an ant-hill that had just been kicked over. We were only one of half-a-dozen free shows going on at the same time. There was nowhere any sign of hostility to us or the Russians.

As soon as I began to take stock of my surroundings, I felt we had been rather hardly done by when Teheran was divided between us and our allies. The Russians had undoubtedly been allotted the more pleasant residential parts of the city, while our sector sported much more than its share of tanneries, soap factories, gas works and other necessary but not salubrious industrial undertakings. Most of the cemeteries seemed also to be in our area.

Next day at an inter-allied conference at the Russian Legation, I suggested to Novikov some adjustment of areas. Over a map of the city, he asked me what alterations I would like. I told him and, to my surprise, he at once agreed. The only hesitation he showed was over the rifle factory which I had asked for as a billet for my troops. I understood that some of its newly installed machinery was wanted for workshops in Russia. However, this difficulty was surmounted and Novikov there and then issued the orders for the moves of his troops made necessary by the redisposition. Incidentally, the changing of the guard at the main gate of the rifle factory between troopers of the Household Cavalry, average height about six feet, and riflemen of the Gurkhas, average height five feet four inches, became one of the daily sights, drawing considerable crowds.

If you confined yourself to the main streets, looked at the buildings only from the front and never peered behind them, Teheran was an attractive and almost imposing city. A great range of mountains, its snow-capped peaks towering up to 18,000 feet, stretched across the northern horizon, and against this magnificent back-drop the city played its drama of wealth and poverty, power and misery. But to us it appeared more as a comedy, not very true to life but colourful and gay. Anyway, as far as gaiety was concerned, all the night-clubs and cabarets reopened with a bang the day we arrived and in a little while every legation was vying with its fellows in cocktail parties and entertainments. That is, all except the Japanese who, still nominally neutral, kept themselves very much to themselves and busily hid and helped our enemies.

While in Teheran, I saw a good deal of Novikov, but never alone and usually with a watchful commissar in close attendance. I found this rather irksome and, as we seemed on mutually good terms, I took an opportunity on one of the rare occasions when for a few minutes we were alone with only a British interpreter, to ask him to dine with me by himself. After a little hesitation, he said that he would come with one officer, his A.D.C., and I was to come with one only and an interpreter. We agreed on the time and place, and duly met.

My A.D.C. and I on our arrival were a little surprised to find that Novikov's A.D.C. was a lady, a major, in I should say, her middle thirties. Like all Russian women officers, she was very neatly turned out in well-fitting uniform, and she had the advantage of being distinctly good-looking in an Amazonian sort of way. She had clear-cut features and a pleasant smile, rendered slightly startling by the flash of gold. My A.D.C. was ungallant enough to suggest later that, while a Gurkha lady often dangled her dowery from her ears, the Russian custom appeared to be to carry it in the teeth. He also christened her 'The Adjutanta', a name by which she became known to many of my staff who met her at work as the general's secretary.

Our dinner, in spite of the inevitable slowing up of conversation by the need to interpret, was a pleasant affair, and I would have been very happy to repeat it. Unfortunately, I never persuaded the general to accept another invitation of this kind. I was not surprised, for however much he had enjoyed our company—and we certainly enjoyed his—I fear he must have taken enough risk as it was.

My stay in Teheran was not to be long but, while there, I was fortunate again to be the guest of the British minister in his most delightful legation with its friendly and helpful staff. I had plenty of work to do but I managed to enjoy the social, semi-diplomatic life in which I found myself involved. All the same, I was not sorry when my division and I were ordered away to a more spartan and active role.

With typical good-fellowship, General Novikov invited a number of my staff and me to a farewell party which took the form of an evening reception. As usual, the entertainment was extremely well arranged and on a generous scale. The Defence— alias Opera—Company was in evidence and so was an excellent dance band. There were a good many ladies present, some, including the Adjutanta, in Russian uniform and others from the legations.

The general did not dance and, as I am at the best no expert, I was happy to sit with him on a dais, watching those more skilful perform. My friend, the chief interpreter, sat with us translating with his usual fluency and, while not yet exactly hilarious company, he was, I thought, rather less hang-dog than usual. In a rash moment, I said: 'Why don't you dance, General? There's your Adjutanta sitting over there; ask her for a dance!'

He laughed.

'In the Red Army', he explained, 'it is not permitted for the General to dance with his Adjutanta. But', he added, 'that does not apply to the British General. *You* shall dance with my Adjutanta!'

In vain I protested that I was the poorest of performers; that I could not think of inflicting myself on the lady. He brushed all that aside.

'No matter, she will be honoured to dance with the British General!'

I tried another line. The band at the moment was playing some stirring Russain dance which I noticed had got all but our most dashing young officers into difficulties.

'I don't know your Russian dances,' I pleaded. 'I couldn't possibly dance this!'

In no way perturbed, the general at once stood up and clapped his hands imperiously; the band stopped in mid-bar.

'Play something English,' he ordered.

After shuffling and juggling with music sheets, the band struck up what I thought might be a tango or some, to me, new kind of dance that was no more within my compass than the wildest Russian mazurka.

'Good!' said General Novikov with great satisfaction, and he beckoned to the Adjutanta, seated in a group a few yards away.

She came at once and the general spoke to her. She turned to me, clicked her heels together and gave a little military bow. There was nothing for it. I got up and led her on to the floor and, holding her rather gingerly at arms-length, launched out.

I had been quite right; I had no idea how to dance to this infernal tune. The poor Adjutanta, who I am sure like most Russians, was a good dancer, never had a chance with me to show that she was. Then to my consternation, I realized that the other couples were drawing away to the edge of the floor, leaving a wide space in which my partner and I, the centre of all eyes, gyrated alone. Now and then the Adjutanta, determined at all costs to be polite, flashed a golden smile at me, which I returned as amiably as I could manage. If only I could have said something to her! At last the music, with a bang on the drum and a clash of the cymbals, stopped. The relief of it! In the silence that followed I thought it only courteous to applaud the band; I clapped.

That was madness! They at once began again. At last, even that encore ended; no claps from me this time! I led the Adjutanta back to her friends and joined them at their table, where I found a young Russian lieutenant who had once acted as interpreter for me. We all had a glass of champange—which I needed—and I rose, thanked the Adjutanta and turned to go back to the dais. Hardly had I taken a step, when the lieutenant asked my late partner a question and I heard the laughter that greeted her answer.

I swung round at once and demanded to know what they had said. My request seemed to cause some embarrassment to the lieutenant and the Adjutanta and a great deal of amusement to the others. The lieutenant hesitated but I pressed him, and, urged to it by his companions, 'I asked her,' he admitted, '"What was it like dancing with the English General?"'

'And what did she say?'

He paused.

'Well, what *did* she say? Out with it!'

'She said,' he confessed, 'she said "It wasn't very *dangerous*!"'

As I walked thoughtfully back to say good-bye to General Novikov, I meditated on the Adjutanta's answer. Whatever interpretation one put upon it—and several were possible—none, I reluctantly decided, could be flattering to the English General.

'Not very dangerous!' Well, that phrase might go for more than dancing. It might for us sum up the joint Anglo-Russian incursion into Persia. Exciting sometimes, amusing often, even, in its wider effects on the war as a whole, perhaps important, but certainly not very dangerous. In fact, among the hard tack of campaigning, a bit of caviar to the generals—and the troops.